MEET THE PROPHETS

A beginner's guide
to the books of the biblical prophets—
their meaning then and now

John W. Miller

PAULIST PRESS
New York/Mahwah

Index prepared by Michael Kerrigan, C.S.P.

Excerpts from the *New Jerusalem Bible*, © 1985 by Darton, Longman and Todd, Ltd., Doubleday & Company, Inc. Reprinted by permission of the publisher.

Library of Congress Cataloging-in-Publication Data

Miller, John W., 1926–
    Meet the prophets.

    Bibliography: p.
    Includes index.
    1. Bible. O.T. Prophets—Criticism, interpretation,
etc. I. Title
BS1505.2.M55   1987   224'.061   87-9208
ISBN 0-8091-2899-3 (pbk.)

Published by Paulist Press
997 Macarthur Boulevard
Mahwah, New Jersey 07430

Printed and bound in the
United States of America

CONTENTS

Section III

The Prophets of the Babylonian and Persian Periods

For Jeanette and Lowell

My trust is in Yahweh
who hides his face
from the House of Jacob;
I put my hope in him.*

*Is 8:17. Unless otherwise noted biblical citations in this volume are from the *New Jerusalem Bible*.

A Note to the Reader

The books of the biblical prophets are among the most provocative ever written, and yet they are by no means easy reading. A first impression is that they are anthologies of sorts, but, lacking as they do "introductions" or "tables of contents," we are often confused as to where a given segment begins and ends, or what its context might be. Even the voracious Luther once complained that in perusing these books we are compelled to jump from topic to topic until we can scarcely endure it! His advice was to read them in small doses.

My hope is that the following pages will help in surmounting these and other difficulties and bring about a meaningful encounter with these unique writings. Other excellent studies attempt to do the same, of course. Why yet another?

Most introductions to the prophets, I have found, concentrate on interpreting their *messages* within the context of the world in which they were initially presented. This is essential, and the following study seeks to do this too. More help is often needed, however, in understanding the prophetic *books* (their compositional histories), as well as the unique prophetic *personalities* referred to by these books as their primary source. Nor, in my opinion, is enough attention generally paid to the ongoing *relevance* of these books for those who transmitted them or for today, or to the overall shape and thrust of the prophetic movement as a whole. If there is anything unique about the following study, it is the degree perhaps to which it addresses this wider range of subjects in a sequentially clear and meaningful way.

I must quickly add, however, that not all of the prophetic books are given equal time and attention in what follows. Most students agree that not all deserve this, for some are more substantive by far than others. To this latter category belong: Amos, Hosea, Micah, Isaiah of Jerusalem (chs. 1–39), Jeremiah, Ezekiel and the so-called Second Isaiah (chs. 40–55). Without totally neglecting the others these then are the writings on which we will be focusing.

Needless to say, a study of this nature will be most useful when adapted to specific needs and expectations. Not all students, for example, will want to concentrate on compositional issues as thoroughly as I sometimes do before proceeding to a study of the prophetic messages. Obviously, too, a resource of this kind is no substitute for the guidance of an experienced teacher.

Since the prophetic books were all written in Hebrew, most English speaking students will require a suitable translation. Fortunately, many such are now available. However, for consistency in citation I

1

thought it preferable in the following study to follow mainly one of these. The reasons for my choice of the *New Jerusalem Bible* for this purpose are given in the appendix (as well as a few recommendations regarding other accessible translations).

My indebtedness to others in preparing this volume is only partially accounted for in the annotated bibliography at its end. Having read, studied and taught the prophets for over a quarter of a century, I am no longer always sure what thoughts are my own and where I have borrowed from others. Wherever possible, however, I have tried to give credit where credit is due. Where a name appears in parenthesis, a full citation of that author's work may be found in the appended bibliography. The helpful suggestions of Fr. Lawrence Boadt in the process of editing this study for publication were much appreciated.

While preparing this manuscript a daughter and son-in-law were on assignment in the land of the prophets, working with displaced peoples. Its dedication is meant as a gesture of recognition, affection, encouragement and hope, both for them and the many like them in our time in whom the spirit of the prophets so manifestly lives on.

SECTION ONE

GETTING ACQUAINTED WITH THE PROPHETS AND THEIR BOOKS

The Law and the Prophets,
and the other writers succeeding them,
have passed on to us great lessons,
in consequence of which Israel
must be commended
for learning and wisdom.
                    Translator's Foreword to
                    Ecclesiasticus (vv. 1–2)

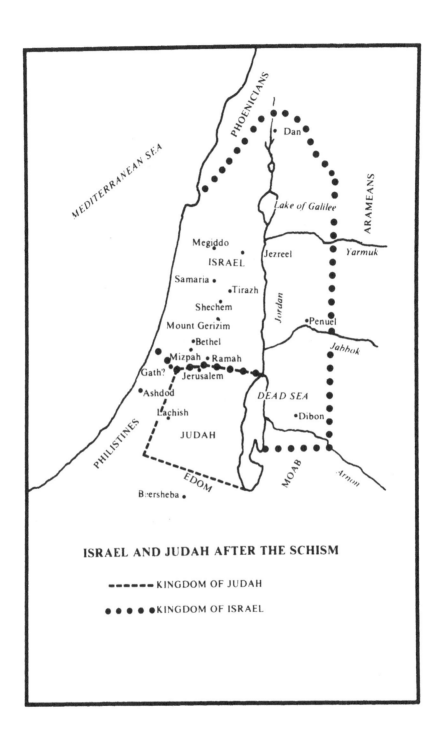

ISRAEL AND JUDAH AFTER THE SCHISM

------- KINGDOM OF JUDAH

●●●●● KINGDOM OF ISRAEL

1

What Prophetic Books? What Prophets?

A. Opening Questions

Before looking at individual prophetic books several questions
need answering:
- what books are we talking about?
- who are the individuals named by these books as their source?
- when and where did they live, in what kind of world?
- what is a prophet?
- what is a prophetic book?
- how and why should we study these books?

These are the questions that will engage us in this introductory section of our study (chs. 1 to 4).

B. A Provisional List

The best way to identify the prophetic books we are going to study
in this volume is to open the Bible you are using to the Book of Isaiah.
If your Bible is a Catholic version of the Bible and you page through it
from there (Isaiah) to the end of the Old Testament (Malachi), the books
you will encounter (with two or three exceptions) are the prophetic
books of the Bible. Should you jot down their names on a sheet of pa-
per, when finished, your list will look like this:
1. Isaiah
2. Jeremiah
3. Lamentations
4. Baruch (not found in Protestant Bibles)
5. Ezekiel
6. Daniel
7. Hosea
8. Joel

9. Amos
10. Obadiah
11. Jonah
12. Micah
13. Nahum
14. Habakkuk
15. Zephaniah
16. Haggai
17. Zechariah
18. Malachi

Simply listing these books in this way poses certain additional questions. Where did these books come from? Who wrote them, preserved them and put them together in this sequence and why? How did they become a part of our Bible?

Answers to these questions are not easy to come by. In fact, only after we have studied the prophetic books themselves, one by one, will the picture of their origins and transmission become clearer to us. But a partial insight into the story of their organization as a *library* of books is given by a chance reference in the intertestamental Book of Ecclesiasticus, a collection of wisdom sayings from the beginning of the second century B.C. There, in the Translator's Foreword, it is said that the author of this volume, Jesus ben Sirach, was an avid student of "the Law, the Prophets and the other books of the Fathers." From this startling bit of information we learn that already 2,200 years ago a collection of books called "the Prophets" not only existed but was held in highest esteem by respected teachers among the Jews of Palestine (where Jesus ben Sirach lived at that time).

But it should also be noted that "the Prophets" were not by any means the only books respected in this manner. Rather they are listed (in the quote from the Translator's Foreword to Ecclesiasticus cited above) as the *middle* group of a still larger collection that included two other collections as well: "the Law . . . and the other books of the Fathers." The "Law" (or Torah), in this instance, refers to the Pentateuch (Genesis, Exodus, Leviticus, Numbers, Deuteronomy) and by "other books" (or "writings") is meant a certain number of additional books in excess of "Law" and "Prophets." These three collections, then (Law, Prophets, Writings), in this order, made up, we might say, the Bible (or sacred Scriptures) of Jesus ben Sirach.

Interestingly, this is exactly the way the Jewish Bible (Old Testament) is organized right down to the present day (books of the Law first, then Prophets, then Writings). On the other hand, as we have just seen, in Christian Bibles the prophetic books appear not in the middle (after the Law) but at the *end* of the Old Testament. To complicate matters still more, the list of prophetic books in Christian Bibles differs slightly from the list in the Jewish Bible. In the Jewish Bible the "Prophets" section begins with six historical books called "Former Prophets" (these are Joshua, Judges, Samuel and Kings), followed by a section called the "Latter Prophets" made up of the books listed above, but *without* Lamentations, Baruch or Daniel. In Jewish Bibles Lamentations and Daniel appear in the "Writings" section and Baruch is missing altogether.

In summary, the arrangement of books in the Jewish Bible is as follows:

Law	Prophets		Writings
	Former	Latter	
Genesis	Joshua	Isaiah	Psalms
Exodus	Judges	Jeremiah	Job
Leviticus	1 Samuel	Ezekiel	Proverbs
Numbers	2 Samuel	Hosea	Ruth
Deuteronomy	1 Kings	Joel	Song of Songs
	2 Kings	Amos	Ecclesiastes
		Obadiah	Lamentations
		Jonah	Esther
		Micah	Daniel
		Nahum	Ezra
		Habakkuk	Nehemiah
		Zephaniah	1 Chronicles
		Haggai	2 Chronicles
		Zechariah	
		Malachi	

How do we explain these differences between Christian and Jewish Bibles in this regard? It seems evident from the Translator's Foreword to Ecclesiasticus that the *earliest* way of arranging the prophetic books was as they appear in the Jewish Bible: immediately *after* the Law (first five books) and Former Prophets (Joshua, Judges, Samuel, Kings), and *before* the Writings. As such they are closely linked to the history recounted in the prior historical writings, and confirm the importance of God's law as revealed in the first books of the Bible.

However, when Christianity arose, the chief importance of the prophets came eventually to be seen in a somewhat different light. It was not so much the way they confirmed the previously given law that gripped Christian imagination, but their visions of the future, and the way these appeared to be coming to fulfillment in the life and mission of Jesus and his followers. As a consequence these books were rearranged to come at the *end* of the Jewish Scriptures (now thought of as the Old Testament)—on the threshold, so to speak, of the Christian New Testament. Thus a close bond was created between Old and New Testament Scriptures.

When the early Christians did this, they eventually added Baruch and Lamentations to the older list of the prophets (perhaps because of the association these books came to have with Jeremiah), and Daniel too, because it also points forward to a new age (see Daniel, chs. 7–12). During the sixteenth century reformation, Protestant Christians adopted the shorter list of canonical writings found in the Jewish Bible, while retaining their traditional Christian arrangement. When doing this they assigned Baruch and several other writings to a separate section called the Apocrypha. In Catholic tradition seven of these so-called apocryphal books (Baruch among them) are regarded as deuterocanonical (a second canon).

C. The List We Will Study

Today the majority of scholars, both Jews and Christians, when teaching courses or writing books about the prophets, concentrate on the fifteen books of the prophets as listed in the middle section of the Jewish Bible (Latter Prophets), rather than the eighteen books at the end of the Christian Bible. They do this not for theological reasons, but because Lamentations and Baruch are clearly not prophetic type books at all and Daniel also is now understood to be quite different in style and outlook from the other books on this list. (I will have more to say about Daniel at the conclusion of our study.)

One more question merits some attention as we conclude our consideration of the list of books we will be studying: Why are several of them—Isaiah, Jeremiah and Ezekiel, in particular—so much longer than the others? Is this because these prophets were more important than the others? Perhaps. But another factor must also be reckoned with, and that is the way in which these books were first written. Initially books of this kind were transcribed on leather or parchment scrolls (see Jer 36:4; Ez 2:8–10). Such scrolls were typically of a certain length, not too long, nor too short. Each of the longer books (Isaiah, Jeremiah, Ezekiel) represents approximately the amount of writing that could easily be contained on one of these scrolls. The shorter books too were originally written on scrolls, not individually however, but together on a single scroll. Because there are twelve of them, they were known as the Book (or Scroll) of the Twelve. Initially then, there were four prophetic scrolls: Isaiah, Jeremiah, Ezekiel and the Scroll of the Twelve.

These are the books that will engage us in the following study.

1. Locale and Date of Each Prophet

We turn now to a second set of introductory questions. A characteristic of the prophetic books is that each of them begins with a short phrase or sentence giving the name of the prophet whose words follow and sometimes informing us of where and when he lived (as well as other matters). As a next step in getting acquainted with these books, I suggest that we do a quick survey of these headings to get some sense of the time period and locale of each prophet and of the prophets as a group. In those instances where this information is missing in the heading, I suggest we scan the book quickly to see if there are hints elsewhere that might help us at this point.

As we do this, be sure to identify the place names on a map (see p. 4). Note too that the dating system used in these headings is in terms of the reigns of certain Judean and Israelite kings. To coordinate these reigns with our modern dating system (years B.C. and A.D.) is not a simple matter. Even the experts disagree at points. The chronology I will be utilizing both here and elsewhere in this study is the one followed by the editors of the *New Jerusalem Bible*.

My summary of data in these headings is as follows (students should study them on their own, then compare their summaries with mine): (see pp. 10–11)

2. Summary Sketch of Prophets as a Group

What have we learned from this first exploratory study of the prophetic figures mentioned in the headings of the prophetic books?

Most lived and prophesied in one small corner of the world: the

Overview of Locale and Date of Each Prophet

Prophet	Where	When
Isaiah 1:1	Nothing is said in 1:1 about where Isaiah lived, but a quick look at the following verses will indicate he was a Jerusalem based prophet.	During the reigns of Uzziah, Jotham, Ahaz and Hezekiah (781–687). Note, however, that in Isaiah 40–55 a new locale and time are implied. The prophet of this section (Second Isaiah) lived in Babylon (43:14) shortly before it was captured by Cyrus in 539 (44:28; 45:1). Scholars conjecture that still another prophet, living in Palestine a decade or so later (Third Isaiah) may have been the author of Isaiah 56–66.
Jeremiah 1:1–3	Anathoth, a village just north of Jerusalem.	From the thirteenth year of Josiah until the "deportation of Jerusalem" (626–587).
Ezekiel 1:1–3	Among the exiles deported from Jerusalem to Babylon.	Began prophesying in the fifth year of their captivity (593).
Hosea 1:1	Locale unspecified, but if place names elsewhere in book are any clue, very likely lived in Ephraim (northern kingdom).	During the reigns of Uzziah, Jotham, Ahaz and Hezekiah (about 750 onward).
Joel 1:1	Locale unspecified, but there are numerous references to Zion–Jerusalem (2:1, 15, 23; 3:5; 4:1, 16f, 20f).	Date also unspecified, but 4:2 suggests a time after the destruction of Jerusalem in 586 and the building of a second temple there in 515 (1:14, 16; 2:17; 4:18).
Amos 1:1	Tekoa, southeast of Jerusalem.	During the reigns of Uzziah of Judah and Jeroboam of Israel (about 760 onward).
Obadiah 1:1	Place unspecified, but references to Zion (Jerusalem) are prominent (verses 16, 17, 21).	Unspecified, but reference to the violence Edom did to Jacob (1:10) may refer to Edom's plunder of Judah after Judah's humiliation by Babylon in 586.

Prophet	Where	When
Jonah 1:1	Place unspecified.	Jonah lived when Nineveh was "a great and wicked city" (Nineveh fell in 612). If this is the prophet mentioned in 2 Kings 14:25, he was active in the northern kingdom (Ephraim) during the days of Jeroboam II (783–743). It should be noted, however, that Jonah is *about* Jonah, not a collection of his words. The writing down of this story might have been much later.
Micah 1:1	Moresheth southwest of Jerusalem.	During the reigns of Jotham, Ahaz and Hezekiah (about 740–700).
Nahum 1:1	Elkosh (precise location unknown).	Date unspecified, but Nineveh's fall appears to be imminent (perhaps in the period 640–612); Nineveh fell in 612.
Habakkuk 1:1	Place unspecified, but references to the temple (2:20) suggest Jerusalem.	Also unspecified, but Babylon is on the rise (1:6); this points to a time soon after 625.
Zephaniah 1:1	Place unspecified, but the northern kingdom is no more; he must be from Judah, possibly Jerusalem.	During the reign of Josiah (640–609).
Haggai 1:1	Place unspecified, but somewhere in Judah, as indicated by references to Jerusalem temple and king.	Second year, first day, sixth month of the Persian monarch Darius (August 520).
Zechariah 1:1	Again place unspecified, but like Haggai his focus on temple and king indicates he is living somewhere in Judah.	Second year, eighth month of the Persian monarch Darius (October-November 520).
Malachi 1:1	Place unspecified, but his concerns for temple and priests (ch. 1) suggests Jerusalem.	Sometime after 515 when the second temple was built.

land of Israel, in and around Jerusalem. The exceptions are Ezekiel and Second Isaiah who though very much focused on Jerusalem were called to their prophetic missions in far away Babylon.

If we exclude Jonah (the book is about him, not by him) only two of these prophets lived *north* of Jerusalem (Hosea, Jeremiah), and only Hosea was from the northern kingdom. The rest were either from Jerusalem itself or the region *south* of Jerusalem (or the southern kingdom, Judah).

With one or two exceptions all of these prophets lived in a three hundred year period between 750 and 450 B.C., and the majority can be dated to a two hundred year period, 750–550.

Amos, Hosea, Isaiah and Micah were contemporaries, living in the last half of the eighth century; Zephaniah, Nahum, Habakkuk, Jeremiah and Ezekiel were also contemporaries living in the last half of the seventh century. Most of the remaining prophets lived during the last half of the sixth century, or a short time thereafter.

In other words the biblical prophets appeared in well-defined clusters in the latter half of each of three centuries. This important point is made visually clear in the following chart:

750–700	650–600	550–500	After 500
Amos	Zephaniah	Isaiah 40–66	Malachi
Hosea	Habakkuk	Haggai	Joel
Isaiah 1–39	Jeremiah	Zechariah	Jonah
Micah	Ezekiel	Obadiah	
	Nahum		

How do we explain this clustering of prophetic activity? Even a provisional understanding of what was happening in the world of these prophets will begin to suggest an answer.

What was happening? It is to this that we will turn in the next chapter.

Questions for Review

1. What is the earliest reference we have to a collection of books called "the Prophets"? Where are these books located in Jewish Bibles? What reasons might there have been for locating them there?

2. Why are the books of the prophets arranged differently in Christian Bibles than in Jewish Bibles? What differences are there

in the list of books included? Which arrangement and list is the older?

3. How many books of the prophets are there in the oldest list? Why are some of these books called "major" prophets and others "minor"? Can you give the names of these books by memory?

4. Where, generally speaking, did these prophets live, and in what time period? More specifically, which prophets were active in which centuries?

2

Historical Setting of the Biblical Prophets

A. The Importance of Historical Setting

Before answering the question posed at the conclusion of the last chapter, it is worth pausing to consider the importance which the Bible itself attaches to historical background in the study of the prophets. As already noted, in the Jewish Bible the prophetic books appear not at the end of the Old Testament (where we find them in Christian Bibles) but in the middle immediately after a group of historical books called "former prophets" (Joshua, Judges, Samuel and Kings). Clearly, one reason for this arrangement was to encourage students of the prophets to become familiar with the history of the people to whom the prophets spoke before turning to the prophetic books themselves. This too, no doubt, was the intent of the references to the reigns of certain kings during which the prophets were active, in the headings to the prophetic books (see previous chapter). This way of introducing these books alerts their readers to the fact that only as they are acquainted with what was actually going on in Israel when these kings ruled (as related in the preceding histories) will they fully comprehend what these prophets were meaning to say.

Today of course we do not need to rely on the Bible alone for historical information of this nature. Through scholarly research our understanding of the ancient Near East in the time of the prophets has been vastly enriched (see the references to modern histories of ancient Israel in the bibliography). But even so the historical books of the Bible are still a valuable, readily accessible resource for those who would study the prophets seriously.

This being so, it will be worth our while to note briefly what manner of histories these are and what in general they tell us about the historical setting of the prophets.

B. The Deuteronomic Histories

The book of the Bible most immediately relevant to a reconstruction of the historical setting of the prophets is 2 Kings. It is here that the historical period specific to most of the prophets is narrated. 2 Chronicles reviews the events of this era as well, but in doing so leans heavily on Kings (although occasionally it too supplements the record in valuable ways). So, it is the book of 2 Kings (which the compilers of the Jewish library have placed at the doorstep of the prophetic canon) that is our most important resource for understanding the historical setting of the biblical prophets. This being so, what kind of book then is 2 Kings and what does it tell us about the history of the times of the prophets?

It should be noted, first of all, that 2 Kings is not a volume standing alone, but is the culminating part of a larger historical narrative that begins in Joshua and continues in Judges, 1 and 2 Samuel and 1 Kings. In fact, striking stylistic and theological similarities between these six books (Joshua, Judges, 1 and 2 Samuel, 1 and 2 Kings) and the book immediately preceding them in the canon, Deuteronomy, have prompted the suggestion that initially Deuteronomy too may have been a part of this sweeping historical overview, serving as a kind of preface or introduction.

In other words, Deuteronomy, followed by Joshua, Judges, Samuel and Kings (many biblical scholars now believe) was initially meant to be read as a single, continuous history telling the story of Israel from the days of its founder-prophet, Moses (thirteenth century), to the point in time when the authors of this historical overview were themselves probably living (the near aftermath of the destruction of Jerusalem in 586 B.C., as narrated in their history's final chapter, 1 Kings 24). Because the Book of Deuteronomy seems to serve as the anchor point for this larger work, not only introducing it, but supplying it with its basic themes, this history as a whole has come to be called the Deuteronomic history.

What were the compilers and authors of this amazing historical overview (the most comprehensive of its kind in antiquity) wanting to say?

C. The Story They Tell

Even a glance at the broad outlines of the Deuteronomic history (which you should take time to scan) will quickly reveal the strong convictions of those who composed it.

To begin with, you will notice that in its opening volume (Deuteronomy) the founder-prophet Moses is the overwhelmingly dominant figure. In fact, virtually the entire book is made up of his speeches to the Israelite people as they stood on the threshold of their new homeland, Canaan—speeches in which he reminds them of the way God led their forefathers, brought them out of Egypt and made a covenant with them at Horeb (chs. 1–11); speeches in which it is emphasized how important it is, therefore, that they love this God and obey his laws (12–26), so that they might truly be his people and he might bless and not curse them in the land to which they are going (Dt 27–28). These are the convictions which undergird the Deuteronomic historical overview.

Two books, Joshua and Judges, trace the follow-up story of Israel's entry into Canaan-Palestine and how marvelously God helped them in doing this. In this part of the story the Deuteronomists hammer home the conviction that Israel is no ordinary people, but a community set apart by Yahweh for a way of life that brings blessing, if followed, but, if forgotten or rejected, can lead to terrible disasters (including expulsion from their land).

Another set of convictions of the Deuteronomists begin to emerge in the stories they relate in 1 and 2 Samuel. These books are largely devoted to the beginnings of kingship in Israel and the astonishing rise to prominence of David and the Davidic monarchy. Through David, the Deuteronomists inform us, Yahweh not only delivered Israel from the Philistines and brought them unprecedented prosperity and power, but graced his people with yet another covenant (in addition to the one made through Moses at Sinai)—this one, not with the people as a whole, but with David and his descendants only. "Your dynasty and your sovereignty will ever stand firm before me," God promised, "and your throne be for ever secure" (2 Sam 7:16). With David, the Deuteronomic historians seem to imply, Israel's long history had reached an unimaginable apex of blessing and success.

This, however, was by no means the culmination of the story the Deuteronomists had set out to tell. Two more books, 1 and 2 Kings, were needed to describe and analyze the totally unanticipated developments that occurred next. From this pinnacle of power and promise, during David's reign (around 1000), Israel gradually declined and then fell in abject defeat. Why? Already upon the death of David's son and successor, Solomon, due to his oppressive measures, civil war broke out (931) and the ten Israelite tribes to the north of Jerusalem broke away from the Davidic monarchy and formed an independent monarchy of their own (1 Kgs 12:16–19). Israel now existed as a people divided against itself in two often contentious kingdoms. A century of strife and intermittent war followed during which the admonition of Moses centuries earlier to follow the way of Yahweh was all but forgotten by leaders and people alike, it seemed (1 Kgs 14–2 Kgs 13).

It was right at this juncture, the Deuteronomists inform us (around 750 B.C. according to our modern reckoning), that a series of truly catastrophic events occurred. Already a century earlier to the northeast of Israel, along the Tigris River at Nineveh, a people calling themselves the Assyrians (after their god Asshur) had begun establishing themselves and harassing their neighbors. But now, around 750, they began moving westward in force (2 Kgs 15:19, 29), conquering Syria-Damascus first of all and then, a few decades later (in 721), the northern Israelite state, turning its territory into a province of their now rapidly expanding empire (2 Kgs 17). At this time Judah narrowly escaped the same fate (2 Kgs 19:35–37), largely by forfeiting its sovereignty, but then was destroyed a century and a half later (586) by another superpower of a similar type, the Babylonians (2 Kgs 25).

D. The Place of the Prophets in This Story

It is this tragic account of great beginnings under Moses and David, but then precipitous spiritual decline and devastating military invasions by pagan superpowers, that the Deuteronomists relate as a backdrop to the prophets. And from what they tell us we can begin to sense the reason for that clustering of prophetic activity noted in the previous chapter. The prophets did not speak in a vacuum. Their missions were attuned to the international events and upheavals of their times. Their calling as prophets is related to the rise of political superpowers in the ancient Near East during the eighth to sixth centuries and to the life and death decisions posed by this development.

More specifically, it was the Assyrian rise to power during the latter part of the eighth century to which Amos, Hosea, Isaiah and Micah responded. The decline of Assyria and the rise of Babylon, a century later, set the stage for the prophetic activity of Nahum, Habakkuk, Zephaniah, Jeremiah and Ezekiel. Although beyond the scope of the Deuteronomic historians (who concluded their account with the rise of Babylon), the advent of Persia, during the latter part of the sixth century (at a time when virtually all that was left of the Israelites was a small refugee community in Babylon), marked the opening of still another wave of prophetic activity (that of Second Isaiah, Obadiah, Haggai, Zechariah, Malachi, possibly Jonah).

It is sometimes said that stories have a beginning, middle and an end. The beginning of this one, in summary, was in the days of Moses and the settlement and rise to power of the Davidic dynasty in Canaan-Palestine. Its middle was Israel's apostasy and destruction by international superpowers, after the breaking apart of the Davidic kingdom. Its end was that period when, with the help of Persia, an Israelite remnant returned to its homeland, chastened and fiercely determined to begin life over again in the land God had given them.

The prophets we are about to study belong to the middle and end of this story. In the midst of their people's spiritual decline and the mysterious rise to power just then of destructive superpowers (Assyria and Babylon), they warned of dangers ahead. But even more, they interpreted *why* these catastrophes were occurring. And then, as the disasters descended, they sought to awaken hope in a new and better future (and especially so as Persia took charge of their ancient Near Eastern world).

This story and the prophets' place in it may be outlined as follows:

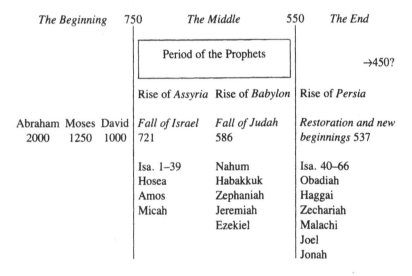

The Beginning	750	The Middle	550	The End
		Period of the Prophets		→450?
		Rise of *Assyria* Rise of *Babylon*	Rise of *Persia*	
Abraham Moses David		*Fall of Israel* *Fall of Judah*	*Restoration and new*	
2000 1250 1000		721 586	*beginnings* 537	
		Isa. 1–39 Nahum	Isa. 40–66	
		Hosea Habakkuk	Obadiah	
		Amos Zephaniah	Haggai	
		Micah Jeremiah	Zechariah	
		Ezekiel	Malachi	
			Joel	
			Jonah	

Questions for Review

1. What hints or indications do the editors of the prophetic books themselves give us as to the importance of history for a correct understanding of these books?

2. Why are the historical works they have provided for reconstructing the background history of the prophets referred to by modern

scholars as "the Deuteronomic history"? What books of the Bible make up this history, and what in outline is the story they tell?

3. Where do the prophets fit into this story? How does this historical background begin to clarify why these prophets appear in clusters at the times that they do?

3

What Is Prophecy?

A. Inductive Divinizing

Having identified the prophetic books we are going to study, having located the date and place of the men referred to in their headings (and having also now discussed their historical setting), a few words about prophecy as such may be in order. What is a prophet? What did it mean in the time of the prophets to prophesy?

In answering, it is important to recall, to begin with, how intensely religious the age was during which these prophets lived. Not only in Israel, but throughout the ancient world it was simply taken for granted that divine forces were at work influencing and shaping all aspects of human existence. It was an urgent matter therefore to find out, if one could, what these forces were like and how to deal with them. The various ways employed for contacting this realm, or influencing it, can be referred to as "divinizing." Students of divinizing in ancient cultures classify the various techniques and approaches followed as either "inductive" or "intuitive" (see Koch, I, p. 7). A brief description of each of these will help us locate Hebrew prophecy in its wider cultural context.

By far the most prevalent mode of divinizing in the world of the prophets was by means of "inductive" divinizing. By "inductive" is meant the direct study or observations of concrete objects, in this case with the goal in mind of obtaining divinely revealed knowledge. In ancient Mesopotamia, for example, if one wished for divine guidance regarding some matter, an expert in liver divinization might be consulted. After listening to the request, the diviner would sacrifice an animal, then examine the creases of its liver for clues to the will of the god whose advice had been sought (see Ez 21:26 for a biblical reference to this practice).

Similarly, patterns of oil on water, or smoke rising from an incense burner, or birds in flight, or dreams, or stellar events were also thought to yield divine revelations when studied by an expert in this way. Peculiar daily events such as tears in the eyes of an ox, or a scorpion lurking in one's bed, or pigs gnashing their teeth might also yield divine meanings to those aware of their true significance. It has been estimated that thirty percent of the twenty to thirty thousand extant tablets from the library of King Asherbanipal at Nineveh have to do with omens of this nature—an indication of the fascination people had in that culture for this mode of divinizing.

Examples of divinizing practices of this type are to be found worldwide in almost every culture (see *Oracles and Divination* by Loewe and Blacker). Even today in our supposedly enlightened modern cultures palm readers and astrologers are still popular, the assumptions being that supernatural knowledge may be obtained through the study of objects by experts who know how to interpret them. Inductive divinizing is thus viewed as a science of sorts by its practitioners.

B. Intuitive Divinizing

However, this was not the only way people of the ancient Near East believed contact might be established with the realm of the divine. The gods might also on occasion take the initiative, it was thought, and *speak* through the "intuitions" of chosen messengers. So, for example, in letters from eighteenth century Mari (a city of the Mesopotamian region) we read of "ecstatics" or "speakers" who heard the voice of their god speaking to them while in ecstasy, or at night through dreams. Insights received in this manner would then be conveyed to those for whom they were intended in the form of "messages" of the god who had so spoken. As we shall soon see, this is a speech-form that occurs often in the Bible, and in the books of the prophets especially. It will be worth our while, therefore, to examine it more carefully.

It was not of course just diviners who received and delivered "messages" in the world of that time. The bearer of messages was an important figure generally in ancient Near Eastern societies. Being without telephones, to communicate at a distance one had either to send a letter or summon a "messenger." If a messenger was used, the message would be spoken and memorized, then carried orally to those to whom it was being sent. A peculiarity of this mode of transmission was that the message would then be delivered as though the sender of the message was *himself* present and speaking.

This required that the messenger begin by identifying the one who had sent him. If, for example, it was a certain king, he might say: "King So-and-so says this!" Then would follow the message, spoken as though the king himself were speaking: "I request that you come at once to the palace to give account of your conduct!" (the message of the sender). Again at the close of his message, the messenger might repeat the name of the one who had sent him: "says King So-and-so!"

A vivid portrait of such a secular messenger at work is afforded by a report in 2 Kings 18:17–37. There we read of the servant of an Assyrian monarch who had been sent to Jerusalem to persuade the leaders there to surrender. To the representatives of King Hezekiah of Judah who came out to meet him, he began by saying: "Say to Hezekiah, 'The great king, the king of Assyria, says this' " (identification formula). This is followed by a recitation of the king's message spoken as though the king himself were present:

> What makes you so confident? Do you think empty words are as good as strategy and military strength? Whom are you relying on, to dare to rebel against *me*? . . . And lastly, have *I* marched on this place to lay it waste without warrant from Yahweh? Yahweh himself said to *me:* March on this country and lay it waste (2 Kgs 18:20–25).

Note too, in this instance, how, when rebuked for speaking such provocative words in the hearing of the people who were listening from the walls (2 Kgs 18:26), this skillful messenger boldly repeated his message in a slightly revised form to make it even more forceful (2 Kgs 18:28–35). From this we can see how autonomous such messengers were in the carrying out of their missions. As personal representatives of the one who sent them, they acted on their sender's behalf with all the intellectual and intuitive powers at their command.

It was in precisely this way, seemingly, that intuitive diviners of the ancient Near East viewed their experiences with their gods. The "thoughts" that would come to them from time to time, while in ecstasy or asleep, were experienced as divine messages to be delivered to those with whom they had to do. Thus in delivering them, they would be spoken in the same "messenger-speech" form used by secular messengers—that is, in the name of the god who had inspired them, in the first-person of that god, as though the god were present and speaking. From the sources available to date, however, it appears that compared to inductive divinizing, this intuitive mode of divinizing was relatively rare in the cultures of the ancient Near East.

C. Israelite Prophecy

Just the opposite was the case among the Israelites, it seems. There inductive divinizing was rare, while intuitive divinizing appears to have been the predominant mode of contacting God—and from Israel's earliest period of history onward.

The outstanding example of *inductive* divinizing in Israel was the use of certain material objects called "urim" and "thummim" (Dt 33:8). These, it seems, could be manipulated by experts (in this instance Levitical priests) to obtain what were believed to be "yes" or "no" answers from God. David is said to have made frequent use of this divinizing technique during the early stages of his career (1 Sam 23:6, 9–12; 30:7–10). Later on, however, even this mode of inquiry disappears, for we read of it no more after the fall of Jerusalem in 586. It may have never been widely employed.

Instead, when divine help or advice was needed, a more typical response among the Israelites appears to have been to call upon a "prophet" or "seer" (1 Sam 9:6–11). These were diviners of the *intuitive* type, as the terms themselves imply. The Hebrew word translated "prophet" (*nabi'*) means either "one who is called" or "one who calls" (proclaims). In Jeremiah 18:18 it is said of such a person that whereas priests teach and wise men give advice, a prophet (*nabi'*) speaks a "word" or message. Thus a prophet in Israel was thought of as someone who received divine messages which were then spoken to those to whom the prophet was sent. Even a glance at the books of the Hebrew prophets will reveal (as already noted) that the biblical prophets did this in precisely the same manner as intuitive prophets generally in the ancient Near East (that is, as "messengers" bringing first-person divine messages; see Am 1:3–2:16, for example). Because prophets of this kind were thought to be especially close to the God who sent them, they were sometimes also referred to as "men of God" (1 Sam 9:6, and elsewhere).

Another term for "prophet" in Israel was "seer" (Hebrew: *ro'eh* or *chozeh*—1 Sam 9:9, 11; 2 Sam 24:11; Am 7:12). This expression hints at the way prophets of this type typically received the divine words that flooded their consciousness. This might happen, as in the case of Jeremiah, as they were gazing at an almond tree blossoming (Jer 1:11–12), or a potter at work (Jer 18:1–12). An especially graphic account of such a "seer" in action can be found in Numbers 23–24 where we are told of a certain Balaam whom the king of Moab had hired to curse Israel, just prior to its entry into Canaan (Num 22:5–6). But as he gazed upon Israel's tents so beautifully spread out before him, it was not curses that flooded his mind, but intimations of Israel's future greatness.

As the frequent references to such prophet-seers in our biblical sources indicate, the divine insights of such men were as seriously attended to in Israelite society as were the thoughts of wise men and priests—indeed, in many instances, more so. Some prophet-seers of this kind were affiliated with worship centers where they could be regularly consulted on matters as trivial as finding lost donkeys (1 Sam 9). Others were isolated figures who, prompted by the voice within them, acted alone and with complete autonomy to anoint kings (1 Sam 10), or divide kingdoms (1 Kgs 11:26–39), or challenge an entire people to put away false gods (1 Kgs 17). Then again we read of them living in separate communities with other prophets (2 Kgs 2), or in groups associated with kings' palaces (1 Kgs 22).

All, however, seem to have had one thing in common. They were not inductive divinizers of the type common in the ancient world, but rather "heard" God speaking and on this basis brought "messages." Indeed, in at least one famous text, Deuteronomy 18:9–12, the point is made that the kind of inductive divinizing in vogue among Israel's neighbors is "detestable" by comparison with the wonderful way Israel's God, Yahweh, speaks through his prophets. Here the founder-prophet Moses is singled out as the model figure. Yahweh, it is said, will "raise up" a prophet like him "from among your own brothers" and that is the kind of prophet to be heeded, not the other kind. Elsewhere it is said of this same Moses that Yahweh spoke to him "plainly," "face to face," and not in riddles or dreams (Num 12:6–8). Where such prophets are present (and the promise is given in Deuteronomy 18:18 that such prophets will be available to Israel in each generation) alternative-type diviners and soothsayers are not only detestable; they are superfluous.

What manner of persons then, in summary, were the Israelite prophets? They were diviners of the intuitive type. Their messages came to them not by deciphering obscure objects, but as inspired thoughts. The more precise conditions for the reception of such thoughts, in their case, will become clear as our study proceeds. It might be noted in a preliminary way, however, that they do not seem to have valued ecstatic moods to the same extent as the Mari prophets, for example. *Their* messages were born, it seems, in a quieter frame of mind, while meditating or at prayer. Indeed, Jeremiah tells us in one of his more revealing self-disclosures that at times divine thoughts forced their way into *his* consciousness even when he did not want them to (20:8–9). This suggests that the greatest of Israel's prophets might be thought of as messengers of *unsolicited* thoughts that broke in upon their consciousness in spite of themselves, sometimes.

D. The God of the Prophets

But who was it who inspired these prophets of Israel in this way? In the world of the prophets there were many gods, many religions. Seen in this context, it is not enough to know simply *that* they were prophets, or what kind of prophets they were (prophets of the intuitive type). One must also ask what God it was these prophets believed had summoned them to be his messengers. His name appears on virtually every page of their books. Indeed, their revelations regarding him are among their most urgent and substantive messages. Who was he, and what did he mean to them?

Two observations may help us in beginning to get acquainted with this preeminent feature of the prophetic world: the God who spoke to the prophets was understood by them to have (1) a quite specific name, and (2) a quite well-defined character.

1. God's Name

The name of the God of the prophets faces us on almost every page of their writings. It is not to God in the abstract that they refer so repetitiously and eloquently as author of their messages, but to a God bearing a unique and particular name: Yahweh (not "Lord," substituted for this name in most translations; see below). This, of course, is the same name for God found elsewhere throughout the Old Testament Scriptures. It is the name repeatedly invoked in prayer in the psalter. It is the name of the one who is regarded as the giver of the laws in the law codes of Exodus, Leviticus and Deuteronomy. It is the name pointed to in the Book of Proverbs as the source of true wisdom ("the fear of Yahweh is the beginning of wisdom"). It was the divine name given to Moses when at the burning bush he wished to know who it was that was speaking to *him* there (Ex 3:16). It is the name of the God who subsequently guided Moses in bringing Israel out of slavery and in whose name they settled in their new Canaanite homeland.

So important was this name to the devout in Israel that protecting it from abuse or misuse was one of the three most important religious duties (Ex 20:3–7). In fact, in the course of time so holy did it become that the Jewish people stopped using it altogether, even when reading their sacred Scriptures. It was they who began the tradition of substituting a title for this name, *Adonai* or "Lord" instead of Yahweh. Since then most Christian translators have done the same, the outstanding exception being the *Jerusalem Bible.*

A title, however, is no substitute for a name. The title "Lord" (in Hebrew: *Adonai*), for example, points to a role or function and can be applied interchangeably to a variety of people. As a result it is somewhat abstract (like King, Queen, President). A *name* on the other hand is unique to the person bearing it (even if the same name is used for a variety of people). Individuals become closely and emotionally associated with their names. Hence, to know the names of people is to have access to their inner being. It is a preeminently personal way of establishing a bond with them.

Moreover, names may have meanings symbolic of the qualities of the people who bear them. In any event such was the case in the world of the prophets where children's names were frequently chosen with an eye to unique circumstances or characteristics of the children involved (see Gen 21:4; 25:25–26; 30:24; 1 Sam 4:21). This is why in a study of the prophets it is by no means irrelevant to note the meaning of their names (as we shall).

What then is the meaning of "Yahweh"? What flooded the minds of those who invoked it in prayer or praise or received messages from the one bearing it (as did the prophets)? We cannot be certain of this, but some think the name itself, in Hebrew, may be a third-person causative form of the verb "to be." If so, its meaning would be: "He causes to be" (or creates). Hence, it may be conjectured that Yahweh was revered above all as a God who "causes to be" or creates.

If we ask *what* it was he had created to have merited this attribution, the answer seems to be: he had created a people! This, in any case, is what is explicitly stressed about him in the Deuteronomic Song of Moses: "Is this [Yahweh] not your father, who *made* you, by whom you subsist" (Dt 32:6). Psalm 100 says the very same thing:

> Acclaim Yahweh, all the earth,
> serve Yahweh with gladness,
> come into his presence with songs of joy!
> Be sure that Yahweh is God,
> he *made* us, we belong to him,
> his people, the flock of his sheepfold (Ps 100:1–3).

For the prophets then, God was no abstraction, but a living reality bearing a name that itself bears testimony to his father-like power and grace in creating a people (see Is 1:2; Hos 11:1–4; Is 63:16).

2. God's Character

But the God of the prophets not only had a name. He was also viewed as having a well-defined character, one marked by two qualities especially: compassion and zeal (or "jealousy" as it is sometimes referred to).

Christians are especially vulnerable to mistaken notions at this point. They are prone to think of the Old Testament God as an angry deity who is quick to punish his people when they sin. Many believe that it was Jesus who first taught us that God is compassionate and loving. On the contrary, if the Israelites generally, and the prophets in particular, were certain of anything, it was that Yahweh was kind and gracious. For had he not delivered the Israelites from slavery in Egypt (Ex 20:2)? And had he not given them good laws to live by (Ps 19:7–11)? And had he not brought them to a wonderful land and delivered them again and again from their enemies there (Jgs 5; Am 2:9; Ps 33)? "Yahweh, Yahweh, God of tenderness and compassion, slow to anger, rich in faithful love and constancy . . ." (Ex 34:7). These are the words Moses heard regarding Yahweh his God when he passed before him early one morning on Mount Sinai (34:1–5). If we are going to understand the prophets, it is essential that we remember that for *them* Yahweh was first and foremost (and above everything else) a God of compassion.

However, compassion and tenderness were not his only qualities. For it was also said of him that he was a zealous (or "jealous") God (Ex 20:5; 32:16; 34:14) in the sense that he wanted his people to have *no other gods* (Ex 20:3; Dt 5:7). It was this unique quality that prompted the Israelite people to proclaim his "oneness" (Dt 6:4), and then eventually that he *alone* is God and there is no other (Is 45:14).

In summary then: the God of the prophets had a name, Yahweh. It characterized him as the exalted Father-Creator of his people. In addition, he was regarded as kind, forgiving and good, but also as jealous in his desire to be his people's only God.

Obviously, these few comments regarding the God of the prophets do not exhaust the subject. Perhaps they will help us begin our study with some sensitivity to the importance of this facet of their experience for the messages they were inspired to bring.

Questions for Review

1. What is meant by divinizing? How would you differentiate between "inductive" and "intuitive" modes of divinizing?

2. How did prophets of the "intuitive type" regard their insights? Why might it be said that they were "messengers"? How did messengers go about performing their task in the world of that time? What form was followed in presenting their messages to those to whom they were sent?

3. What comparisons can be drawn between Israelite "divinizers" and those of the ancient Near East generally? What words does the Bible use for prophets? What do these terms suggest regarding the kind of divinizers they were? Indicate how the forms of divinizing mentioned in Deuteronomy 18:9–12 may be viewed in the light of our discussion of the two types of divinizing that prevailed in the ancient Near East generally?

4. Indicate two key characteristics of the God of the prophets. To what extent do these qualities correspond to your own views of God?

4

A Prophetic Book
and How To Study It

A. What Is a Prophetic Book?

For the most part, so far, our discussion has been focused on the prophetic *figures* whose names are referred to in the headings of the prophetic books. These were the men whose prophetic activity gave rise to these books. But now we want to turn to a consideration of the prophetic *books*. What kind of books are these?

As already intimated (see our opening ''Note to the Reader''), they appear to be anthologies—that is, collections of shorter literary units into larger compendia. However, if that is the case, it is by no means obvious who created these, or why, or on what basis, for upon opening a prophetic book we note immediately that apart from their brief headings there are no introductions or tables of contents to assist us in answering such questions. Furthermore, even when we get more closely acquainted with these books, we are often baffled by their seeming lack of organization. Why is this? By what process *were* these books assembled and preserved?

As a first step in answering these questions it should be recalled that none of the prophets referred to in the headings of these books were writers or authors of books. Rather (as just noted), their task was to be ''messengers'' of the God who inspired them. This means that their initial goal was to transmit messages or ''words'' in an oral mode to quite specific individuals or groups. It is possible, of course, that some of these ''words'' may have been jotted down either before or after their oral delivery. One has the impression, for example, that Hosea and Jeremiah may have kept a journal of sorts (see our introductory comments to their books). Also, occasionally, we read of the prophets being told quite explicitly to write down their messages (see for example Is 8:1–4, 16; Jer 29:1–23; ch. 36). So the prophets did also write, but this writing was always in the service of their role as divine messengers to particular peoples, times and places. Only as a *second step* were their messages preserved and assembled into larger books or scrolls.

This simple fact alone helps to explain several outstanding features of the prophetic books. With this in mind we can now begin to understand, for example, why individual literary units are often so tersely focused and yet, seemingly, unrelated to what precedes or follows them. This is because they were not initially composed for inclusion in a book, but were spoken or addressed to particular audiences, one by one, at specific times and places. Those who organized these books did not themselves know, in many instances, precisely when and where these individual units were first spoken.

But how then, if that were the case, *did* it happen that messages that were at first spoken on specific occasions came to be written down and collected in this way? The answer is nowhere given in so many words. We must guess at it on the basis of many small observations. In some instances, it would seem, the prophets themselves may have begun this process (see again Is 8:16; Jer 36). But, from early on, others would have become involved as well. These would be those who had come to recognize a given prophet as an authentic messenger of God. Stories *about* the prophets (biographical anecdotes) are to be found in many of their books (Am 7:10–17; Hos 1:2–9; Is 7, for example). Such were no doubt originally from persons like this and their very existence testifies to the role that "friends" of the prophets may have had in the process of preserving, writing down, collecting and editing their messages.

We must not think, however, that even those initial "friends" (or disciples) were the only ones to have had a hand in shaping these collections. When reading a prophetic book we must put aside our modern notions of how books are published and circulated. At the time these books were composed, as noted in chapter 1, documents of this kind were written on scrolls. These had to be *re*written periodically if their contents were not to be lost. Each such occasion presented the custodians of these documents with a new opportunity for reediting, correcting, clarifying and supplementing them. This would naturally be done with an eye to improving their value for the community for which they were being preserved. The hand of such transcribers and editors is evident, for example, in the headings of these books (some of which may have been added decades or even centuries after the books first began to circulate).

A prophet, we have said, was a messenger of God to a particular person or group at a specific time and place. What then, in summary, is a prophetic *book?*

The comments just made confirm the impression that they are anthologies of messages of the men whose names they bear. But we have also become aware of the possible contributions of those who preserved them. Friends of the prophets had a hand in adding prophetic anecdotes and notes. Later readers and transcribers may have also shaped them in certain ways. A prophetic book is thus not only an anthology of the words of a certain prophet. It is a collection of his words as edited and amplified by those who preserved them for the benefit of future generations.

To be more specific, a prophetic book typically contains at least four types of material (as we shall soon discover): (1) prophetic *messages* (often in the form of first-person God-speeches of the type earlier discussed); (2) words of the prophet *regarding himself* and his experiences (autobiographical memoirs or reports, they might be called); (3) third party *stories* or reports (from friends of the prophet); (4) explanatory *notes* of one kind or another from the hands of editors or transcribers, often of an historical or interpretative nature (such as the headings to these books).

B. How to Study These Books

It goes without saying that the nature of a book determines how to go about studying it. A volume of poetry is approached differently than a book of history and a book of history differently than a novel. In the light of all that we have learned so far about the prophets and their books how shall *they* be studied?

From what has just been said it should be clear that the prophetic writings themselves elicit a dual focus. Some of the texts or passages we encounter there will have us concentrating our attention on a specific prophet and the relevance of *his* messages for the people of *his* time. Other passages or texts will turn our thoughts toward those who edited these books and *their* thoughts as *they* interpreted these writings for their time and place.

What shall we do with this double focus?

Our primary interest as we read these books, I suggest, is the same as that of those who first preserved and edited them. Like them, we want above all to hear and understand the messages of *those whose names these books bear*. It is they who originated the tradition preserved in them. It was their prophetic mission that these books are intent upon preserving for the benefit of future generations. Of course, the editorial additions and supplements of those who did this preserving interest us as well, but mostly insofar as these prod us to do in our time what they sought to do in theirs: that is, to try to capture the *ongoing* relevance of these prophets for our own time and place.

An initial task, therefore, as we take up our study of these books will be to distinguish, if we can, between those texts in these collections that are from the prophets whose names the books bear and those that have been added by the compilers and editors. This will require, as a first step, that we look at a given book *as a whole* in order to get some sense of its *compositional history*. Because the editors of these books were not always careful to maintain such distinctions (as would modern editors, for example), this will not always be easy to do, and the results of our efforts in this regard will therefore not always be as satisfying as we might wish. Nevertheless, the attempt to do this is mandatory and often worthwhile. It will also be discovered that once this step is taken further study is definitely made easier. For then, in most instances, we will have gotten some sense of a book's overall organization and will have begun as well to locate the types of literature referred to above. In short, our way into and around a prophetic book will have become significantly easier.

Then too we will be ready for a next step in our study: to discover *what can be known about the prophet named by that book as its point of origin*. As noted earlier, these prophets were no mere conduits of the messages they brought, but personal representatives of the one who sent them. Eloquent testimony is born to the dignity and importance of their role in this regard by the preservation of their names. The authors of many biblical books are totally unknown to us. But we *know* the names of almost all of the prophets, and in some instances much more—details about when and where they lived, what work they were engaged in at the time of their call, and how they were commissioned to their task.

To become acquainted with what can be known about these prophets is therefore a most essential next step, for only then will we be able to turn to a study of a prophet's *messages* and understand them as they were meant to be understood by those who first heard them. And when we have done that, then we can take a final step as well and reflect on their *ongoing relevance* both for those who edited these books and for us today.

These then, in summary, are the steps that the prophetic books themselves invite us to take in studying them:

(1) First, lacking as they do their own introductions, we must in-

itially scan them as a whole to become acquainted with their overall organization and compositional history.

(2) Second, following the lead of their editors (and their headings), we turn next to what can be learned about the prophets themselves whose missions gave rise to these books.

(3) Third, we look then more carefully at their messages within the setting of the times in which they were initially given.

(4) Finally, we pause to reflect on the ongoing relevance these books have had both for those who preserved them and today.

It is with these steps in mind that I have adopted the following outline for my approach to the prophetic books we will be studying: (a) the book as a whole, (b) the man behind the book, (c) his message, and (d) the ongoing relevance of that message. I would only emphasize yet that *prior* to reading what I will have to say in this regard students should themselves read the book being studied and form their own impressions. Then what I have written can serve as a stimulus, not a substitute for first-hand independent study.

C. Why Study Them?

How might we expect to benefit from such a study? The importance of this literature will, I trust, become evident as our study proceeds. But I have been suggesting that the reading of these books can be difficult at points. It is worth asking, therefore, already here at the threshold of our study, why we should put forth the effort to do so. We might answer by pointing to the fact that these books are, after all, in the Bible. But this would still leave us wondering why *this* is so. What is it that prompted those who preserved these books to single them out in this way? Why even today, apart from this fact, do they elicit the respect they do and merit our serious attention?

An outstanding characteristic of the prophetic books is the way they focus on Israel's future—and then increasingly on the future of the world. As noted, the world of the prophets was a turbulent one. During their time military superpowers were ravaging the smaller nations of their region. What was happening? One after another these men arose with an answer. Yahweh, Israel's God, was behind these developments, they said. The nations of this region were being punished because of their sins. But what then of the future? Would there even be a future? Could a people who had lost its way as badly as Israel had ever recover? If so, how and when? And what about the world generally? Is there any hope of things ever getting any better anywhere in this sin-prone, tumultuous universe? These were some of the questions that increasingly preoccupied the prophets we will be studying.

As such, they may be characterized as inspired interpreters of history, as pioneering social analysts and futurologists—among the first in history to take a hard look at what is *really* wrong with our world and to begin thinking about what might be needed to set it right. We are of course still intensely concerned with such questions, perhaps more so than ever before, faced as we are with the possibility of global self-destruction through war or pollution. Is it possible that individually and as a group these prophetic classics might still have something to teach us in this regard?

But there is yet another reason for studying them. Since Karl Jaspers' pioneering study of world history (*The Origin and Goal of History*), we have become conscious of the fact that these prophets were part of an intellectual awakening that was worldwide. At about the same time that they were speaking in Israel, Socrates and Plato were teaching on the streets of Athens, Gautama Buddha was beginning his mission in India, Confucius and Lao-tze were spreading their teachings in China, and in Persia the prophet Zoroaster appeared. A characteristic of all these figures was their critique of the prevailing nature religions and the mythological thought structures that sustained them. This contributed to the decline or death of these older faiths, and in some instances to the fading of religious consciousness altogether.

The prophets too, as we shall soon see, brought a critique to bear upon the religions of their time, but in their case, certainly, this did not result in the fading of faith in their God. On the contrary, as the primary source of their insights God became even wiser, stronger and greater in their eyes. And the confirmation of these insights through the fulfillment of their prophecies in the destruction and restoration of Israel (in the eighth to sixth centuries) gave rise to the conviction that their God was alone God. In this way "ethical monotheism" was born, and *reason and faith* emerged together in a synthesis that has proven to be exemplary for the religion of the Bible, and subsequently for western consciousness.

This too is an issue that remains with us. Indeed, in our time especially faith and reason often threaten to go separate ways. The relevance of the prophets lies not only in *what* they say about the world and its future, but in the intelligence with which they say it—the way they help us *think* about present and future in the *light of God*.

Why then study the prophets? There are many reasons, but these certainly are two of them: as a stimulus to our putting reason and faith back together and as a provocation to think seriously about the future of *our* world and what might be required for it to become a better place for all.

This we will attempt to do in the chapters that follow, beginning with Amos, chronologically the first of the prophets.

Questions for Review

1. Why is it misleading to think of the prophets as the authors of their books? What bearing does an understanding of how a prophetic book originated have for the approach we take to its study? Why is it important to begin the study of these books with an analysis of their compositional histories? What justifies our also spending some time studying who the prophets were as individuals before looking at their messages?

2. What questions are uppermost in your mind as you begin this study? What motivates you in pursuing it? In what sense might the prophets be regarded as part of a worldwide intellectual awakening? How might we characterize them as thinkers? On what issues were they focused? What role did faith play in their thought?

SECTION TWO

THE PROPHETS OF THE ASSYRIAN PERIOD

Woe to those who call what is bad, good,
and what is good, bad,
who substitute darkness for light
and light for darkness,
who substitute bitter for sweet
and sweet for bitter.

Is 5:20

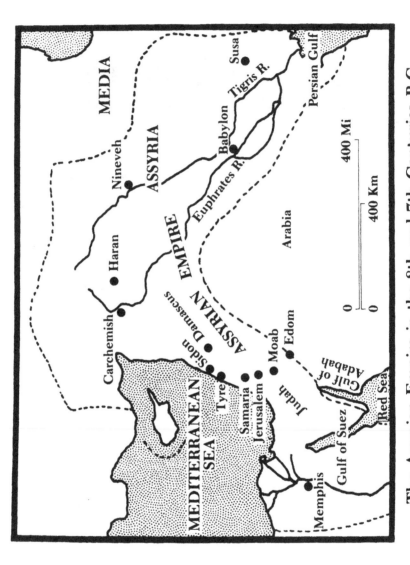

The Assyrian Empire in the 8th and 7th Centuries B.C.

5

Amos of Tekoa

It is generally recognized that Amos was the first of the Israelite prophets whose words were assembled in a scroll, although three others (Hosea, Isaiah and Micah) were his near contemporaries. In getting acquainted with his book the steps outlined in the previous chapter will be followed: we will look first at the book as a whole (its organization and compositional history), then at the prophet (the man behind the book), then at his message, and finally at the ongoing relevance of his message. However, before looking at my comments on these topics, be sure to read the book yourself and form your own impressions.

A. The Book as a Whole

Compared with other prophetic books the Book of Amos is well organized. There are hints, however, that it too (like the other prophetic books) was compiled by "friends" and grew by stages. It is not the product of Amos alone.

A good place to begin an analysis of the book's compositional history is with its heading: "The *words* of Amos one of the shepherds of Tekoa. The *visions* he had about Israel in the time of Uzziah king of Judah and Jeroboam son of Joash, king of Israel, two years before the earthquake" (1:1). The observation has been made (Wolff) that we seem to have here not one but two headings: the first referring to "*words* of Amos" and identifying his background ("one of the shepherds of Tekoa"); the other referring to "*visions*" he had and when he had them (during the reigns of certain kings or, more precisely, "two years before the earthquake"). Is it possible that each of these headings (awkwardly linked in Hebrew) may have once stood at the head of originally independent collections: one a collection of Amos' words, the other a collection of his visions?

This possibility is supported by what we observe when we scan the book as a whole. There appear to be at least three distinct parts:

Part 1 opens with a relatively long series of messenger speeches, in 1:3–2:14 (note the short oracles introduced and concluded with the messenger formula, "Yahweh says this . . . Yahweh says."

Part 2 extends through chapter 6 and begins with the phrase, in 3:1: "Listen, Israelites, to this prophecy . . ." followed by additional admonitions to "listen" (3:13; 4:1; 5:1, "Listen to this word which I utter against you").

Part 3, chs. 7 to 9, includes a rare biographical anecdote and appears to be organized around personal reports of five visions: 7:1–9; 8:1–2; 9:1–4.

How might the titles to the book noted above, in 1:1, relate to these three sections? Clearly, the second title (with its reference to "the visions" Amos had) would be appropriate as a heading for the collection of five visions, in 7:1–9:4.

Wolff (Amos commentary) has suggested that likewise the first title (with its reference to "words of Amos") would be well suited as a heading for Amos 3 to 6. While it is true that some "words" in this section are, strictly speaking, not "words of Amos," but "words of Yahweh," all were spoken by him and many are presented in the form of insights of Amos himself, not as Yahweh oracles (for example, 3:3–8; 5:1–3, 7–15, 18–20; 6:1–7, 12). In other words, in this section an unusual number of Amos' own thoughts and observations are located, in addition to certain Yahweh prophecies. One also notes that peculiar to this section is the repetition of his personal admonition to: "Listen!" (3:13), "Listen to this oracle . . ." (3:1; 4:1), "Listen to this word which *I* utter against you . . ." (5:1). Wolff's suggestion that Amos himself may have had a hand in assembling this section of his book is therefore worth considering.

Thus, originally, there may have been two independent collections of Amos materials: a collection of his visions (chs. 7–9) and a collection of his words (chs. 3–6).

But what then shall we make of the long passage that opens his book, in 1:3–2:16? Was this perhaps, at some point, yet another collection independent of the other two, or shall we think of it as perhaps part of either Amos' collected "words" or "visions"? Notice that this section differs significantly from the "words of Amos" collection immediately following, in that here it is stressed throughout that these are "words of Yahweh" (note the messenger formula, "Yahweh says this," in 1:3, 6, 9, 11, 13; 2:1, 4, 6). It seems unlikely therefore that they were originally linked to the collection that follows.

Are they related then in any way to chs. 7–9 (the visions collection)? An allusion at the end of this section to an earthquake ("I shall crush you where you stand"; 2:13) may hint of this—it seems to parallel the one in the fifth vision (9:1–4) where Amos hears "the Lord" summoning an earthquake that will topple a temple on the heads of its worshipers. So both sections, chs. 1–2 and 7–9, culminate in an allusion to an approaching earthquake, perhaps the one alluded to in the heading to the visions collection (1:1b). Wolff conjectures that 1:3–2:16 and chs. 7–9 were both assembled in the approximate form we now have them at about the same time by disciples of Amos who believed that his predictions of an approaching catastrophe were in part fulfilled when an unusually powerful earthquake struck their region just two years after Amos first prophesied (I will be saying more about this earthquake a bit later).

The book of Amos appears then to have existed originally in two independent collections: one entitled, "words of Amos one of the shepherds of Tekoa" (chs. 3–6); the other, "the visions he had . . . two years before the earthquake" (7:1–9:4 and 1:3–2:16). Amos himself may have been responsible for assembling the "words-of-Amos" collection. However, the "visions" collection bears the marks of having been put together by disciples of Amos who actually experienced the earthquake referred to in the heading. In any case, they, not Amos, must be thought of as responsible for the third-person anecdote, in 7:10–17. These same disciples were also, no doubt, the ones to whom Amos transmitted his "words" collection (chs. 3–6). This they eventually expanded by adding at the front and back their own collections (combining the headings of each collection, as they did so).

This stage of the developing book may be diagrammed as follows:

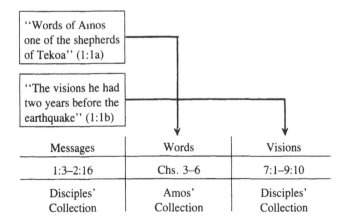

"Words of Amos one of the shepherds of Tekoa" (1:1a)		
"The visions he had two years before the earthquake" (1:1b)		
Messages	Words	Visions
1:3–2:16	Chs. 3–6	7:1–9:10
Disciples' Collection	Amos' Collection	Disciples' Collection

Some commentators believe that a final stage in the development of this book occurred when the time reference in the heading, "two years before the earthquake," was coordinated with the Book of Kings (note the references to the reigns of Jeroboam and Uzziah in 1:1) and there was also added an introductory caption (1:2), referring to God's presence in Zion ("Yahweh roars from Zion . . ."), and a concluding prophecy referring to God's promise to restore the Davidic dynasty (9:11–15)—as well as a few supplementary words, here and there, within the body of the book itself: the Judah oracle, in 2:4–5; the remnant oracle, in 9:8b–10; and the three notable doxologies, in 4:13; 5:8–9; 9:5–6. With these supplements, it has been suggested, editors of the book living in the aftermath of the destruction of Israel (721) and Judah (586) linked the book to theological ideas current among those for whom they edited it. As we shall soon see, Amos addressed *his* messages primarily to Israel during the middle of the eighth century B.C. The third-person anecdote, in 7:10–17, informs us that when he was called to prophesy, he went not to Jerusalem, capital of Judah, but to Bethel, chief worship center of Israel. In other words, although Amos lived in Judean territory, for reasons we will discuss later, he was not at all focused on Judah-Jerusalem as such. Yet this is the focus of these editorial additions (see our discussion of the traditions unique to Jerusalem in chapters 2 and 9).

Thus these final editors of Amos, it seems, were persons of the Judaean-Jerusalem theological tradition who added the oracles at the beginning and end to render the book more meaningful to fellow students who shared their theological outlook (we will have more to say regarding these oracles at the conclusion of our study of Amos).

Looked at again, as a whole, the book of Amos may now be diagrammed as follows:

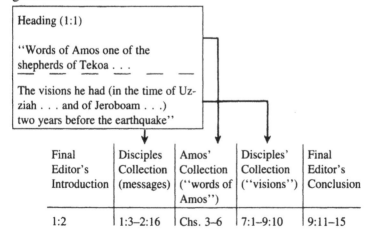

Heading (1:1)
"Words of Amos one of the shepherds of Tekoa . . .
The visions he had (in the time of Uzziah . . . and of Jeroboam . . .) two years before the earthquake"

Final Editor's Introduction	Disciples' Collection (messages)	Amos' Collection ("words of Amos")	Disciples' Collection ("visions")	Final Editor's Conclusion
1:2	1:3–2:16	Chs. 3–6	7:1–9:10	9:11–15

Students of Amos differ on some of the points just made regarding the compositional history of this book. These differences are not as important, however, as the fact that through careful study of this kind we can begin to sharpen our understanding of its leading features. Having gone through this exercise, we now have a better understanding of how it is organized, the types of literature it contains (visions, words, oracles, third-person anecdotes, editorial supplements and the like), as well as some feeling for how, possibly, it began with a "core collection" (chs. 3–6) that Amos himself may have assembled, then was enlarged by the collections of disciples, and then was preserved by editors who wanted to make sure its readers would not miss its relevance for them.

It will also be easier now to know how to approach the book so that Amos' own words and messages will be our primary focus rather than the book's editorial supplements. But before turning to that, we should note what the book tells us about the man Amos himself.

B. The Man Behind the Book

What impressions are you forming of Amos and his world? As noted, it is typical of a prophetic book to have a heading which gives us at least some information about the man through whom the words assembled there were delivered. This is significant. It indicates how important the editors of these books felt it was that we, their readers, are conscious of the fact that the prophetic words they assembled did not just fall from the skies. They were spoken by specific people under particular circumstances in unique times and places. The more we can know therefore about a given prophet the better we will be able to understand his message.

To assist us in our study of Amos the editors of his book have provided, first of all, the data in the book's heading (1:1), but also the story of his expulsion from Bethel, in 7:10–17. We have in addition Amos' own personal reports of certain visions (7:1–9; 8:1–2; 9:1–4). From these and other hints and suggestions in the messages themselves it is possible to gain a fairly vivid picture of Amos and his world.

1. Name

The name of this prophet is itself worth pondering. We encounter it right off in the heading (1:1), and it recurs in the accounts of his visions (twice he hears Yahweh asking him by name, "What do you see, Amos?"—7:8; 8:2), and then again in the story of his expulsion from

Bethel (7:10, 11, 12, 14). A highly individualized person bearing a quite specific name is an important "presence" in this book.

Even today personal names and their meanings are important. This was much more the case in the world of Amos. In fact, names given to Israelite sons can be translated into meaningful phrases or sentences. For example, Elkanah, father of Samuel (1 Sam 1:1), means: "El [God] has created [this son]." Elisha means: "El [God] is saviour," a confession of faith. Needless to say such names bear testimony to the spiritual world in which those bearing them lived and moved and had their being.

The name "Amos" is found only here in this book, in the Hebrew Bible, although it might be a shortened form of "Amasiah" (2 Chr 17:16). Amos means "carried" (or "he has carried"); Amasiah means: "Yah [or Yahweh] has carried" (the "-ah" at the end standing for "Yah," a shortened form of Yahweh). Does it then allude to the way Yahweh "carried" or "cared for" Amos, in bringing him to birth?

2. Occupation

We are not always told what a prophet did professionally before becoming a prophet (or even what he did to make a living thereafter). But where this is known, it too may shed light on the kind of person he was. In Amos' case, not only are we told what he did, but that he himself wanted this known to counteract false judgments regarding his motives. To the order that he leave Bethel and earn his living prophesying elsewhere, Amos replied in effect that this is not at all how he earned his living. He was a "herdsman and dresser of sycamore-figs" (7:14). Thus, he had no reason to prophesy for money, since he already *had* an occupation. His only reason for prophesying, he declared, was because God had summoned him to do so (7:13).

What then, more precisely, was it that Amos did to make a living? His statement, in 7:14, that he "was a herdsman and looked after sycamores" could be misleading. To most of us the word "herdsman" evokes the image of a lowly shepherd watching over a few sheep. Also, to tend sycamores is sometimes thought of as a poor man's job, for the sycamore is a fig tree whose fruit had to be scratched, one by one, before it would ripen properly—a tedious, dirty job done usually by day-laborers.

However, the parallel term, in 1:1, in Hebrew, to that of "herdsman," in 7:14, means "sheep-master" and refers to owners and managers of a very special kind of dwarfed sheep (bred and raised from ancient times in the Near East), and famous for its wool. In 2 Kings 3:4

this same term is used to describe the vocation of King Mesha of Moab ("Mesha King of Moab was a sheep-breeder and used to pay the King of Israel a hundred thousand lambs and a hundred thousand rams with their wool in tribute").

Far then from being a poor herdsman of sheep, Amos may have been one of the more substantial men of his region, and especially so in that he appears to have had a second source of income. The sycamore groves referred to would likely have been some distance from where Amos lived, for to grow properly they required the warmer climate of the Jordan valley where he would have taken his flocks for pasturing when the hills of Tekoa were barren.

3. Where He Lived

A third bit of information in the book's heading has to do with where Amos lived. He is referred to as belonging to the shepherds of *Tekoa*. Adding knowledge of where a person lived to our information about his work may afford us an even sharper focus on the kind of person he might have been. The archaeological remains of Tekoa lie some twelve miles southeast of Jerusalem, on a high hill (2800 feet above sea level), right at the point where the cultivated land ends and the uncultivated lands begin that slope down to the Dead Sea. Tekoa is mentioned elsewhere, in 2 Chronicles 11:6, as one of several cities that King Rehoboam (Solomon's son and successor) rebuilt and fortified after the breaking away of the ten northern tribes and the founding of the northern kingdom Israel (in 931). Rehoboam did this, the text says, "to keep Judah and Benjamin under control" (1 Chr 11:12). From the heights of Tekoa the world Amos refers to in his book was spread out before him like a gigantic map: Gilead, Ammon, Moab and Edom to the east, Jerusalem, Samaria and the regions of Damascus and Phoenicia to the north, Beersheba to the south, his own people Jacob, looking "so small" (7:2,5), right below him. Small wonder that in his times the heights of Tekoa served as a watch tower from which a warning could be sounded in advance of an approaching enemy (Jer 6:1).

This suggests that our picture of Amos must be enlarged a bit. He may have been a sheep-breeder, but he also lived in a strategically located fortified walled village that had strong ties to Jerusalem administratively and defensively. He might have had a house in this village to which he returned at night, even if he spent his days out with his herds. He would also, of course, have had to travel to larger cities (Samaria, Beersheba, Jerusalem, for example) to sell his produce there.

Others in his village were no doubt also managers of flocks and lived as he did (see 1:1), although some might have been more involved with farming than herding.

4. Lifestyle and Theology

What might life have been like among "the shepherds of Tekoa" (1:1)? What experiences did they have in their daily lives? What was their outlook on life? Amos' own words give us numerous hints.

For example, in Amos 3:3–6a we read:

> Do two people travel together
> unless they have agreed to do so?
> Does the lion roar in the forest
> if it has no prey?
> Does the young lion growl in his lair
> if it has caught nothing?
> Does a bird fall on the ground in a net
> unless a trap has been set for it?
> Will the net spring up from the ground
> without catching something?
> Does the trumpet sound in the city
> without the people being alarmed?

Each one of these questions (leading up to an explanation of why Amos felt he had to prophesy, in 3:8) offers a glimpse into the kind of world he lived in. It is one of wide open spaces where men meet only by appointment (3:3). The sound of lions growling over their prey is commonplace (3:4; 3:12). Bird-traps are set for unsuspecting fowl (3:5). Occasionally a trumpet blares, warning of danger (3:6). In another passage Amos likens the disasters that he is convinced are about to come upon his people to what happens "when someone runs away from a lion, only to meet a bear; he goes into his house and puts his hand on the wall, only for a snake to bite him" (5:19). Amos must have lived every day with dangers of this kind.

What a contrast such a life was to what Amos saw when he visited the bigger cities of his region! A shepherd only rarely ate one of his own sheep (their wool was too valuable), and drinking wine was an even greater rarity. In fact, some nomadic groups eschewed wine altogether (Jer 35). But in the cities Amos saw people dining regularly on stall-fattened veal and lambs from the flock and drinking wine by the bowlful (6:4, 6). Furniture in Tekoa, no doubt, was of the very simplest sort, if there was any at all, but in the cities Amos saw people lounging on couches and beds inlaid with ivory (6:4). Houses in his village were mostly built of burned brick or rough stone, but city dwellers, Amos observed, were building country houses for themselves with elaborately "dressed stone" (5:11).

Such marked differences in lifestyle must have grated on Amos' moral sensibilities long before God took him from following his flocks and said, "Go, prophesy . . ." (7:15).

It can be assumed that Amos' vigorous speech patterns were also rooted in the culture of this region (see Wolff, *Amos the Prophet*). The shepherds of Tekoa were not far removed from Israel's earlier clan life where elders transmitted the tribal legacy in a vigorous stylized pedagogy that made frequent use of questions and answers, repetitions, lists, aphorisms, comparisons, admonitions and exclamatory "woes" (warning of the consequences of foolish behavior)—as did Amos himself in conveying his messages.

Theologically too, it seems, the "sheep-breeders" of Tekoa were unique. Like others elsewhere in Israel, they were of course devout Yahwists and believed themselves to be a part of Yahweh's peculiarly known and loved people (Am 3:2; 7:15). But there is no evidence that Amos thought, as did the Yahwists of Jerusalem, that Yahweh was somehow especially present at Zion (Ps 132:13–14) or with the Davidic dynasty (Ps 132:12). Nor, strangely enough, does he ever mention the covenant Yahweh made at Sinai (as other prophets do). On the other hand, he is aware of the wonderful way Yahweh had helped Israel escape from Egypt (2:10; 9:7) and conquer Canaan (2:9). It is also absolutely evident to him that Israel's life in this land was to be guided and controlled by certain firm standards of right and wrong (2:6–7; 3:2).

In this light, what was happening at the Israelite shrines was especially abhorrent to him (4:4–5). In fact, Amos seems to view the sacrificing of animals going on there as a senseless novelty without precedent. "Did you bring me sacrifices and oblations those forty years in the desert, House of Israel?" he asks, implying, "No, you did not!" (5:25). Not at the shrines, but at the village "gates," he says—there where the elders meet to decide what is right and wrong (5:15)—*that* is where Israel's fate will be decided. But even there, he declares, justice is being turned into wormwood and uprightness thrown to the ground (5:7). When that happens, nothing else matters, for justice above all is what Yahweh requires of his people (5:24).

Where did Amos get ideas such as these? Wolff (*Amos the Prophet*) points to the fact that Amos alone among the prophets refers to Israel as "the House of *Isaac*" (7:16; see also 7:9). He is also the only prophet who mentions the Yahweh shrine at Beersheba (5:5; 8:14) which was founded by Isaac (see Gen 26:23, 33; 46:1–4). Isaac was the father both of Jacob (forefather of Israel) *and* of Esau, forefather of the Edomites (Gen 25:29–30), and they in turn were semi-nomadic neighbors of the Tekoans to their immediate south. Wolff conjectures that Amos may have had a special regard for these Edomite neighbors of his, perhaps even thinking of them as "brothers" (as they are called in Numbers 20:14 and Deuteronomy 23:8). The oasis at Beersheba would have been one of their meeting places. Moreover, Wolff observes, the Edomites were highly regarded in Old Testament times for their clan "wisdom" (1 Kgs 4:31; Jer 49:7; Ob 8; Job 2:11), as were the Tekoans (see the story of the wise woman of Tekoa in 2 Samuel 14:1–24).

Wolff concludes from all this that the breadth of Amos' outlook, his moral fervor, trenchant speech patterns and astute observations, may spring in part from his close associations with Tekoan *and* Edomite wisdom traditions.

5. Prophetic Call

And yet, this alone does not explain how Amos became a prophet. That happened, his disciples inform us, when Yahweh "took" him from herding his flocks and said: "Go and prophesy to my people Israel" (7:15). These words point to a divine intervention as the sole basis of his mission. What was true of Amos in this regard was true of all the prophets we are studying. They were not born prophets, but were called to this task by a highly personal summons from Yahweh himself.

What this experience entailed for Amos is alluded to by him in his first-person reports of five visions (see 7:1–9; 8:1–2; 9:1–4). In the first two of these he conveys something of the shock he felt when it was revealed to him that Yahweh was about to send locust plague and drought upon "Jacob" to destroy him (7:1–6). Locust plague and drought are among the worst disasters that can befall a people of that region. This experience brought Amos to the crushing realization that Yahweh was contemplating the destruction of his own people—an almost unimaginable thought for someone raised in a tradition that had emphasized Yahweh's compassion and goodness (see our comments on this point in chapter 3).

Amos' initial response was to plead for forgiveness (7:2) and ask Yahweh to "stop" (7:5). His fear was that Jacob "being so small" would be totally annihilated (7:2, 5). Astonishingly, his cry was heard. "Then Yahweh relented; 'It will not happen,' said Yahweh" (7:3, 6).

But these first two visions were followed by a third that left him speechless. What he saw this time was a man standing by a tottering wall, symbolic, we imagine, of the moral condition of Israel. In the man's hand was a plumb-line (held up to the wall). A voice was heard calling Amos by name. He was asked to identify what he was seeing. When he did so, a terrifying revelation suddenly flooded his consciousness: "Look, I [Yahweh] am going to put a plumb-line in among my people Israel; never again will I overlook their offenses" (7:8).

Then came this shocking sequel: an even greater catastrophe than locust plague or drought was about to befall Israel—a military invasion would soon sweep through the land! "The high places of Isaac will be ruined, and the sanctuaries of Israel laid waste, and, sword in hand, I will attack the House of Jeroboam" (7:9). Amos now knew that the frightful destruction of his region by war was imminent.

Visions four and five (8:1–2; 9:1–4) confirmed this frightening premonition. In vision four Israel was likened to a basket of rotting fruit "ripe" for destruction (8:2). In vision five the shadowy figure of Yahweh himself was seen already at work destroying a temple and slaughtering its visitants (9:1–4).

It is these visions of an impending catastrophe brought about by Yahweh through war, because he cannot any longer "overlook" Israel's offenses, that transformed the Tekoan sheep-breeder Amos into a prophet and compelled him to go to Bethel, chief shrine of the northern kingdom (7:14) with a shrill cry of warning on his lips (7:16).

6. Historical Setting

Seldom was a prophet so out of step with his times. Not since the days of King David had Israel been as powerful or prosperous as right then. King Uzziah of Judah and King Jeroboam of Israel were the rulers at this time (1:1). More precisely, it was two years before a certain earthquake (1:1b; see also the allusions to this quake in Amos 9:5 and Zechariah 14:5) which has been dated to the year 760 on the basis of archaeological evidence from the north-Galilean city of Hazor. This would locate Amos in the middle years of the long, exceptionally prosperous reigns of these kings. By then they had succeeded in extending the boundaries of their kingdoms northward and southward to an unprecedented degree (see 2 Kgs 14:25; 2 Chr 26; also Am 6:14). Small wonder that the "notables" in Zion and Samaria were as proud and self-confident as Amos describes them to be (see 6:1–7). Many believed Yahweh was blessing Israel as never before: a "day of Yahweh" must be imminent when Israel would triumph gloriously over all its foes (5:18).

These developments were made possible, however, by a set of rather peculiar events to the northeast where a people called the Assyrians (after their god Asshur) was becoming increasingly powerful. However, after a century of periodic military forays into Palestine, these Assyrians had become temporarily inactive in this region due to troubles on their own northern frontiers. Furthermore, Israel's more immediate neighbors to the north, the Syrians (Arameans), were also at this time quiescent because of a state of fatigue from earlier wars with Assyria. Thus, for the first time in centuries Israel had no one to contend with on its northern boundaries. This alone was the reason for the prosperity and ease with which at this time her northward borders were expanded.

But how long would this state of affairs last? What would happen, for example, were the Assyrians to overcome their northern enemies and return to this region as they had done so often before? Could Syria-Damascus possibly survive yet another Assyrian onslaught? And if Syria were to fall, where would it end? Would Israel be next?

Others in Israel may have been entertaining such questions as these as Amos began his prophetic mission. For most, however, the Assyrian menace to the north was out of sight and out of mind. It was Amos' calling to challenge this thoughtless, self-confident mood of his people and wake them up to the dangers facing them.

Questions for Review

1. Why is it thought that the heading to the Book of Amos may be a composite of two headings? To what other major segments of the book do these headings relate? What basis is there for regarding the opening caption, in 1:2, as well as the concluding prophecies, in 9:11–15, as editorial additions rather than words of Amos?

2. How important is it to know something about the prophet before considering his message? Of the information available to us regarding Amos, what would you regard as possibly the most significant? How does knowing that he was a sheep-breeder from Tekoa help us in understanding his reactions to certain developments in his culture?

3. Why was Israel as prosperous and powerful as it was when Amos first began to prophesy? Explain the meaning of Amos' first three "visions," in 7:1–9, in the light of the Assyrian menace that lurked in the background. Why would the message conveyed to Amos through his third vision have been an especially shocking one for both him and his people?

6

His Message and Its Relevance

A. Message

The relative brevity of the Book of Amos is deceptive. Within its few pages are assembled a surprisingly wide and complex range of prophetic insights. The comments that follow are by no means exhaustive. They should be viewed as no more than a stimulant to the student's own independent reading and study.

1. Opening Proclamation (1:3–2:16)

A good place to begin a study of Amos' prophecies is with the oracles that the editors of his book have placed at its forefront: 1:3–2:16. Some interpreters suggest that the words here may be a transcript (roughly speaking) of the words Amos actually spoke in his famous speech at Bethel soon after God called him to be a prophet (7:10–15). If so, we can understand why the priest in charge of that sanctuary, upon hearing it, quickly informed King Jeroboam that "Amos is plotting against you . . ." (7:10).

In any case, a brief review of these oracles will take us to the heart of the message this prophet felt called upon to bring to the people of his time.

(a) Danger Ahead!

The war of judgment Amos was himself forewarned of through his visions (7:9) is here publicly proclaimed. Yahweh is about "to hurl fire" on Israel (2:4–16), Amos declares, but not only on it, but on *all* the petty kingdoms of this region: from Damascus (1:3) and Tyre (1:9) in the north, to Gaza (1:6) and Edom (1:11) in the south, to Ammon (1:13) and Moab (2:1) in the east. "Hurl fire" is the prophet's metaphor for the "sword in hand" he had earlier been told would soon sweep through this region (7:9), breaking into walled cities and setting them ablaze (1:3, 7, 12; 2:5). Only one nation in that time would have been able to mount an invasion of this magnitude: the dreaded Assyrians! It is they his audience would immediately have thought of as he spoke. But for Amos *which* nation would do this was almost incidental. It is that *Yahweh* is doing this that fills him with dread. It is Yahweh, he declares, who is sending this fire of judgment.

(b) Why?

But why? Why is Yahweh doing this? Amos charges each nation of that region with having committed a *multiplicity* of crimes ("for the three crimes, the four crimes"—an idiom for "many"; see Prov 30:15–31). However, a notable difference exists between the charges brought against Israel (2:6–12) and the crimes of the others.

(i) Crimes of the Neighboring Kingdoms (1:3–2:3)

In his critique of the neighboring kingdoms, in each instance, after stressing that it is for many crimes (not just one) that disaster is coming upon them, Amos cites only *one* example. All of these fall into a single category. They are all instances of what today would be called *war crimes.* This is understandable. The nations of this region had been fighting one another almost continuously for over a century. It is to be expected that during these wars atrocities of all kinds would have occurred. It is of these that Amos speaks in his gruesome recitation of merciless slaughter of civilians (1:3, 11, 13), genocide (1:6, 9), flagrant treaty violations (1:9) and desecration of the dead (2:1).

Even in war, his words here imply—even among kingdoms that do not worship or acknowledge Israel's God—even under these circumstances there are *limits* to what is permissible. The God of Amos is witness to these atrocities and they are abhorrent to him—no matter who did them or what their rationalization might be. *Judgment by war* is coming upon the petty kingdoms of this region, Amos proclaims, because of their repeated *atrocities in war* over many years.

What then of Israel? Why is disaster coming upon it?

(ii) Crimes of Israel (2:4–16)

The Judah oracle at the head of this section (2:4–5) may stem from an editor. It does not appear that for Amos himself Judah had any independent significance. For him "Israel" was a single people inclusive of both kingdoms (3:1; 5:1; 7:8). Hence, what he had to say regarding Israel, in 2:6–16, applied to Judah as well. However, after *northern* Israel fell in 721, only Judeans remained. This oracle was intended for *them* to make sure they would realize that Amos' scathing critique was not meant only for the northerners. The Judeans too, during this period, had rejected Yahweh's Law (2:4).

It is the longer Israelite oracle (2:6–12) then that constitutes the climax of this sweeping proclamation. Here not just one but *four* instances of criminal behavior are cited. None of them, however, are war crimes of nation against nation (as was the case with the previously cited examples), but crimes of *individual Israelites* against each other. Yet, it is suggested, Israel's moral condition is even worse than its neighbors' because of the way this behavior flies in the face of prior privileges and opportunities: the miraculous way it had received its homeland (2:9); before that, its liberation from Egypt (2:10), and the guidance it had received (2:11). From all this the impression is given that Israel is being measured by a higher standard than that of the surrounding nations.

But what standard, more specifically? The four quite explicit crimes cited by Amos in 2:6–8 are worth noting carefully if we wish to begin getting inside of his critique of developments within the life of his people. Briefly stated these are:

• First (2:6), that basically good people ("the upright," "the poor") are being sold into debt-slavery for piddling sums ("for silver," "for a pair of sandals"). 2 Kings 4:1–7 provides a concrete example of the kind of thing Amos might have had in mind in making this charge. There we read of a poor widow (in the time of Elijah) who was being forced to sell her children into slavery in payment of her deceased husband's debts.

• Second (2:7a), that certain "oppressed" ones who prior to this time had been living on small ancestral estates (a house and an acre or two of land) were now being forced to sell under pressure from an upper class elite who were taxing and cheating them to death ("they have crushed the heads of the weak into the dust and thrust the rights of the oppressed to one side. . . ." See also 5:11 and 8:5–6 for some indication of the economic malpractices being perpetrated).

• Third (2:8), that in flagrant violation of quite specific legal traditions (see Ex 22:25; Dt 24:12–13, 17) cloaks taken in pledge from the desperately poor as collateral for small loans were being held beyond nightfall (when a cloak would have been essential for warmth while sleeping). Even worse, these same cloaks (together with other unjustly obtained wealth) were being used by those who acquired them for religious celebrations ("in the house of their god").

• Fourth (2:7b), that sexual morality and respect for others had broken down to the extent that a father and son had no shame about consorting with the same servant girl.

A nation divided against itself in this manner, Amos prophesied, cannot survive. It cannot survive because the God who brought this community so graciously into existence (with a totally different goal in mind) will not permit it to survive. A disaster is coming that will "crush" the elite who are perpetrating these crimes (2:13). "Even the bravest of warriors will jettison his arms and run away, that day!—declares Yahweh!" (2:16).

From this amazing speech (1:3–2:16) it is evident that in the eyes of Amos Yahweh is sovereign over all nations and all are accountable to him. Israel, however, is measured by a higher standard. This point becomes explicit in a trenchant statement at the beginning of the following section of his book: "You alone have I intimately known of all the families of earth; that is why I shall punish you for all your wrongdoings" (3:2). Israel alone of all nations is on intimate terms with Yahweh. It alone has knowledge of Yahweh's divine will for upright living. But the crimes being daily perpetrated in its midst are a flagrant violation of this special relationship. This is why punishment is coming.

But once again, what *does* Yahweh require of a people so "intimately known" by him? Once again, what *is* the sin, essentially, that infects the lives of those whom Amos singles out in 2:6–8 as chiefly responsible for his people's downfall?

2. The Root of the Problem

We do not need to guess at Amos' answer to the questions just posed. Elsewhere in his book sayings of Amos are recorded that summarize in no uncertain terms what he thought was the crux of the problem afflicting the Israelite society of his time. There is no "justice," he says (Hebrew: *mishpat*), and, even more alarming, there is no "uprightness" (Hebrew: *tsedakah*). These two terms occur together in several key passages and serve to illuminate the heart of Israel's moral dilemma as Amos viewed it.

> Can horses gallop over rocks?
> Can the sea be ploughed with oxen?
> Yet you have changed justice [*mishpat*] into poison,
> and the fruit of uprightness [*tsedekah*] into wormwood (6:12).

> They turn justice into wormwood,
> and throw uprightness to the ground (5:7).

. . . but let justice flow like water,
and uprightness like a never-failing stream (5:24).

What, more concretely, is Amos referring to when he so repeatedly laments the demise of justice and uprightness and calls for their restoration?

(a) No Justice

The word *mishpat* (justice), in Hebrew, may be used of what is just and right in general, but also of specific rulings regarding right and wrong. It is these latter that convey the more concrete meaning of this term in the world of Amos. So for example in the ancient covenant code we read: "If you take someone's cloak in pledge, you will return it to him at sunset. It is all the covering he has; it is the cloak he wraps his body in; what else will he sleep in?" (Ex 22:25–26). This can be called a *mishpat*, a "ruling" (it is the one in fact that Amos had in mind in his charge against Israel in 2:8; see above). It states what is reasonable and right in a quite specific matter having to do with lending and borrowing. "You will accept no bribes, for a bribe blinds the clear-sighted and is the ruin of the cause of the upright" (Ex 23:8). This too is a *mishpat*, one directed to those responsible for the judicial process. Collections of "rulings" or laws of this kind were referred to in Israel as *mishpatim* (see Ex 21:1).

It could be said therefore that a society that turns *mishpat* (justice) into wormwood and throws uprightness to the ground, as Amos stated his did, is one that has no concern for such rulings and either ignores or subverts them.

(b) No Uprightness

But not only is *mishpat* increasingly missing in his society, Amos declares, but also *tsedakah*. While their meanings overlap, *tsedakah* refers not so much to the deed as to the *attitude* that produces the deed. A ruling over what is right or wrong, as noted, can be called a *mishpat*. The man who fosters *mishpat* is called a *tsadik* in Israel. Ezekiel, for example, writes that such a man, among other things, "oppresses no one, returns the pledge on a debt, does not rob, gives his own food to the hungry, his clothes to those who lack clothing, does not lend for profit, does not charge interest, abstains from evil, gives honest judgment between one person and another . . . someone like this is truly upright . . ." (Ez 18:7–9). The inner drive that motivates a person to live in this way is what is meant by uprightness (*tsedakah*). When "just decrees'' (*mishpatim*) are violated and "turned to wormwood" a society suffers. When the very *desire* to live justly (*tsedakah*) is dissipated and "thrown to the ground" (5:7) a society dies.

This, Amos believed, was what was happening to the Israelite society of his day. Upright men whose responsibility it was to uphold justice were being pushed aside by a greedy elite (5:10). As a result they were becoming demoralized and silent (5:13). In this way not just justice, but the emotional capacity for justice was being destroyed. The fabric of Israel's life as a people was disintegrating, like a crumbling wall (7:7–8).

3. The Failure at the Gate

The one institution in Israel most severely affected by this loss of integrity was "the gate" (5:10). "The gate" referred to is the place of entry and exit to a walled village or city where the elders of that city gathered periodically to make decisions (Ru 4:1–12) or dispense justice (Am 5:10). It was in these meetings at the gate that the needs of the weak and poor were heard and defended against the whims of the wealthy and powerful (5:11).

For Amos this assembly of elders at the gate was more important than the gatherings for worship at the Yahweh shrines. Indeed, in one of his rare admonitions he states that *here,* not there, is the place where those should gather who *truly* "seek" Yahweh. "Seek me out and you will survive" (5:4), but "do not seek out Bethel, do not go to Gilgal, do not journey to Beer-sheba" (5:5); rather "seek good and not evil . . . hate evil, love good, let justice reign at the city gate" (5:14–15). Only if this is done, Amos warns—and even that is not certain—"it may be that Yahweh, God Sabaoth, will take pity on the remnant of Joseph" (5:15).

In short, if there is any hope at all of salvation from the disasters now approaching, it is among those who restore justice at the gate. That is how highly Amos regarded this institution. Its corruption was the source of all evil, its renewal the only hope.

4. Once Again, Why?

But why was all this happening? Could nothing be done to avert it? Might not Amos himself, through his words, bring about a change for the better? If Amos at some point had thought so, it seems evident from the oracles now available to us that he soon thought differently. His experience quickly taught him otherwise. The elite of his community were impervious to challenge and change. Even though repeatedly warned by a whole series of nature catastrophes, he observes in one oracle (4:7–12), it was to no avail (". . . and still you would not come back to me—declares Yahweh").

Why was this so? Why were the elite of his time so oblivious to their own moral decay and so resistant to rebuke and repentance? Amos' critique of this recalcitrant condition of his people is a powerful one. It centers on three issues: complacent theology; soporific worship; a callously affluent lifestyle.

(a) Complacent Theology

The elite to whom Amos spoke were by no means godless or apostate (as might be imagined). On the contrary, they appear to have been devout Yahwists whose faith had seldom been stronger. Recent success in regaining lost territory to the north and northwest and the resultant prosperity (as noted in the previous chapter) had confirmed them in this faith. More than ever they were confident that Yahweh was "with them" (5:14) and that, Yahweh being who he is (the greatest of gods), they were the "first of nations" (6:1). Indeed, there appears to have arisen at this time an expectation that Yahweh might soon act on a certain "day" to bring them as a people to a position of unprecedented preeminence over all others (5:18). A religiously inspired optimism reigned as never before among the Israelite elite of this period.

It is this complacent theology which comes under attack in several of Amos' most memorable words:

Are not you and the Cushites all the same to me,
children of Israel?—declares Yahweh.
Did I not bring Israel up from Egypt
and the Philistines from Caphtor,
and the Aramaeans from Kir? (9:7).

You alone have I intimately known of all the families of earth,
that is why I shall punish you for all your wrong-doings (3:2).

Disaster for you who long for the Day of Yahweh!
What will the Day of Yahweh mean for you?
It will mean darkness, not light . . . (5:18–20).

Other nations too, Amos declares, have been led and helped by Yahweh. Therefore, Israel should not pride itself in thinking that it alone is the apple of his eye. Yet, it is true that Israel has been intimately known and loved by Yahweh to a special degree. For this very reason its behavior is especially reprehensible. The Israelite elite have no excuse for behaving as they do. They know better! Disaster, therefore, not triumph lies ahead. Yahweh is by no means the soft-hearted, morally neutral deity the Israelite upper class suppose him to be.

(b) Soporific Worship

From complacent theology comes soporific worship. This is the second characteristic of the life of the elite that Amos singles out as contributing to the neglect of justice.

Again, there is no indication that the worship practices he attacks are pagan or hypocritical. On the contrary, the items listed in his satirical catalogue of activities at the Yahweh shrines, in 4:4–5, are in themselves innocuous, if not commendable: morning sacrifices; tithes; thank-offerings of leaven; free-will offerings. And the people are said to be doing all this joyfully ("for this, children of Israel, is what makes you happy").

Yet in describing these practices Amos "exhorts the congregation in a shocking parody of ecclesiastical language that must have sounded like irreverent blasphemy" (Mays, *Amos*). "Go to Bethel, and *sin,* to Gilgal and sin even harder!" (4:4). Amos' abhorrence of these practices, both here and in his famous diatribe against "solemn assemblies," in 5:21–26, is transparent.

> I hate, I scorn your festivals,
> I take no pleasure in your solemn assemblies,
> When you offer me burnt offerings . . .
> your oblations, I do not accept them
> and I do not look at your communion sacrifices of fat cattle.
> Spare me the din of your chanting,
> let me hear none of your strumming on lyres . . . (5:21–23).

Such worship, he implies in 5:25, is without precedence in Israel ("Did you bring me sacrifices and oblations those forty years in the desert, House of Israel?"). And this is what's wrong with it. In and of itself it may be all right, but it distracts from doing what is really important, what Yahweh *really* wants, what he had really taught his people to do "those forty years in the desert." It lulls people into thinking that the relation to Yahweh is intact, when what Yahweh wants of his people is missing.

But let justice flow like water
and uprightness like a never-failing stream (5:25).

(c) Affluent Lifestyle

But it was not only theology and worship that were subverting justice in Israel. A callously indifferent lifestyle among the elite in the cities was an equally important factor, Amos declared. Indeed, this was the paramount factor, as Amos viewed it. The link between the two is drawn with poetic sharpness in his biting portrait of an indolent wife, in 4:1, who calls to her husband to bring her yet another drink, while elsewhere the poor are crushed and oppressed. In 6:1–7 the same is said regarding the luxury-loving husbands of such women. While "Joseph" is being "ruined," they lie about on expensive ivory-inlaid furniture eating sumptuous meals and drinking wine by the bowlful (6:4–6). Elsewhere, he writes, "they cram their palaces with violence and extortion" and "little they know of right conduct" (3:10).

5. Is There No Hope?

Is there no hope then for this people? If the elite are so set in their ways, does this mark the end? Will the disaster that is coming completely annihilate Israel? Is the story now over that had begun so wonderfully with Israel's liberation from Egypt and settlement in Canaan?

We have already noted the reasons for thinking that the oracles of hope at the book's conclusion—those predicting that a remnant will survive the coming ordeals and be gloriously restored to a kingdom as great as the one David himself once ruled (9:8b–15)—are not from Amos but from later editors (see above, "The book as a whole"). The most, it seems, that Amos himself could say regarding a more hopeful prospect for Israel is, as noted above, that "it *may* be that Yahweh, God Sabaoth, will take pity on the remnant of Joseph" *if* there were those who would take courage in hand and speak up for justice at the gate (5:14). But, as also noted, that *this* would happen was far from certain. The only thing *Amos* seems to have been sure of is that a terrible "blackness" lay ahead for his people (5:20).

She has fallen down, never to rise again,
the virgin of Israel.
There she lies on her own soil,
with no one to lift her up;

For Lord Yahweh says this:

The town which used to put a thousand in the field
will be left with a hundred,
and the one which used to put a hundred
will be left with ten, to fight for the house of Israel (5:2–3).

As the shepherd rescues two legs or the tip of an ear
from the lion's mouth,
so will the children of Israel be salvaged
who now loll in Samaria in the corners of their beds, on their
    divans of Damascus (3:12).

The days are coming—declares the Lord Yahweh—
when I shall send a famine on the country,
not hunger for food, not thirst for water,
but famine for hearing Yahweh's word.
People will stagger from sea to sea,
will wander from the north to the east,
searching for Yahweh's word,
but will not find it (8:11–12).

Look, Lord Yahweh's eyes are on the sinful kingdom,
I shall wipe it off the face of the earth . . . (9:8).

Amos as prophet said what he was given to say—no more, no less.
Others would be called upon to envision the future *beyond* the disaster
that now loomed. *His* calling was to forewarn of the catastrophe itself,
and say why it was coming. Then those who came after would understand that this occurred not because Israel's God was weak or irration-
ally angry, but because of his justice and integrity, and his compassion
for those who suffer and are wrongfully oppressed. There come times
when even a God of grace and forgiveness can no longer "overlook"
a people's offenses (7:8b). Something had to be done.

B. Ongoing Relevance

The very fact that the words of Amos were written down, collected, edited and reedited through the centuries is itself testimony to
their ongoing significance for at least some of its readers.

For those who lived when that earthquake struck "two years" after
Amos had prophesied (1:1), it must have seemed that already then his

dire predictions of catastrophe were being frighteningly fulfilled. But even later, when both Israelite states had been destroyed by the war Amos had prophesied, the book's relevance was even more apparent, as can be seen by the way its Judean readers supplemented its heading with appropriate dates (cross-referenced with the Deuteronomic history of this period). Yet others added those oracles that declare that the Yahweh who spoke through Amos is the one who "makes his voice heard from Jerusalem" (1:1). By this they alerted the book's readers to their conviction that this prophet's words were as relevant for them, Jerusalemites though they might be, as for Amos' original audience at Bethel (see also their comments regarding Judah, in 2:4–5).

Still others wanted the book's readers to remember (especially as they came to the book's end) that while all Amos says in it about sin and catastrophe is true (and must be taken to heart), his was not the final word regarding Israel's future. While the "sinful kingdom" Israel did have to be destroyed (9:8), "the House of Jacob," they declared exuberantly, is going to endure (9:8b) and Israel's "fortunes" will one day be magnificently restored (9:14). These particular editors, being who they were (heirs of Jerusalem theology), could envision this restoration in no other way, apparently, than as a restoration of the Davidic empire to its former greatness (9:11–15).

Such were a few of the responses, thoughts and addenda of earlier generations of readers as they studied the words of this prophet. What are ours? What is the relevance of this book for us today?

Answers will vary. Each of us will hear different things. I will try to gather a few of my own reflections as I complete this study, mainly as a stimulus for others to do the same.

Amos' words about atrocities in war as a major reason for the impending judgments he predicted would soon befall his region (1:3–2:3) caught my attention on this reading. It is difficult not to think of the wars and atrocities that continue to afflict the nations of this very same part of our world, even today. Wars may be necessary, even justified under certain circumstances, but even in war, not everything is permissible. There are limits.

As I read this section, on this occasion, my thoughts turned to those bombs that were dropped at the end of World War II on Hiroshima and Nagasaki—without warning, without recourse, without pity. Was this necessary? Were there no alternatives? Will this very first (and so far only) use of these horrendous weapons return to haunt us? "The race had been won," James Agee wrote of World War II's traumatic ending (*Time* magazine, August 20, 1945), "the weapon had been used by those on whom civilization could best hope to depend; but the demonstration against living creatures instead of dead matter created a bottomless wound in the living conscience of the race" (quoted by Peter Ellertsen, "James Agee, the Bomb and Oliver the Cat," *Christian Century*, July 31–August 7, 1985, p. 709). Is this a modern Amos speaking? Are we listening?

Unfortunately, excessive violence in war is not our only problem. Are we becoming addicted to violence? In 1980 there were 10,012 hand gun murders in the United States, eight in England. Between 1963 and 1973 the war in Vietnam took 46,212 lives; firearms in America killed 84,644 (see William Fore, "Media Violence: Hazardous to Our Health," *Christian Century*, Sept. 25, 1985, p. 834). Having so long lived by the sword, are we now dying by the sword—"on her own soil with no one to lift her up" (Am 5:2).

The unregulated economic conditions in Israel in Amos' time, and the gravitation of economic power into the hands of a few elite, are strikingly similar to conditions that existed in modern times during the early stages of the industrial revolution. They still exist today in many underdeveloped countries. The social results are catastrophic: growing numbers of people without house, land or job, and a massive split between rich and poor—with some becoming so wealthy they don't know what to do with it all, and others so poor they can scarcely survive. Even the more advanced nations must constantly do battle with the greed that fosters and permits such conditions. Modern history is rife with examples of how dreadfully easy it is to ignore the plight of the destitute, if you are wealthy. Tragically, only too often religion continues to buffer and protect rather than challenge the decadent lifestyles of these privileged elites.

A fear of revolutionary communism repeatedly grips our western populations—not without reason. A third of the world's peoples have undergone social upheavals of this nature during this century. Is this our Assyria? Has God anything to do with this? Were there a prophet in our midst would he warn us of yet additional upheavals and catastrophes should we fail to muster the will to rectify our most obvious inequities? Is there still enough uprightness left to even want to do so?

Reading Amos is a potent antidote to the poisonous lethargy those of us repeatedly fall prey to who are among the world's more fortunate ones.

Questions for Review

1. Compare and contrast the criticisms Amos brings against Israel's neighboring nations and those brought against Israel itself, in 1:3–2:16. Why does he seem to be measuring Israel by a finer, higher standard? What is implied regarding Yahweh in the charges he brings? How, according to Amos, will Yahweh execute his judgment against the peoples of this region?

2. What would you say is the crux of Amos' critique of his society? Explain what is meant by the terms ''justice'' and ''uprightness'' that recur so often in his book. What institution of his society was of very special concern to him? Why that one? What did he see happening there that was so reprehensible?

3. Summarize how lifestyle, theology and worship practices of an elite in Israel were contributing to the downfall of Israelite society according to Amos. How serious did he believe the deterioration had become? Did he have any hope at all for the future?

4. In what sense might the supplements to the book be regarded as testimony to its vitality and ongoing relevance? What do these supplements suggest were points of interest and concern of its earliest readers? Identify for yourself what you would consider its most important points of relevance to be.

7

Hosea, Son of Beeri

About a decade after Amos appeared at Bethel with his somber warning and critique another prophet appeared in Israel, one who not only prophesied in northern Israel but *lived* there. His name was Hosea son of Beeri and we will seek to "meet" him as we did Amos by first looking at his book, then at the man himself, then at his messages and their relevance for subsequent times, including our own.

A. The Book as a Whole

Looking at the Book of Hosea as a whole (as again you should before proceeding), one division is immediately evident: that between chs. 1–3 and 4–14. Chs. 1–3 are clearly marked off from the rest of the book by their unique contents (third-person reports, 1:2–9; messages, ch. 2; first-person memoirs, ch. 3), and a new heading occurs at 4:1 ("Israelites, hear what Yahweh says [literally: hear the word of Yahweh]"). This heading is almost identical to the one at the beginning of the book ("The word of Yahweh which came to Hosea . . ."). Both characterize the contents that follow as "*word* of Yahweh" (1:1; 4:1). Elsewhere this phrase ("word of Yahweh") is used by the prophets to introduce fairly short, specific words, spoken on particular occasions (Is 1:10; Jer 1:4). Here "word of Yahweh" is a *title* for a collection of such words.

The identical title recurs in the headings of Joel, Zephaniah, Micah, Ezekiel, Jonah, Zechariah, Haggai and Malachi. There too, as in Hosea 1:1, it is followed in some instances by references to certain kings during whose reigns these prophets prophesied. This feature of these headings links these books to the Books of Kings and suggests that the same Deuteronomic historians who edited Kings (see chapter 2 above) had a hand in editing these books as well. For them these books were, each one, a divine "word" or revelation! From this we

65

can see how the books of the prophets were becoming sacred to those who preserved them.

In summary, Hosea (like Amos) appears to have once existed in two independent collections (chs. 1–3 and 4–14). It is possible that the Deuteronomists whose editorial fingerprints are apparent in the titles of both collections may have spliced them together. This initial overview can be shown graphically as follows:

First Collection (chs. 1–3) 1:1 "The word of Yahweh which came to Hosea"			Second Collection (chs. 4–14) 4:1 "Israelites, hear the word of Yahweh"
1:2–9 biography	ch. 2 messages	ch. 3 autobiography	Messages

The subdivisions of the "First Collection" (chs. 1–3) are fairly obvious and have already been noted. But what of the "Second Collection" (chs. 4–14)? Are there no subdivisions there as well?

As we have seen, prophetic messages are usually introduced or concluded by a simple phrase indicating the source of the message: "Yahweh says this," or "says Yahweh" (see Am 1:3–2:16). Unique to this section of Hosea is the almost total absence of such identifying phrases, even though many of the words here are obviously meant to be understood as words of Yahweh. Indeed, after the opening summons to "hear the word of Yahweh," in 4:1, we do not encounter another explicit reference to Yahweh as speaker until we reach the end of chapter 11. There we read: "—declares Yahweh" (11:11). This gives the impression that *everything* from 4:1 to 11:11 is one long Yahweh-speech!

Reading through these chapters, however, it is quite obvious that there are many longer and shorter units of discourse having to do with a great variety of subjects. It is hardly possible, therefore, that they were all spoken on one occasion in one speech. They also do not seem to be as carefully crafted as prophetic messages generally are. The text of this portion of Hosea is exceptionally difficult to translate. Several suggestions have been made as to why this is so (see Anderson and Freedman). Perhaps the contents of this section of Hosea are not a record of what the prophet actually said but more like a journal of his experiences and thoughts—notes that he jotted down either before or after appearing in public.

The closing off phrase at 11:11 ("—declares Yahweh") alerts us to the possibility that an initial collection of Hosea's words may have ended at this point and that with 12:1 a third collection begins. The self-disclosure in 12:1 suggests this as well. There Hosea alerts us to the fact that a new and dangerous period in his mission was beginning ("Ephraim besieges me with lying, the House of Israel with duplicity"). Furthermore, a careful study of the *contents* of chs. 4–14 indicates that a chronological factor may have been at work in the way this entire collection was initially shaped—with his earliest words appearing in the early chapters of this section (chs. 4–14) and the latest in the latter ones (this would be an additional indication of the journalistic nature of these jottings). It is possible therefore that 12:1–14:9 may come from the very last period of Hosea's mission.

In summary: there appear to be not just two main divisions to this book, as our initial analysis indicated, but three: chs. 1–3, 4–11, and 12–14. It has been observed that each of these begins with words of warning, but concludes with words of hope. There is also not just a heading to this book (1:1), but an epilogue (14:10), perhaps from the hand of some later teacher who wished to encourage his students to read it with the care and intelligence it deserves.

With these fresh observations in mind the book as a whole may now be diagrammed as follows:

Heading 1:1					Epilogue 14:10
Section 1		Section 2		Section 3	
Judgment	Hope	Judgment	Hope	Judgment	Hope
1:2–2:25	3:1–5	4:1–11:6	11:7–11	12:1–14:1	14:2–9

One final feature of the book should be noted before turning to Hosea himself. Just as certain *Judean* readers added oracles of hope to Amos (9:8b–15), so they appear to have done the same in Hosea. For example, the restoration of the Davidic dynasty is predicted in 3:5 (compare Amos 9:11–12), and in 1:7 and 12:1b the point is made that while Ephraim (northern kingdom) is corrupt, Judah is still faithful and will be saved. As a resident of Ephraim, Hosea's own hopes for the future take a rather different form, as we shall soon see. Like Amos the division of Yahweh's people into two kingdoms has no real significance for him. From his point of view they are still essentially one people, with a single destiny (see especially what he has to say regarding this in Hosea 2:16–25).

B. The Man Behind the Book

Having considered his book, we turn now (as a next step in our study of this prophet) to discovering what can be learned about Hosea himself. Chief among the passages available for doing so, thanks to the editors of Hosea's literary legacy, are the heading (1:1), the third-person report which follows (1:2–9)—where we learn of the rather unusual experiences that prompted this prophet to *be* a prophet in the first place—and Hosea's own terse personal report of certain related experiences in ch. 3.

1. Name

Both *Hosea's* name and that of his father are mentioned in the heading of his book (1:1). He was remembered as "Hosea son of Beeri" (his own name without the father's name appears in the following verse—1:2). Hosea means "he has helped" or "saved" (the "he" referring to Yahweh) and was popular in the north where we assume Hosea to have lived. According to Numbers 13:8 the famous Ephraimite leader Joshua once bore this name; it was also the name of Israel's last king, a contemporary of Hosea's (see 2 Kgs 17:6—there transliterated as "Hoshea").

2. His Country

We are nowhere told precisely where Hosea lived, but all the place names in his book are in the north. Not once, for example, is the Judean capital Jerusalem mentioned, while there are frequent references to Samaria, capital of Israel, and to Ephraim, the largest of the northern Israelite tribes. The northern shrines at Bethel and Gilgal are also often referred to (6:10; 5:15; 8:5), as is the ancient tribal center, Shechem (6:9). Indeed, the suggestion has been made by Wolff that this latter may have been his home, a suggestion we will examine more closely after we have looked at his occupation. It seems apparent, in any case, that he both lived and prophesied in the northern kingdom. If so, he was the only prophet we will be studying to have done so (Amos prophesied at Bethel, but lived in Judah).

3. Occupation

As we have seen (ch. 5), *Amos* was a herdsman and custodian of sycamore trees when Yahweh called him to be a prophet. As noted, this was not incidental to the kind of prophet he became. His way of expressing himself, his theology and the character of his messages were all rooted in his daily life. What might be said of Hosea in this regard? What kind of life was he leading at the time Yahweh called him?

The answer is nowhere given in so many words, but hints here and there in his book enable us to make a few educated guesses. In ch. 3, for example, Hosea relates how he paid out a sum of money to buy back his wife (3:2). Half of the sum was paid in silver (fifteen pieces), the other half with a homer of barley (about twelve and a half bushels) and a skin of wine. The impression given by this is that Hosea had insufficient cash to pay the whole sum in silver, so the remainder was paid in what he did have plenty of: barley and wine. Perhaps, then, he was a small farmer.

More important than this, however, is Wolff's suggestion that he may have been a member of the Levitical priestly groups that we know were living in scattered settlements in the north at this time. To appreciate the significance of this fascinating possibility it will be necessary to review briefly the checkered fate of this important Israelite subculture. At one point in Israelite history these Levites were *the* leading priestly group in Israel (see Dt 18:1–8). In fact, according to Exodus 32:25–29 (see also Dt 33:8–11) Israel's founding prophet Moses himself had appointed them to this role as reward for their loyalty during an especially grave crisis. Furthermore, early during the Israelite settlement in Canaan it was one of their number, the famous Eli, who presided as priest over all Israel at the central tribal shrine at Shiloh (1 Sam 1:3).

But it was right then in their history that tragedy struck. In the wars between Israel and the Philistines this important shrine was destroyed and its most sacred object, the ark of the covenant, fell into Philistine hands (for details, see 1 Sam 4–6). When this happened, Israel was for a period without any central shrine at all. When, however, David brought the ark of the covenant to Jerusalem and housed it there in a new tent shrine (2 Sam 7), one of their number, Abiathar, was again installed as one of two priests in charge of the worship there (see 2 Sam 8:17; for Abiathar's Levitical lineage, see 1 Sam 14:3; 22:20–23).

But, then, tragedy struck a second time. Soon after David's death Abiathar and his family were expelled from Jerusalem by Solomon (David's son) for having opposed him in the struggle for the succession (1 Kgs 2:26–27), and when the northern shrines were established under Jeroboam (after the breaking away of the ten northern tribes and the founding of the northern kingdom of Israel), the Levites were bypassed in favor of "ordinary families" (1 Kgs 12:31). So it came about that the Levitical families of the north, despite their venerable heritage, were without any official role as priests at any of the state shrines of either kingdom—and so it had been, at the time of Hosea, for almost two centuries!

If then Hosea was in fact a member of these Levitical groups, it is quite possible that he made his living by farming, since they were not at that time in charge of any of the state sponsored shrines. But they *were* still priests, nevertheless, and that in itself is significant for understanding Hosea. Later on, in fact, during the Josiah reforms in 621, their priestly role would be restored to them in part (it was at this time, we conjecture, that they were re-installed as subordinates to the presiding Aaronite priests of Jerusalem; see 2 Kgs 23:8–9; Num 3:6).

But what are the reasons for thinking Hosea was at all related to this Levitical tradition? The key to this conjecture is the affinity of Hosea with the biblical Book of Deuteronomy which many scholars regard as Levitical in origin (note how Deuteronomy takes for granted, in 18:1–8, that the Levites are the only Yahweh appointed priests). The following are a few examples of this:

● both Hosea and Deuteronomy view Israel as a people related to Yahweh by a covenant mediated by Moses (Dt 5; Hos 8:1–3; 12:14);

● both point to the decalogue as the basic outline of what Yahweh requires of his covenant people (Dt 5:1–22; Hos 4:1–3);

● both stress the importance of knowing Yahweh and not forgetting his laws (Dt 4:9; 6:6–13; 8:11–20; Hos 4:6b);

● both believe that to forsake Yahweh's covenant by breaking these laws will have disastrous consequences (Dt 28; Hos 8:3);

● both characterize the role of true priests as primarily that of "teachers" of this law, not sacrificers (Dt 33:10; 31:9–11; Hos 4:6; 8:12);

● both are critical of the institution of kingship and regard a particular king as legitimate only if appointed by Yahweh (Dt 17:14–15; Hos 8:4);

● both regard the calf image at Bethel (even though of Aaronite origin) as a totally invalid symbol for Yahweh (Dt 9:15–21; Hos 8:5–7).

A likely interpretation of these and other striking similarities is that they point to a common background. One has the impression that both Deuteronomy and Hosea originated in northern Levitical communities. Bearing this in mind—and also the fact that these Levites were excluded from the official shrines—helps us understand why Hosea is as critical as he is of the established priesthood (see Hos 4:4–11, among others). The priests he is criticizing are not Levites, but those "ordinary families'' Jeroboam is said to have installed at the official shrines of the north (1 Kgs 12:31). Note too how Hosea's criticisms are exactly of the kind we would expect Levites to make—the priesthood he is critiquing favors sacrificing over teaching with the result that ''my people perish for want of knowledge'' (4:6).

In summary, Hosea may have been a farmer, but as a member of the disestablished Levitical priesthood we can also imagine him as someone who was very involved in studying and maintaining this venerable counterculture (see 8:12 for his possible role in helping to preserve the teachings of this heritage in writing).

4. His Town

As earlier noted, once having established what Hosea might have done (his occupation and cultural milieu), we might also be able to be a little more specific regarding where he might have lived. In any case, it is worth noting that there was one particular town in the north that was especially sacred to the Levitical priests. This was Shechem, located between Mount Ebal and Mount Gerazim, where, according to Deuteronomic tradition (Dt 11:29; 27:11–14), Moses commanded that a great covenant renewal ceremony of the Israelite tribes take place after their entry into Canaan (and where indeed such renewal ceremonies did take place; see Jos 24:1 and Dt 31:10–13). It was here too, we are told, that the tribes of Israel gathered in the time of Rehoboam to protest his father's over-taxation (1 Kgs 12:1), and this was the first temporary capital of the northern tribes when they broke away to form an alternative kingdom to that of Judah (1 Kgs 12:25).

There is only one reference to this sacred place in the Book of Hosea. This occurs in Hosea 6:9 where mention is made of a ''gang of priests'' who committed murder ''on the road to Shechem.'' However, the very fact that Hosea alludes here to a crime perpetrated by priests and that this crime was against those *on the road* to this city suggests a crime against pilgrims by rival priests. This together with the fact that he nowhere criticizes Shechem as he does other Israelite cities and towns of his region (Bethel, Mizpah, Tabor, Samaria) leads one to suspect he had some special regard for it. Did he live there, as Wolff has suggested? Entertaining this possibility heightens our consciousness of him as a person steeped in Deuteronomic traditions stretching back to the days of Moses and the first entry of his people into Canaan.

5. Prophetic Call

Whether priest or farmer or both, how did Hosea become a prophet with a mission to all Israel? Unlike Amos, Hosea himself has left us no personal report that might help us answer that question. Fortunately, however, his friends (or disciples) have filled in this gap. Right after his book's heading (1:2–9) they relate how at the time "when Yahweh first spoke" to Hosea (1:2) he was the recipient of four distinct revelations. The implication is that it was these that thrust him into the prophetic role and were foundational for all of his subsequent messages.

In the first of these, at the very beginning of Hosea's mission, he was prompted to "go, marry a whore, and get children with a whore, for the country itself has become nothing but a whore by abandoning Yahweh" (1:2). That Hosea acted on this revelation and actually did this cannot be doubted, for his disciples proceed to inform us who it was, quite specifically, that he married: Gomer daughter of Diblaim (1:3).

It is not clear, however, that Gomer was a whore in the usual sense of that word, for the term in Hebrew, literally translated, is not "whore" but "woman of whoredoms," and this is similar to the phrase, "spirit of whoredoms," which Hosea uses elsewhere to characterize what was happening *generally* in the society of his time (4:12; 5:4). *Many* Israelite women of that day, it seems, were "prostituting themselves" (Hos 4:13), not as professional prostitutes, but in sexual activities that were a feature of the worship at the Canaanite shrines of that era (more about this later).

When then Hosea was asked to marry a "whore" and have children with a whore, the point may have been, not that he was to take to wife a professional prostitute, but rather that he was to marry one of the numerous girls of his time who were worshiping at the Canaanite shrines.

That Hosea did even this must have been shocking to the families of the conservative Levitical community to which we think he belonged—comparable, for example, to a young man of *our* time from one of the more conservative rural communities or churches marrying a modern, sexually liberated woman of the city. But that of course was its purpose: to produce a jolt that would wake his contemporaries up to the fact that because of the encroaching breakdown in sexual morality, Israel had now, for all intents and purposes (regardless of how this conduct might be rationalized), become "nothing but a whore by abandoning Yahweh" (1:2).

To this marriage three children were born (1:3–9). At the birth of each child three subsequent revelations flooded his mind as he sought to name them.

The first child was to be called "Jezreel" (1:3–5), he was told—not a personal name, but the name of a city that had become famous because of a bloody massacre that had occurred there a century earlier (2 Kgs 9 and 10)—hence, similar in sound to the words "Hiroshima" or "Buchenwald" today. Thus, the name itself symbolized catastrophe and could serve as a potent sign that "it will not be long before I [Yahweh] make the House of Jehu pay for the bloodshed at Jezreel and I put an end to the sovereignty of the House of Israel" (1:4–5).

Surprisingly, the focus of this second revelation was not Israel's "whoredom" (as was the initial one), but the excessive *violence* used by an Israelite king (Jehu), a century earlier, in founding the dynasty of which King Jeroboam II (Hosea's contemporary) was the reigning representative. That Hosea was at all critical of this "bloodshed at Jezreel" is itself surprising, for this had been a political purge carried out with *prophetic* backing in retaliation against a previous dynasty for its persecution of Yahweh loyalists (see 2 Kgs 9:1–10). But even more surprising is the fact that he regards it as such an evil that Israel would have to itself suffer the violence of war because of it ("When that day comes, I shall break the bow of Israel in the Valley of Jezreel"—1:5).

In summary, it would appear that at this moment (at the birth of his first child) Hosea became conscious of that awful truth that had earlier broken in upon Amos through his plumb-line vision: namely, that a catastrophic invasion of Israel was imminent, because of Israel's deplorable moral condition.

The births of two additional children (and the revelations that accompanied them) only served to intensify this awareness. One of these was to be called "Lo-Ruhamah" (not pitied—1:6) and the other "Lo-Ammi" (not my people—1:8). These names simply underscored what was already implicit in the initial two oracles: because of the depths of whoredoms and violence that now characterized Israel's existence, Yahweh could no longer be their gracious guardian. The covenantal relation with this people established at Sinai was now terminated. "You are not my people and I do not exist for you" (1:9). This was the core of what Yahweh said when he first began speaking "through Hosea" (1:2).

The story of Yahweh's personal dealings with this prophet does not end here, however. There was, it seems, a surprising sequel to the events alluded to in this brief account of the birth of his children. A tragic rupture in the relation of Hosea and his wife is alluded to in his allegorical denunciation of Israel for adultery, in 2:4–5.

> To court, take your mother to court!
> For she is no longer my wife
> nor am I her husband.
> She must either remove her whoring ways from her face
> and her adulteries from between her breasts,
> or I shall strip her and expose her
> naked as the day she was born . . .

The possibility that a personal experience of some sort lies in the background of this verse is reinforced by Hosea's intimate account, in ch. 3, of a command that came to him from Yahweh to "go again, love a woman who loves another man, an adulteress . . ." (3:1). While we are not told, in this instance, the name of the woman to be loved "again" in this way, it is hard to imagine that it was anyone but the wife he had previously loved, since the very reason for asking him to do this, it is explained, is because Yahweh too is now going to love again those *he* had previously loved ("the Israelites"), even though they have forsaken him (3:1b).

It seems likely, therefore, that sometime after the birth of his three children Gomer left Hosea and became involved with other men. That he was able to buy her back for a sum roughly equivalent to the price of a slave (Ex 21:32; Lev 27:4) indicates how far she had fallen. Needless to say, in doing this, Hosea once again created shock-waves among his more conservative contemporaries, for the traditions of his Levitical community specified that an adulterous wife should be executed (Dt 22:22), not restored in this manner. How wrenching this action might have been for Hosea himself will become evident as we examine those aspects of his message that show him wrestling with the question of his people's future (ch. 11 especially).

Regarding how then Hosea became a prophet, these texts point relentlessly to the prophet's domestic situation as the key factor. It was within the setting of a marriage that he entered into at the prompting of Yahweh that Yahweh's words began flooding his consciousness: first, during the marriage itself, then on the occasion of the birth of each of three children, and then again after his wife had left him for an adulterous affair. In this way the most intimate aspects of Hosea's existence were incorporated into his prophetic mission.

6. Historical Setting

When, precisely, did Hosea live and under what circumstances? The editorial heading to the book (1:1) dates his mission to the reigns of Uzziah, Jotham, Ahaz and Hezekiah of Judah, and of Jeroboam son of Joash in Israel. This is not too helpful, since the reigns of these kings span almost a century (783–687). The fact that nowhere in his book is there a reference to the Assyrian conquest of Samaria (which took place in 721) suggests that Hosea's mission had *ended* sometime earlier. The oracle prophesying the collapse of Jehu's dynasty (of which Jeroboam II was the heir), in 1:4, is proof that it *began* prior to the death of Jeroboam in 743. Very likely Hosea's prophetic mission opened not long before that, however, since the background of his prophecies is clearly one of social chaos of a kind we know prevailed during Jeroboam's *final* years and the two decades that followed, and not earlier. It was then that the Assyrians began their relentless advance into this region.

An outline of the events leading up to the decline and fall of the northern kingdom, during these decades, is given in 2 Kings 15:8–17:6. In summary, from the time of Jeroboam's death in 743 until the destruction of the Israelite kingdom in 721, six kings reigned, two of them (Zechariah and Shallum) for less than a year. Four of these kings were assassinated by their successors—one symptom among many of the disarray and confusion that prevailed in the face of the now ever present threat to Israel's existence posed by the Assyrians under their new and powerful leader Tiglath-pileser III (the biblical "Pul"; see 2 Kgs 15:19). Neither hefty ransoms (see 2 Kgs 15:19) nor military alliances (Is 7:1–9) could stay his advance (we will have more to say regarding this in our discussion of Isaiah). The end came at the conclusion of a relentless three year siege of Samaria, in 721 (2 Kgs 17:5–6).

Just prior to the end, we conjecture, some in Israel (perhaps Hosea himself, or disciples of his) fled south into Judah. This would explain how a record of Hosea's prophecies survived this ordeal. However, for many Israelites Assyria's conquest meant being uprooted and deported to distant places, while foreigners were brought in to take their place (2 Kgs 17:6, 23–34). For all intents and purposes, Israel (northern kingdom) had now ceased to exist. Judah alone survived, and this only as a puppet of the now gigantic Assyrian empire.

The following chart outlines the most important background events of this period:

Events during Hosea's mission

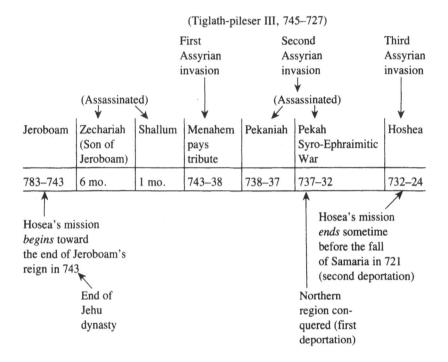

(Tiglath-pileser III, 745–727)

	(Assassinated)		First Assyrian invasion		(Assassinated) Second Assyrian invasion	Third Assyrian invasion
Jeroboam	Zechariah (Son of Jeroboam)	Shallum	Menahem pays tribute	Pekaniah	Pekah Syro-Ephraimitic War	Hoshea
783–743	6 mo.	1 mo.	743–38	738–37	737–32	732–24

Hosea's mission *begins* toward the end of Jeroboam's reign in 743

End of Jehu dynasty

Hosea's mission *ends* sometime before the fall of Samaria in 721 (second deportation)

Northern region conquered (first deportation)

Questions for Review

1. Why has the suggestion been made that chs. 4–14 of Hosea might have originated as a "journal" of sorts? Compare this section of the book with its opening section, in chs. 1–3. What significance is there in its editors referring to the book as a whole as the "word" of Yahweh?

2. Why is it thought that Hosea both lived and prophesied in the northern kingdom, rather than in Judah, and that he may have belonged to the venerable Levitical groups of that region? What role had these Levites played in the history of Israelite religion? What role were they playing at the time of Hosea? How might the recognition that Hosea belonged to these groups contribute to a better understanding of his stance as a prophet?

3. What part did his personal life play in Hosea's becoming a prophet? Who was his wife? What is likely meant by the characteri-

zation of her as a "whore"? Why did he marry her? How many children did he have and what names were given them? What evidence is there that Hosea's wife left him for another man? By what means did he get her back? What impression might these actions have made on those among whom he lived and prophesied?

4. During what period of time was Hosea active as a prophet? How in general would you characterize the political circumstances of this period?

8

His Message and Its Relevance

A. Message

Hosea's messages, like those of Amos, are more complex and subtle than may be apparent at first. *Un*like Amos he spoke unequivocally of both disaster *and* hope. Indeed, so important was this added theme that his book's editors carefully arranged his messages to reflect it in all its parts. As noted (in the previous chapter), in each of his book's three major sections (chs. 1-3, 4-11, 12-14) warnings of disaster come first, followed by oracles of hope. I suggest that we observe this division as we examine more closely the messages of this prophet.

1. Danger Ahead!

From the day of the birth of Hosea's first child, a son, it was clear to him that a catastrophic invasion was about to sweep through the "House of Israel" (1:4). Amos too had foreseen this, but from afar, so to speak. To Hosea it was revealed that this disaster was imminent: "in a little while" (1:4). In fact, in the background of many of his oracles we sense that this catastrophe is already happening. Already the war trumpets are blowing (5:8), already diplomats are scurrying from capital to capital to avert this disaster if they can (5:13; 7:11).

Yet, in spite of the gravity of the situation, the nation's governing elite are optimistic, it seems. Their God might punish them, they are quoted as saying, but surely he will never forsake or destroy them (6:1-3). He is far too gracious and kind for that.

> Come, let us return to Yahweh.
> He has rent us and he will heal us;
> he has struck us and he will bind up our wounds;
> after two days he will revive us,
> on the third day he will raise us up

and we shall live in his presence.
Let us know, let us strive to know Yahweh;
that he will come is as certain as the dawn . . . (6:1–3).

Hosea does not share this optimism. On the contrary, he is almost in-
sane over what is about to happen (9:7). Far from returning to heal,
Yahweh has become an enemy of his own people. Danger, terrifying
danger, lies ahead on the *near* horizon, and with every poetic resource
at his command he seeks to warn his people of it.

For I shall be like a lion to Ephraim,
like a young lion to the House of Judah;
I myself shall rend them, then go my way,
shall carry them off, beyond hope of rescue (5:14).

My God will cast them off
and they will become wanderers among the nations (9:17).

Then they will say to the mountains, "Cover us!"
and to the hills, "Fall on us!" (10:8b).

Like a leopard I shall lurk beside the road,
like a bear robbed of her cubs I shall meet them
and rend the membrane of their heart . . . (13:7–8).

The wind from the East will come,
Yahweh's breath blowing up from the desert
to dry his spring, to dry up his fountain,
to strip his treasury . . .
They will fall by the sword,
their little children will be dashed to pieces
and their pregnant women disemboweled (13:15–14:1).

The last of these oracles points to the terrifying literal reality Hosea
is warning of in this flood of poetic images: a *war* was about to sweep
over Israel. The *Assyrians* were coming (a "wind from the East")! Israel was about to be engulfed and enslaved as it once was in Egypt
(8:13b). The calf image of Bethel (in which the bogus priests in charge
there put so much stock) was about to be carried off (10:6) and it was
Yahweh himself, the prophet declares in no uncertain terms, who was
ultimately responsible for all this.

But why? What had happened in Israel to merit such a catastrophic train of events?

2. Why?

Again, we do not need to guess at the answer. Like Amos, Hosea was not content merely to *warn* his people of these disasters, but saw it as his duty to *interpret* why they were occurring and so justify the ways of Yahweh.

(a) The Heart of His Critique

Hosea's critique of his culture is a particularly trenchant one. Its starting point was his rock-bottom certainty (a legacy of his Levitical heritage) that Israel was and is a unique people by virtue of a special covenant with Yahweh its God that was fashioned centuries earlier through Moses in the wilderness of Sinai at the time of Israel's escape from Egypt (12:14). That is where Israel was "found" by Yahweh (9:10). That is when Israel was "loved" by Yahweh as a father tenderly loves his infant son and teaches him to walk (11:3). That is when Yahweh became Israel's God (12:10) and Israel became a people pledged and committed to live by Yahweh's covenantal law (8:1–3).

The single, encompassing reason for the disaster that is coming, according to Hosea, is that Israel (its protestations to the contrary) has brought about the annulment of this covenant by its failure to uphold its laws.

> Because they have violated my covenant
> and been unfaithful to my Law,
> in vain will they cry, "My God!"
> In vain, "We, Israel, know you!"
> Israel has rejected the good,
> the enemy [Assyria] will pursue them (8:1b–3).

But what "good" more specifically is it that Hosea is talking about in this text? What Law is it that he sees as being so flagrantly violated? The specifics at stake in these charges are alluded to in the indictment the editors of the book have placed at the forefront of its second collection (chs. 4–11). There we read:

> There is no loyalty, no faithful love,
> no knowledge of God in the country,
> only perjury and lying, murder, theft,

adultery and violence,
bloodshed after bloodshed (4:1b–2).

This catalogue is reminiscent of the second half of the decalogue: you shall not kill, commit adultery, steal, bear false witness, covet (see Dt 5:17–21; Ex 20:13–17). Hosea appears to be saying (by implication) that it is quite simply Israel's failure to uphold such basic, elementary values as these (as it was pledged to do) that is the core reason for the catastrophic invasion now so imminent.

However, in the messages that follow, two crimes especially are singled out as especially rampant in his community and hence of particular importance in coming to an understanding of what is about to happen. These are the sins of promiscuity and violence already alluded to in his disciples' report of the revelations that came to Hosea when Yahweh first spoke through him (see again 1:2). To understand why Hosea thought a war of judgment against his people was inevitable attention must be paid to what he said regarding these crimes in particular.

(b) Sexual Promiscuity

In 4:12 the prophet declares that "an urge to go whoring [a prostituting spirit]" has taken hold of his people and is leading them astray. What is he referring to? Clearly, not what we in modern times might make of such words, for in the verses that follow he goes on to describe a situation quite different from anything most of us are familiar with:

> . . . and whoring they go and desert their God;
> they offer sacrifice on the mountaintops,
> they burn incense on the hills,
> under oak and poplar and terebinth,
> for pleasant is their shade.
> So although your daughters play the whore
> and your daughters-in-law commit adultery,
> I shall not punish your daughters for playing the whore
> nor your daughters-in-law for committing adultery,
> when the men themselves are wandering off with whores
> and offering sacrifice with sacred prostitutes,
> for a people with no understanding is doomed (4:12–14).

From this it is evident that the sexual promiscuity Hosea is speaking of is of a quite specific type. It had to do with an activity associated with sacrifice and offerings (4:13) and "*sacred* prostitutes" (4:14). What is being alluded to here is *cultic* promiscuity of a type known to us from other sources as commonplace in the Canaanite religion of that area and period. Its rationale, briefly stated, was the belief that *human* sexual activity in a sacred place could stimulate *divine* sexual action and thereby foster fertility and prosperity throughout the natural realm.

When the austere worshipers of Yahweh entered Canaan from the wilderness of Sinai and first encountered such practices at Baal Peor, they were both shocked and intrigued (see Num 25; Hos 9:10). Their God Yahweh was not thought of in sexual terms and the notion of worshiping him in this manner must have been initially abhorrent to the Israelite majority. However, after having lived in Canaan for many years, this initial shock wore off. Indeed, from reading Hosea we get the impression that in his time many had accommodated themselves to these practices to the extent that they no longer made a sharp distinction between worshiping the Canaanite Baal and worshiping Yahweh (see Hos 2:18–19). Yahweh too, therefore, might have been worshiped in this manner (Hos 6:10 alludes to cultic prostitution at Bethel). We can imagine such a development being encouraged by the use in the north of a popular Canaanite fertility image, the bull-pedestal, as a symbol of Yahweh (1 Kgs 12:30; for the prophetic critique of this artifact see Ex 32; Hos 8:5–7; 10:5–6).

Thus, for many of Hosea's contemporaries sacred prostitution had become a commonplace. To Hosea, however, rooted as he was in the older wilderness traditions, it was still a "shameful" and "loathsome" thing—a practice that had enormously destructive consequences ("they devoted themselves to Shame and became as loathsome as the thing they loved"—9:10b). Not only did it bind Israel to a pagan cult and a pagan deity (4:17), but it fostered a promiscuity that was destructive of the family (4:14a), multiplied the numbers of fatherless children (5:7), and resulted in a moral blindness that must inevitably lead to destruction (". . . a people with no understanding is doomed"—4:14b).

While his contemporaries, therefore, still viewed themselves as Yahweh worshipers (6:1–3), still swore oaths in his name (4:15) and professed faith in him (8:2), in reality they were "wedded to idols," Hosea charged (4:17), and Yahweh had withdrawn from them (5:15). "Their deeds do not allow them to return to their God, since an urge to play the whore possesses them and they no longer know Yahweh" (5:4).

(c) Violence

A second theme that is focused on repeatedly in the messages of Hosea is that of violence. "They break all bounds and blood touches blood" (4:2, literal translation). This was a feature of Israelite society with a long history to it, according to Hosea. The bloodbath perpetrated by Jehu at Jezreel, highlighted by him in the naming of his first child (1:4), was only one example among many. Long prior to that in the days of the judges there was a similar atrocity at Gibeah (Jgs 19), and it has been like that ever since, more or less, he implies in 10:9. This violent side of Israelite society is especially manifest in the bloody coups perpetrated by its rulers, he suggests ("They consume their rulers"—7:7). But violence was rife elsewhere as well. A murder by priests on the road to Shechem is mentioned in 6:9, and in 7:1 he speaks of houses being broken into by thieves. It is as though, like noxious weeds, sexual promiscuity and violence, growing up together, were threatening to choke out the very life of this community.

(d) The Failure of the Priests

Yet, conditions in Israel were not always this bad, Hosea suggests in several passages. In spite of certain characterological flaws (12:3–5), Israel was once a luxuriant vine bearing fruit (10:1)—a powerful people in whose presence others trembled (13:1). Who then was responsible for Israel's tragic descent into promiscuity and violence, and the current weakness? While various influences may have played a role in this development, such as corrupting wealth (10:1), Canaanite influence (9:10), and lawless kings and princes (5:11; 8:4), it was Hosea's firm conviction that the lion's share of responsibility for the widespread decadence in Israel during his time rested squarely on the shoulders of certain priests.

This seems to be the point of his analysis in 4:4–9 where a particular priest or priesthood is addressed, perhaps the one at Bethel (compare Am 7:10–17). There he charges that "you stumble in broad daylight" (4:5) in that "you have rejected *knowledge* . . . and forgotten the *teaching (torah)* of your God" (4:6). For this reason, he adds, "so I [Yahweh] shall reject you from my priesthood; since you have forgotten the teaching of your God, I in my turn shall forget your children" (4:6). For Hosea this matter is crucial. It is precisely because these priests are rejecting "knowledge" (Hebrew: "*the* knowledge") that "my people *perish* for want of knowledge" (4:6).

Here then is the core of Hosea's analysis of the spiritual decline of his people: the priests in charge of the official shrines, whose duty it was to teach the people that "knowledge" of God that might have prevented their moral decay, have themselves rejected it.

But what "knowledge," more specifically, is Hosea speaking of? A trilogy of phrases appearing at key points in his book suggests an answer. In 4:2, for example, the charge is made that "there is no *loyalty*, no *faithful love*, no *knowledge of God* in the country, only perjury and lying, murder, theft, adultery and violence, bloodshed after bloodshed." Here "no loyalty," no "faithful love" or no "knowledge of God," and the violation of a cluster of decalogue-type laws are equated.

Similar terminology is used again at the climax of a piercing analysis of the shallowness of Israel's attitude toward Yahweh, in 6:1–6. The people whom Hosea refers to in this passage are quoted as wanting to return to Yahweh to "know" him, since even though he has "rent" them and "struck" them, he will "heal us" and "bind up our wounds" (6:1–3). Hosea's reply pinpoints his overriding criticism of the contemporary religious attitude. "For your love is like morning mist," he writes, "like the dew that quickly disappears" (6:4). It lacks substance and staying power. The people bring sacrifices and holocausts in the confidence that Yahweh will be gracious to them, when what Yahweh really wants is not sacrifice, but "faithful love" (Hebrew: *chesed*), not "burnt offerings," but "knowledge of God" (6:6).

In summary, what Hosea believes is missing in this community is any real understanding of the basic covenantal stipulations that have heretofore guided Israel or the willingness to be loyal to them. And the chief reason this is missing is because the priests in charge of the Yahweh shrines are busy sacrificing instead of teaching—fostering a notion of "cheap grace," rather than that "knowledge of God" that leads to right living.

To Hosea this degradation of the priestly office was the ultimate tragedy of his people. Because of it "my people perish for want of knowledge" (4:6).

3. Hope for the Future

What then of the future? Unlike Amos, this question was clearly an agonizing one for Hosea, and especially so perhaps during that time of his life when his wife had left him. Was this the end—the end not only of his marriage, but of his people (whose relation to Yahweh the marriage had symbolized)?

An intimation of the personal struggles Hosea went through in arriving at an answer to this question is afforded us in ch. 11, in a soliloquy of wrenching pathos and beauty. What this chapter suggests is that his hope for the future was derived, not from an analysis of political or social conditions, nor by reflecting on prior theological traditions, but from an unmediated intuition regarding something transpiring within the personality of Yahweh himself!

In this passage Yahweh is characterized as someone who is himself inwardly so distraught and perplexed over his people's persistent disloyalty that he entertains the possibility of wiping them off the face of the earth (11:8). But he finds that he cannot do this. His love for Israel is just too strong.

> My heart within me is overwhelmed,
> fever grips my inmost being.
> I will not give rein to my fierce anger,
> I will not destroy Ephraim again,
> for I am God, not man,
> I am the Holy One in your midst,
> and I shall not come to you in anger (11:8–9).

Thus it was revealed to Hosea that there *was* a future for his people. Yahweh's compassion had triumphed over his "fierce anger" (11:9a). In the approaching catastrophe Israel would be decimated, but not annihilated.

It must have been in the wake of this revelatory breakthrough that Hosea was told to find his wife and love her once again.

> Go again, love a woman
> who loves another man, an adultress,
> and love her as Yahweh loves the Israelites
> although they turn to other gods . . . (3:1).

The novelty of taking back an adulterous wife (who by law should have been executed) corresponded exactly to the novelty of his revelation regarding God and the future. In this way he was commissioned to publicize his newly found truth. At the same time this new experience with Gomer seems to have prompted a flood of yet additional insights into what, more precisely, would be happening in the wake of the Assyrian invasion.

Elsewhere in his book, this approaching devastation is viewed as a consequence of sin and divine anger. In ch. 2, however, it begins to be seen as an act of grace whereby the artifacts of a falsely trusted culture are removed (especially those associated with Canaanite religion), so that Israel will be inwardly free for a new courtship and a new covenant between itself and its true Lord (2:16–17). Here destruction and cultural deprivation are preliminaries to a second wilderness experience (like that of the earlier Sinai event) during which the bond between Yahweh and his people will be restored "in uprightness and justice, and faithful love and tenderness," and true knowledge of Yahweh will once again prevail in the land, for ever (2:21–22).

This too Hosea was told to publicize, by the manner in which he restored his wife. Just as Israel will have to spend many days "without king or leader, without sacrifice or sacred pillar, without *ephod* or domestic images" (3:5), so he and Gomer are to live together "a long time" in sexual abstinence. But there will come a day when this deprivation will cease, just as there will come a day when "Israel will return and again seek Yahweh their God . . ." (3:5).

So sure of this was Hosea that in eager anticipation of that day he composed a liturgy of repentance and renewal for use by his people when all these things will have come to pass:

> Assyria cannot save us [he wrote],
> we will not ride horses anymore,
> or say "Our God!" to our own handiwork,
> for you are the one in whom orphans find compassion (14:4).

To this Yahweh replies:

> I shall cure them of their disloyalty,
> I shall love them with all my heart,
> for my anger has turned away from them (14:3).

In summary, the hope that burned in the heart of this prophet was grounded in an unmediated, revolutionary perception and conviction of the ultimate graciousness of Yahweh. Yahweh's love for Israel is so great that he cannot permit her to die "on her own soil, with no one to lift her up," as Amos had prophesied (5:2b). Judgment must come, but even this will be seen as but a preparation for that day when Israel will be restored once again to its land and reunited with Yahweh with the tenderness of a man winning back the affections of an estranged wife.

The way private and public domains may intersect in the experience of a prophet is nowhere more dramatically illustrated than here.

B. Ongoing Relevance

The first Judean editors of Hosea's literary legacy clearly did not feel that what he had said about the rupture between Yahweh and Israel applied to them (see 1:7 and 12:1). As they viewed it "Judah . . . is [still] faithful to the Holy One" (12:1). Yet, having preserved the book as they did, they must have thought that its warnings were valid (especially in that they were fulfilled in the fall of the north in 721), and that they could serve as a warning to the south as well. They must have also valued the book's religious insights. In fact, it is not inconceivable that it was brought south during the collapse of the northern kingdom and contributed quite directly to that reformation in Judah that occurred there in the reign of Hezekiah (see 2 Kgs 18:3–7). Later Deuteronomists (to whom we are indebted for the heading with its dates) were obviously of a similar mind, as was the man who penned the book's concluding admonition counseling the wise of every generation to ponder the relevance of its words (14:10).

As we try to do just that today, in twentieth century North America, certain analogies between what *we* are facing and what Hosea writes of in his book are only too apparent. In the late 1960's and early 1970's, for example—during a single decade—a massive shift occurred in North American sexual values. Prior to that a substantial majority in our culture thought of sexual relations outside of marriage as a sin; today this majority is a minority. Thus an "urge to go whoring" has progressively infiltrated *our* society as well, with consequences that are only too obvious and tragic: an unprecedented increase in out-of-wedlock pregnancies, abortions on demand, divorce, single parent families, and wave after wave of venereal diseases. Was Hosea not right when he targeted such a "spirit of fornication" as one of the worst things that can befall a society—a root cause of its decline and fall, if uncorrected?

A link may exist between sexual promiscuity and crimes of violence. Where promiscuity increases, families are destabilized and more and more children grow to adulthood in environments marked by emotional deprivations, stress, abuse and violence. Psychologists note with alarm the inner rage or lack of conscience that may result. It is no accident that many criminals come from homes of this kind. With promiscuity and infidelity a vicious cycle of disturbance is begun as one generation fuels the disorders of the next.

In morally confused times like these, prophets like Hosea who can sound a warning are a godsend. Their words which may appear harsh at times are essential to stab us awake. "This is why I have hacked them to pieces by means of the prophets, why I have killed them with words from my mouth . . ." (Hos 6:5a). It is a double tragedy, however, when even those who should be teaching us a better way are themselves bogged down in the moral morass. Then truly there is little hope of recovery. The ideals themselves disappear. We "perish for want of knowledge" (Hos 4:6a), "for a people with no understanding is doomed" (Hos 4:14b).

Yet, Hosea encourages us to think that even such a bleak condition may not be the final word. He was the first of the Hebrew prophets we know of to look beyond the chaos and catastrophes of the present into the longer range future and foresee something enormously hopeful on the more distant horizon. From his time onward issues related to the realization of that more distant hope would engage the prophets like few others. These issues are, of course, still with us—perhaps as never before: Does our world have a future, a good future? Can we survive the personal, national and international disorders that afflict us, avoid an atomic war, and build a better world?"

Such questions will engage us repeatedly in the remainder of this study. Hosea's contribution to their answer is a resounding affirmation of faith in the character of the God who he believes is guiding the human historical process, *and* a growing sensitivity to the possibility that disasters too may be redemptive (not simply punishment). Is it not true, even today, that it is sometimes only "in the wilderness" (Hos 2:16) that renewal can come to us—only when all that we have falsely trusted in has been taken away and we are quieter and more open again to hearing the whispers of our God, our ideals, the good "words" that lead to life (Hos 14:2–9)?

Questions for Review

1. Hosea uses a great variety of images to characterize the catastrophe that he believes will soon befall his community. List a few of these. To what one historical reality do they all point? What in general does he see as having gone wrong in his community to merit such a judgment? What in particular? Who in his community does he feel is primarily responsible for this deplorable state of affairs? Why?

2. On what basis did Hosea come to believe that in spite of everything that had happened a good future lay ahead for his people? What was the nature of this future and in what way did he communicate his

convictions regarding it to his community? How might this fresh outlook on the future have altered his understanding of the judgment that was imminent?

3. Formulate your own summary of how the life and messages of this prophet might be relevant to our time. If you wanted to remember one verse or passage from this book, what would it be? May judgments even today be necessary as a prelude to a better future?

9

Isaiah, Son of Amoz

Isaiah is the first of three larger prophetic volumes sometimes referred to as "major prophets" because of their size. The other two are
Jeremiah and Ezekiel. It will be quickly noted that these three books
are many times longer than the minor prophets we have been studying
to this point. The reason for this, in the case of Jeremiah and Ezekiel
(as we shall see), was the extraordinary length of their prophetic careers
and the unusually large legacy of words and stories they left behind.

However, this is not why the Book of Isaiah is as large as it is. Its
size is more a product of the *influence* Isaiah had on subsequent generations and the way those who preserved his oracles were challenged
to supplement them with yet additional words from later prophets. In
other words, more than one prophet speaks in the pages of this volume—a point that becomes evident as we begin scanning the book as
a whole.

A. The Book as a Whole

A good first approach to this book, I have found, is to leaf through
it slowly, noting first of all some of the more obvious editorial headings
and captions that appear from place to place.

As always in the writings of the prophets a simple heading faces
us as we open this book: "The vision of Isaiah son of Amoz, concerning
Judah and Jerusalem . . ." These same words recur in 2:1. Perhaps
the book's final editors found them there and decided they would make
a good caption for the book as a whole. They characterize this collection
as a "vision" or revelation which Isaiah "received in the reigns of Uzziah, Jotham, Ahaz and Hezekiah kings of Judah" (1:1). With these
references to certain kings we encounter once again the handiwork of
those anonymous Deuteronomists who have given us the Books of
Joshua through Kings.

Leafing on, one notices content divisions and breaks of one kind or another (the memoirs and anecdotes of 6:1–8:20 stand out, for example), but so far as additional *editorial* headings or captions are concerned, there are none after 2:1, until we reach 13:1. There we read: "Proclamation about Babylon, seen by Isaiah son of Amoz." This is then followed, in the next ten chapters (13–23), by a number of similar captions all having to do with "foreign nations" (14:28; 15:1; 17:1; 19:1; 21:1, 11, 13; 22:1; 23:1; note too the prophetic story in ch. 20). But then, as suddenly as these headings began, they cease. From ch. 24 onward there is not another caption of this kind in the remaining forty-two chapters! In other words, from this point on, if we wish to identify additional subdivisions, we must rely completely on an analysis of literary forms and content.

When that is done, one subdivision that immediately stands out is the rather extensive historical narrative in Isaiah 36–39. Strange to say, this section of the book is almost identical to 2 Kings 18:13–20:19, and indeed may have been copied from there. In fact, it appears that these chapters may have once served as an historical appendix to an earlier edition of Isaiah that ended at this point (note that a chapter from 2 Kings was also used in this way to close off the Book of Jeremiah—Jeremiah 52 being a slightly modified version of 2 Kings 24–25).

An examination of the chapters that follow, in Isaiah 40–66, would appear to confirm this hypothesis. In this section of Isaiah we look in vain for a single reference to the Isaiah referred to in chs. 1–39. Furthermore, the Isaiah of chs. 1–39, as the heading to the book already suggests (1:1), was a Judean living in Jerusalem during the latter part of the eighth century, while the author of the prophecies in chs. 40ff. appears to be living in Babylon (43:14) at a time when Jerusalem was in ruins (64:9–11), and a Persian ruler by the name of Cyrus was on the march (44:28; 45:1). This latter event took place in the sixth century (546), a full two centuries after the events alluded to in Isaiah 1–39. In other words, the prophet who speaks in these chapters must be someone quite different from the eighth century Isaiah of Jerusalem.

A still more careful analysis of the *contents* of these chapters indicates that a further distinction must be drawn between chs. 40–55 and chs. 56–66. Most scholars are convinced that chs. 40–55 are virtually all from the hand of a single prophet who lived in Babylon in the immediate aftermath of the first wave of Persian conquests in that region in 546. The name of this prophet is no longer known to us, but because his prophecies have been added to those of the eighth century Isaiah of Jerusalem, scholars have come to refer to him as "Second Isaiah."

Chs. 56–66, on the other hand, seem to reflect the activity of still another prophet, even though his message is quite similar to that of "Second Isaiah." He is no longer situated in Babylon, but is among those who returned to the land of Israel when the Persians conquered Babylon in 539 and released the captive peoples there (note especially 56:8). Isaiah 64:9 suggests that he was living at this time in the vicinity of a Jerusalem that was still a "wasteland," but that plans were afoot for rebuilding the temple there (66:1). This was finally accomplished in 515 B.C. (Ezra 6), so his mission would need to be dated to a point prior to that event. Again, we do not know the name of this prophet, so we call him the "Third Isaiah."

From all this the idea begins to suggest itself that the Book of Isaiah preserves the legacy of not just one, but *three* major prophetic figures, each of whom lived and prophesied during a quite distinct and unique time period.

Our observations to this point can be charted as follows:

The Three Books of Isaiah

Book 1	Book 2	Book 3
Messages of Isaiah of Jerusalem	Messages of an unknown prophet in Babylon	Messages of an unknown prophet in Judea
740–700	546–538	537–520
Chs. 1–39	Chs. 40–55	Chs. 56–66
First Isaiah	Second Isaiah	Third Isaiah

At this point in our study of Isaiah we will be focusing on the life and message of First Isaiah only (chs. 1–39). Later on, in subsequent chapters, we will take a closer look at Second and Third Isaiah.

A more careful survey of chs. 1–39 will suggest that even here not everything can be attributed to the Isaiah of Jerusalem mentioned in the heading (1:1). We have already noted two well-defined blocks of content in this opening section of the book: a collection of foreign nation oracles, in chs. 13–23, and an historical appendix, in chs. 36–39. Because of the new heading, in 2:1, as well as the composite character of the opening chapter, in ch. 1, this latter is generally regarded as an editorially arranged introduction to the collection as a whole.

The chapters that immediately follow, in 2–12, may well contain some of the earliest and most important of Isaiah's messages. However, several peculiarities of this block of chapters should be noted. One is the way a personal description of the prophet's call, and then a collection of oracles and reports of his actions during the Syro-Ephraimitic War (6:1–9:6), have been spliced into the middle of a collection of his criticisms and warnings (for evidence of this, note the way the phrase, "After all this, his anger is not spent. No, his hand is still raised!" in 5:25, is repeated in 9:7–10:4).

The following chart indicates some of the major content divisions of these chapters (1–12):

Isaiah 1–12

			Independent collection spliced in ↓			
Ch. 1	2:1–4:6	5:1–23	6:1–9:6	9:7–10:4	10:5–34	11–12
Introduction	Early oracles	Warnings	Oracles during Syro-Ephraimitic War	Warnings	Assyria	New Age

With this we have now identified three of the major sections of Book 1 of Isaiah: chs. 1–12, the foreign nation oracles, in 13–23, and the historical appendix, in 36–39.

What of the remaining chapters?

The four chapters following the foreign nation oracles (13–23), chs. 24–27, are generally regarded as a late addition to the book because of their cosmic end-of-the-world focus—an outlook that is quite different from that of First Isaiah, as we shall soon see. Chs. 34 and 35 remind us of the messages of the Second Isaiah and for this reason are also generally regarded as late additions to this section. Only chs. 28–33 contain material comparable to that in chs. 1–12. These may come from the latter period of Isaiah's prophetic activity.

If we wish then to study and understand the life, activities and messages of the eighth century Isaiah of Jerusalem, it is to three sections of his book in particular that we must turn: chs. 1–12, 13–23 and 28–33.

Our analysis of chs. 1–39, to this point, may be charted as follows:

Isaianic in part	Isaianic in part	Late Additions	Isaianic in part	Late Additions	Historical Appendix
1–12	13–23	24–27	28–33	34–35	36–39
From early period	Foreign Nation Oracles		From late period		

It must be kept in mind, however, that even the prophecies of chs. 1–12, chs. 13–23, and chs. 28–33 may not all be from the hand of Isaiah of Jerusalem. Many commentators consider the following passages to be later additions:

(a) in the first 12 chapters: 2:2–5; 4:2–6; 11:10–16 and all of ch. 12;

(b) in chs. 13–23: the oracles against Babylon (13:1–14:23; 21:1–11) and Moab (15:1–16:14), as well as certain additions to the Egypt and Tyre oracles (19:16–25; 23:5–11, 15–16);

(c) in chs. 28–31: 28:5–6; 29:17–24; 30:19–26. Chs. 32 and 33 may also represent an amalgam of the words of Isaiah and those of his disciples, rather than Isaiah's words only.

Looked at more carefully, then, the Book of Isaiah turns out to be a highly complex mosaic of prophetic words and reports, emanating from an *ongoing* tradition of prophetic activity and spanning a period of centuries. However, this tradition clearly had its point of origins in a certain unique individual living in the eighth century B.C. Why was it that his words were taken up, preserved and expanded upon in this way?

An answer is hinted at in Isaiah 8:16–18 where we are told that at a critical moment early in his prophetic career Isaiah did something that, so far as we know, no other prophet before him had done: he bound up and sealed his "instruction" from God "in the heart" of his disciples—that is, he had a group of his followers memorize his messages and thereby established what might be termed an Isaianic group or "school," one that must have felt itself responsible for preserving the spiritual legacy of its founder. It was this group, we imagine, that edited and supplemented this legacy and from which other prophets may have arisen whose messages were then appended to it as well.

B. The Man Behind the Book

We turn now from the Book of Isaiah to a consideration of those texts that tell us something of the founder of this tradition: Isaiah of

Jerusalem. Who was this man whose messages were regarded as worthy of being preserved and elaborated in this remarkable manner?

Although personal information about him is scanty, we *are* informed as to his name, when he lived and how he became a prophet. We can also be fairly certain *where* he lived. From this we can piece together a good bit about his cultural and theological background. We can also make a few educated guesses about his occupation. Once again, to assemble what the various relevant texts say about the man behind the book can be an important step in coming to terms with his message and beginning to sense its possible significance for his time and ours.

1. Name

"Isaiah," in Hebrew, is a compound of two words, one meaning "save" or "salvation," and the other a shortened form of Yahweh—the two together meaning: "Yahweh saves" or "Yahweh is salvation." Isaiah's father's name was "Amoz" (not to be confused with the prophet Amos). For this reason he is often referred to as "Isaiah-son-of-Amoz" (1:1; 13:1; 20:2; 38:1).

2. Where He Lived

Although it is nowhere stated in so many words, there are few things more certain about Isaiah than that he lived and prophesied in Jerusalem, capital city of the southern Israelite kingdom of Judah. Jerusalem is the target of virtually all of his criticisms, warnings and hopes (see for example 1:21–28). The Davidic kings in Jerusalem, as well as their advisors, appear to have been well known to him (see chs. 7 and 28–31). The Jerusalem temple is the backdrop for that shattering vision that launched him on his prophetic career (ch. 6). The fate of this city and its temple were at the center of his thoughts from the beginning of his prophetic mission (see chs. 7 and 8), right up to its end (see chs. 36–39).

The importance this Jerusalem context had for Isaiah clearly distinguishes him from the previous two prophets we have studied. Amos, as noted, was a Judean, but lived some distance south of Jerusalem among the sheep-breeders of Tekoa; Hosea lived in the Israelite kingdom to the north. Neither appear to have regarded Jerusalem as having any special or unique importance in and of itself—religiously, politically or otherwise. *Their* focus was on *Israel,* conceived of as a single people, or on the northern kingdom, primarily, and the cultic centers at Bethel and Gilgal. When they spoke of the history of their people, they alluded to the exodus from Egypt, the wilderness covenant (at Sinai), and the gift of Canaan, not to traditions associated with Jerusalem.

Isaiah too viewed Israel as a unified people (1:3) and is aware of its exodus origins (10:26). But far more important for *him* than this is the role he believes *Jerusalem* has been singled out to play in Yahweh's plan for Israel and the world. For him and his contemporaries this city was far from being just like any other.

For one thing, Yahweh had chosen it to be his dwelling place on earth. This had happened shortly after David had captured it and made it his residence (2 Sam 5:6–12). Then it was that he arranged to have brought to this city that ancient symbol of Yahweh's rule and presence: the ark of the covenant (see 1 Sam 4–6; 2 Sam 6). The train of events that made this possible was so uncanny that the conviction emerged that not just David, but Yahweh himself had been active in bringing this to pass. It was not David, but Yahweh who had "chosen Zion," saying (as the point is put in Ps 132:13–14), "Here shall I rest for evermore, here shall I make my home as I have wished." This being so, Jerusalem was viewed by those who lived there, not so much as David's city, but as the "city of God" (Ps 46:4), the one place on earth where Yahweh was most near and accessible to the prayers of his people (see 1 Kgs 8:30–53).

> Great is Yahweh and most worthy of praise
>   in the city of our God,
> The holy mountain, towering in beauty,
>   the joy of the whole world.
>
> Mount Zion in the heart of the north,
>   the settlement of the great king;
> God himself among its palaces
>   has proved himself its bulwark (Ps 48:2–3).

But Jerusalem was unique to those who lived there for yet another reason. Just as Yahweh had chosen Zion to be his home forever, so also, it was believed, he had chosen the family of David to establish a line of kings to reign there forever (see 2 Sam 7:4–16; 23:5). For each succeeding Davidic king this promise held true that Yahweh would be a father to him and he a son to Yahweh (Ps 89:26). In this way, ideally, each king was empowered to live righteously, represent Yahweh and bring about his rule on earth "from sea to sea, from the river to the limits of the earth" (Ps 72:8). Of course, should individual kings fail to realize this ideal and do evil instead, they would have to be disciplined (Ps 89:30–33). But such failures would never defeat Yahweh's overarching goals, it was believed. Unlike the covenant made at Sinai (a covenant which could be broken), Yahweh's covenants with Zion and with David were *forever.*

> I have made a covenant with my Chosen One,
>   sworn an oath to my servant David:
> I have made your dynasty firm for ever,
>   built your throne stable age after age (Ps 89:3–4).

> For Yahweh has chosen Zion,
>   he has desired it as a home.
> "Here shall I rest for evermore . . ." (Ps 132:13–14a).

These twin convictions (Yahweh's choice of Zion and the Davidic dynasty) were the pillars of "Jerusalem theology" and hence of Isaiah's theology as well. For him too Jerusalem was unique and supremely sacred because Yahweh, the Holy One of Israel, "dwells" there "on Mount Zion" (Is 8:18b). For him too the reigning kings in Jerusalem were also sacred, for they belonged to the "House of David" with whom Yahweh had made his unbreakable covenant (7:13–17). We will not be able to understand the messages of Isaiah adequately unless we keep this fact constantly in mind. He is not only Isaiah-son-of-Amoz, but, even more importantly, Isaiah-of-*Jerusalem,* Yahweh's dwelling place on earth and of his kingly rule through the House of David.

3. What He Did

Unfortunately, neither Isaiah, nor his disciples, nor the editors of his book tell us what his occupation was prior to his becoming a prophet. The fact that his wife is called a "prophetess" (8:3) and that Isaiah himself is accorded an unusual degree of respect and protection by kings and officials in Jerusalem (in spite of his sometimes sharp criticisms of them) has prompted Koch to suggest that he might have been a state appointed "seer" (like the seer Gad, for example; see 2 Sam 24:10–25).

Another equally plausible suggestion is that prior to becoming a prophet Isaiah had been a teacher of some sort. That there were schools in Jerusalem at this time cannot be doubted (even though our sources fail to mention them). In a city as cosmopolitan as Jerusalem civil servants would be needed who were trained in reading, writing, history, morality, languages, manners and diplomacy. For this teachers would be needed and programs of instruction such as we know existed at this time in other major Near Eastern cities (see 2 Kings 10:6 for a possible reference to education of this kind in Samaria). Indeed, it is altogether possible (as has often been suggested) that major biblical documents were originally written for use in such schools (the collection of two-line teachings in Proverbs 10:1–22:16, for example, or the thirty "sayings of the sages" attached to it, in Proverbs 22:17–24:22, or the Book of Ruth and other historical accounts such as the so-called Yahwist epic in the Pentateuch).

A key concept of this "school" literature appears to have been that *human* wisdom or counsel (*'esa* in Hebrew) is fallible (Prov 21:30), but "the counsel of Yahweh stands firm" (Prov 11:21). It is precisely this point that Isaiah brings against his contemporaries. The king and his counselors, he says, are giving advice without consulting Yahweh or paying attention to what *his* counsel (*'esa*) might be (28:15; 30:1; 8:10). Therefore, it shall not "stand firm," he declares (8:10; 7:5; 10:5–15; 14:24–27; 31:1–3). Had Isaiah been a teacher in such schools this would also help to explain his literary versatility. Note especially the superbly crafted allegory of the vineyard, in 5:1–7, and his transparently pedagogical approach in a passage like 28:23–29. This too would explain why he alone of the prophets took the unusual step of binding and sealing his teachings (as would a school master) in the memories of a certain group of students or disciples, as noted above (8:16).

Whether seer or teacher, it seems clear, in any case, that Isaiah was among the elite of Jerusalem, a man of intellect and standing in his community.

4. Prophetic Call

However, neither intellect nor standing was the decisive factor in Isaiah's becoming a prophet. Like his prophetic predecessors, this was the consequence of a traumatic experience with God which he himself took the pains to record, in 6:1–13, and which he informs us occurred "in the year of King Uzziah's death" (6:1). During an awesome vision in which he "saw" Yahweh Sabaoth as king enthroned high above the temple, with fiery seraphs attending him and lauding his radiant power filling "the whole earth" (6:3), he felt "lost," he writes, for in a flash, so to speak, he realized that he was living in the midst of a corrupt, unclean people and was himself a man of unclean lips (6:5). He feared for his life, but then an astonishing thing happened. While still in this visionary state of mind, one of the seraphs whose voice he had heard lauding Yahweh's greatness and power went to the altar of sacrifice (in the temple court), carefully took from it a burning coal and brought it to where he was. This was then pressed to his lips, with the words: "Look, this has touched your lips, your guilt has been removed and your sin forgiven" (6:7).

It was in the wake of these wrenching, transforming experiences, Isaiah goes on to inform us, that he heard a summons from God for someone to serve him as "messenger," and volunteered his services (2:8–9). He was then told to go and say to this people:

"Listen and listen, but never understand!
Look and look, but never perceive!"

Make this people's heart coarse,
make their ears dull, shut their eyes tight,
or they will use their eyes to see,
use their ears to hear,
use their heart to understand,
and change their ways and be healed (6:9–10).

It was through these ironical words that the terrible truth dawned in the heart of Isaiah that had early broken upon the consciousness of Amos, during his third vision (Am 7:7–8), and upon the mind of Hosea at the birth of his children (Hos 1:2–9). With this revelation it had now become clear to him that Yahweh's patience with Israel was at an end— that his people's moral condition was beyond converting or healing— and consequently a terrible catastrophe lay ahead.

"Until when, Lord?" he cried out in despair (6:11). The answer was a shattering one:

Until towns are in ruins and deserted,
houses untenanted
and a great desolation reigns in the land,
and Yahweh has driven the people away
and the country is totally abandoned.
And suppose one-tenth of them are left in it,
that will be stripped again, like the terebinth,
like the oak, cut back to the stock;
their stock is a holy seed (6:11–13).

An invasion was imminent from which only a splintered stump of the tree of Judah would survive!

In summary, three convictions seem to have broken upon the mind of the prophet Isaiah during this awesome vision, convictions which were to remain with him for the rest of his life. These were:

● first, that Yahweh, the Holy One of Israel, is truly on the throne of the universe and "in charge" of all that is happening there ("his glory fills the whole earth");

● second, that the sinful condition of his people is so great that there is no hope for reform short of a devastating invasion that will soon sweep through the countryside laying waste the towns and villages of his people until virtually everything is destroyed;

● third, that not all is lost, however, for had he not heard Yahweh say that a "stock" of the blasted stump of his people would remain (6:13)? Soon after this vision Isaiah had a son whom he named "A-Remnant-Will-Return" (*Shear-Jashub*—Is 7:3). Disaster was imminent, but this was not the end. Out of the ashes of this catastrophe a new people would be born.

Isaiah's entire mission was taken up with expositing and amplifying these seminal insights.

5. Historical Setting

Before looking more closely at the way Isaiah did this, however, something must be said yet about the historical background to his mission.

Isaiah's prophetic career was an unusually long one. Called to be a prophet (as just noted) in the death year of King Uzziah (6:1), about 740, he was still active some forty years later (see chs. 36–39). What in general was happening in Jerusalem-Judah during these four decades and how did Isaiah relate to it?

From our study of Amos and Hosea we have already become acutely aware of the threat posed to the petty nations of this region by Assyria. This threat had now become even more imminent. From Assyrian records we learn that King Uzziah himself, just prior to his death, had been desperately engaged in forming a coalition to stop Assyria's now seemingly unstoppable westward movement. It would be difficult to exaggerate the terror that the Assyrians inspired among the populations of this region. The technological sophistication and discipline of their armies was awesome.

Of these Isaiah himself writes, in 5:27–28:

None of them tired, none of them stumbling,
none of them asleep or drowsy,

none of them with belt unfastened,
none of them with broken sandal-strap.

Their arrows are sharpened,
their bows all strung,
their horses' hoofs you would think were flint
and their wheels, a whirlwind!

Their roar is like that of a lioness,
like fierce young lions they roar,
growling they seize their prey
and carry it off, with no one to prevent it.

Especially frightening was the Assyrian army's uncanny ability to besiege and destroy fortified cities (the ultimate refuge in this time against a takeover by foreign invaders). This involved building massive earthen ramps leading upward to the city walls (see 2 Kgs 25:1), then mounting battering rams and archers—all the while keeping the city continuously surrounded (for Ezekiel's dramatic reenactment of such a siege by Babylon a century later, see Ez 4:1–3).

And yet, despite the Assyrian might and prowess, the petty kingdoms of Palestine were not about to surrender without a fight. Six major episodes may be identified in the background of Isaiah's mission, virtually all of them related, in one way or another, to the struggle of these nations for survival in the face of this imminent threat of destruction by Assyria.

(a) The first was a united attack, strangely enough (since they had been implacable enemies), by the combined forces of Syria and Ephraim against Judah, in 734—referred to in modern studies as the Syro-Ephraimitic War. Its purpose was to force Judah to join them in an alliance against Assyria. King Ahaz of Judah rightly saw their plan as a piece of folly, but in an equally foolish move (stridently opposed by Isaiah) turned to the Assyrians themselves for assistance (regarding this crisis and Isaiah's confrontation with Ahaz, see Is 7:1–8:16).

(b) A second event in the background of Isaiah's mission was Assyria's response to this rebellion on its western flank. In that same year, 734, Assyria launched a sweeping invasion of this region during which Damascus-Syria was roundly defeated and large tracks of territory belonging to Israel on the coastal plain, in Galilee, and east and northeast of Galilee were annexed as Assyrian provinces (see the brief allusion to these events in 2 Kgs 15:29). This invasion is the background for

Isaiah's famous prophecy of hope for "the people that walked in darkness" (9:1).

(c) Even this blow, however, did not prevent Ephraim from continuing its hopeless struggle for autonomy. The price paid for this, however, as we have already learned in our study of Hosea (and this is the third event in the background of Isaiah's mission), was total defeat, in 721, when the Assyrians swept into this region, besieged and captured Samaria, and then annexed the entire northern Israelite state as a province of its now vastly enlarged empire. These traumatic events were only what Isaiah had anticipated (although he may have thought that even worse things would happen), for he too, like Hosea, had been forewarned of precisely such a development in his call to prophesy over a decade earlier (see also his criticism and wrenching lament for Ephraim in 9:7–11 and 28:1–4).

(d) In the immediate aftermath of this disaster, sweeping *religious* reforms occurred in Judah under the leadership of King Hezekiah (see 2 Kgs 18:1–8)—this the *fourth* major historical event in the background of Isaiah's mission. Strangely, there is no reference to these reforms in Isaiah's writings, even though he might have helped to bring them about (see chs. 36–39 for examples of his special relationship with this generally wise and good king). As previously noted (see our discussion of Hosea), Levites from the north, bringing with them their sacred writings (including some version, perhaps, of the Book of Deuteronomy), may have fled south at this time. They too might have had some influence on these religious developments. In any case, a century later, when the temple was being repaired, a book of laws was found there (see 2 Kgs 22) that most scholars agree (on the basis of the laws referred to in 2 Kgs 23) was Deuteronomic in character. This book might well have been deposited there at this juncture. If so, it is understandable why the Deuteronomic historians write of Hezekiah that "no king of Judah after him could be compared with him—nor any of those before him" (2 Kgs 18:5–7). From their point of view he was the first specifically Judean king to adopt the laws of Moses (as preserved by the Levites in the Book of Deuteronomy) as state policy.

(e) Another insurrection against Assyria broke out in Palestine, in 714 (the fifth major event of Isaiah's prophetic career). This time it was centered in the Philistine coastal city of Ashdod (see Is 20). Supporting it was a resurgent Egypt under the leadership of an enterprising Ethiopian named Tirhakah. Isaiah's shocking protest (he walked the streets of Jerusalem, naked) may have been partly responsible for saving Judah from becoming involved in this futile affair. As a consequence Jerusalem was spared when Assyria once again invaded this region and quashed the rebellion, in 711.

(f) However, a decade later Judah could no longer restrain itself. It too had to try its hand at insurrection, it seems. The propitious moment for doing so had finally arrived, it was thought, when in 705 the Assyrian leader Sargon II died and revolts erupted all over the Assyrian empire. Indeed, this may be the purpose of the visit to Judah at this time of envoys from Babylon (see Is 39), for we know from other sources that Babylon too was in a state of rebellion right then.

Sargon II's successor, however, the famous Sennacherib, proved himself every bit as resourceful a leader as his predecessors. After quickly crushing the Babylonian insurgency, he mounted, in 701, a devastating military campaign against Judah. In the annals which archaeologists have recovered from the ruins of Nineveh (his capital city) Sennacherib describes in his own words the destruction he wrought. Forty-six armed Judaean cities were besieged and destroyed and Hezekiah himself, he wrote, was cooped up like a bird in a cage. Jerusalem was spared, but only after suffering a humiliating surrender with ransom (see 2 Kgs 18:14)—and a miracle of some sort about which we will have more to say, shortly, when discussing Isaiah's message.

These six events may be plotted on a time line as follows:

1	2	3	4	5	6
Syro-Ephraimitic War	Fall of Damascus (annexation of Galilee)	Fall of Ephraim	Hezekiah's reforms	The Ashdod insurrection	The Sennacherib invasion
734*	733	721*	715	712*	701*

*Times when Isaiah was especially active as a prophet (see Is 7:1–8:18; 20; 28:1–4; 31; 32; 36–37)

From this outline and the above comments it is apparent that Isaiah's prophetic activities were closely intertwined with momentous political and religious events. He began his prophetic career in the death-year of Uzziah (740); he was especially active during the Syro-Ephraimitic War (734); he became active again some twenty years later at the time of the Ashdod insurrection (714), and again during the Sennacherib invasion (701). He may have also gone public, for a brief time, just prior to the fall of the north (721).

As a resident of Jerusalem Isaiah was confident that his city was unique. Had not Yahweh promised to be present there, with temple and king, forever? And yet, in a moment of searing insight, he had seen as well that his city was endangered. Its leading elite was deplorably "unclean." Terrible consequences would soon be resulting from this. A devastating invasion was imminent from which only a few would escape.

It was these shocking revelations, "in the year of King Uzziah's death," that transformed him and compelled him to enter upon his prophetic mission.

Questions for Review

1. Why is the Book of Isaiah as large as it is? Summarize the evidence pointing to the conclusion that in reality this is "three books in one." To what sections of his book will we turn if we wish to study the life and messages of the eighth century Isaiah of Jerusalem? What might Isaiah of Jerusalem might have contributed to the formation of such an enlarged book?

2. What is the importance for an appreciation of his theological presuppositions of knowing that Isaiah was from Jerusalem and did most of his prophesying there? What employment might Isaiah have had, in that city, prior to (or even while) being a prophet? How might knowing this also enrich our picture of him?

3. To what fundamental convictions did Isaiah come as the result of his visionary call experience (ch. 6)? Why were the Assyrians as feared and dreaded as they were? When did they succeed in conquering Samaria? Why did Judah escape being conquered as well at this time? What factors may have contributed to a religious reform in Judah, after the fall of northern Israel? What happened in 701 when Sennacherib led an invasion of this region? During what events of this period was Isaiah especially active as a prophet?

10

His Message and Its Relevance

What, more concretely, did Isaiah have to say in these troubled times? His messages are generally regarded as "the theological high-water mark" of prophetic literature (von Rad) and lend themselves, as such, especially well to *thematic* treatment. With this in mind I suggest that we organize our approach to his oracles around the core ideas we find there, remembering as we do so the chronology of his mission outlined in the previous chapter.

A. Message

From the beginning of his mission to its end Isaiah was certain that in and through the events of his time Yahweh was doing a "work" and carrying out a "decision" (as he termed it). This divine plan was not an arbitrary one. It had its reasons. It also had consequences for the political realm. Those in power in Jerusalem would act in certain ways if they truly understood and accepted it.

These then are the overarching themes that we encounter, again and again, in Isaiah's writings: Yahweh's plan; the rationale behind this plan; the plan's consequences for public policy. Each needs to be carefully attended to if we are going to understand what Isaiah had to say to the people of his time.

1. Yahweh's Plan

Already at the time of his prophetic call (as noted in the previous chapter) Isaiah came to believe that a devastating invasion was about to sweep through Judah, one that would lay waste its countryside and towns (6:11–13). Although, in this particular passage, it was not explicitly stated that Assyria is to be the perpetrator of this invasion, this clearly is what Isaiah had in mind. However, Assyria's rise to power, as Isaiah came to understand it, was more than an accident of history. Behind this event (as its prime mover so to speak) was the One whom his eyes had seen (in his vision) enthroned over the universe: *the* King, Yahweh Sabaoth (6:5b). Assyria was but an instrument of *divine* action (10:5). This appears to be the reason that Isaiah came to refer to the events unfolding in his time as *Yahweh's* "work" or "decision" or "design" (5:12b, 18–19; 10:12; 14:24–27; 28:21). These events were all planned by Yahweh with certain goals in mind.

But what, more specifically, *was* this work, this plan? The answer is never fully spelled out in so many words in any one passage. It can be readily pieced together, however, by observing what Isaiah says in oracles spanning his prophetic mission. Its outlines are roughly as follows: the approaching Assyrian invasion of Judah, while inevitable and devastating, will *not* be total (6:13; 9:1); at a critical point (before all is completely destroyed) the Assyrians themselves will be defeated (10:5–16; 14:25; 28:21; 31:8) with the result that Jerusalem will be spared (31:4–6) along with a "remnant" there (10:20–21; 28:16); this miracle of deliverance will bring about repentance and cleansing and renewed faith (1:25–28; 28:16–22), and in this way a *new* Jerusalem will arise out of the ashes of the old—a Jerusalem faithful and upright, as in the days of old (1:21; 9:1–6; 11:1–9).

Just how important this conception of Yahweh's plan was to Isaiah, *early* in his prophetic mission already, is indicated by the fact (previously alluded to) that shortly after his call (ch. 6) a son was born to him who was named "A-remnant-will-return" (Hebrew: *Shear-Ja-shub*—7:3). "Remnant" here refers to those who survive a catastrophe. As this son's presence by Isaiah's side during the crisis of the Syro-Ephraimitic War clearly indicates (see 7:1–9), he was already then a very special symbol for him of the certainty that even though Jerusalem might be attacked it would *not* be annihilated. A remnant *would* miraculously survive, even if *only* a remnant.

Thirty years later Isaiah was still proclaiming this very same truth during the final onslaught of the Sennacherib invasion (see Is 36–37). Throughout his mission this appears to have been one of his deepest and most central convictions: that his country *would* in his time suffer terribly from war, but that somehow there would be survivors—there would be a deliverance not by "flesh" (31:3), but by "spirit" (31:1, 3), not by military force of arms, but by Yahweh himself.

> Yes, this is what Yahweh has said to me:
> As a lion or lion cub
> growls over its prey,
> when scores of shepherds

are summoned to drive it off,
without being frightened by their shouting
or cowed by the noise they make,
just so will Yahweh Sabaoth descend
to fight for Mount Zion and for its hill.
Like hovering birds,
so will Yahweh Sabaoth protect Jerusalem;
by protecting it, he will save it,
by supporting it, he will deliver it (31:4–5).

This then is Yahweh's plan, his work, "his mysterious work . . . his deed, his extraordinary deed" (28:21). An Assyrian invasion is imminent. Enormous devastation will result. But before all is lost Assyria itself will be punished because of *its* sins (10:5–19) and a remnant in Jerusalem saved (31:8). And from this ordeal a new Jerusalem would be born.

Yahweh Sabaoth has sworn it,
"Yes, what I have planned will take place,
what I have decided will be so:

"I shall break Assyria in my country,
I shall trample on him on my mountains.
Then his yoke will slip off them,
his burden will slip from their shoulders."

This is the decision taken in defiance of the whole world;
this, the hand outstretched in defiance of all nations.
Once Yahweh Sabaoth has decided, who will stop him?
Once he stretches out his hand, who can withdraw it? (14:24–
    27)

2. The Reason for this Plan

But why is Yahweh doing this? Already in discussing Isaiah's call we encountered the fact that there was something amiss in Jerusalem. "Woe is me! I am lost," Isaiah cried out when the vision of Yahweh broke in upon him, "for I am a man of unclean lips and I live among a people of unclean lips" (6:5). Uncleanness, pollution, estrangement from God characterized his society, Isaiah suddenly realized, and *he* was a part of it. Were it not that a "seraph" had pressed a coal from the altar to his lips, thereby purging him, surely he would have perished right then and there (6:6–7).

But what "uncleanness," more specifically, is Isaiah speaking of here, and how, concretely, does Yahweh's plan (the Assyrian invasion and the miraculous deliverance of a "remnant" in Jerusalem) relate to this problem?

An outline of the answer to both questions is given in the messages of Isaiah that have been assembled in ch. 1. There Jerusalem is likened to Sodom and Gomorrah (1:10) and characterized as a community of rebels (1:2). Why? Because, we are told in 1:10–17, the people of this city are endlessly involved in worshiping Yahweh through an extravagance of animal sacrifices which he hates, while neglecting what he really wants of them: ceasing to do evil, learning to do good, searching for justice, disciplining the violent, caring for orphan and widow.

What makes these conditions in Jerusalem so reprehensible, he continues, is that there *had been* a time when things were different. "Zion, once full of fair judgment, where saving justice used to dwell . . ." (1:21). He is referring here perhaps to the days of Uzziah, or of David. For him the ideal or normative time in the life of his people was not (as for Amos and Hosea) the exodus from Egypt or the time in the wilderness of Sinai, but some earlier moment in the life of Jerusalem. But that is not the way things are now in this city.

> Your silver has turned into dross,
> your wine is watered.
> Your princes are rebels,
> accomplices of brigands.

> All of them greedy for presents
> and eager for bribes,
> they show no justice to the orphan,
> and the widow's cause never reaches them (1:22–23).

It is this lawless greed in Jerusalem (covered by a thin veneer of religiosity) that is the target of the catastrophic events that are now about to occur, Isaiah declared. In this particular chapter these are referred to as actions whose effect will be analogous to the purging of dross with potash (1:25). By this he means that "rebels and sinners alike will be destroyed, and those who abandon Yahweh will perish" (1:28), after which, Yahweh says, "I shall restore your judges as at first, your counselors as in bygone days," so that "you will be called City of Saving Justice, Faithful City" (1:26).

This in general then is the "why" of Yahweh's plan as Isaiah envisioned it. Through the ordeal of the Assyrian invasion and the miracle of deliverance something revolutionary is going to happen to the residents of Jerusalem, he believed. Even as *he* was at the time of his call (6:6–7), they will be purged as by fire. Their pride will be shattered, rebels and sinners will be destroyed (1:28), and judges and counselors will be restored as in bygone days (1:26). In this way there will come into existence a new Jerusalem.

In the remaining messages of Isaiah the profile of this plan is amplified at *two points* especially:

● in chs. 2–5 we learn in greater detail of the *disorders* in Jerusalem that are the target of this purging invasion;

● in three remarkable poems, in 9:1–6, 11:1–9, and 32:1–8, a portrait of the *leadership* that Isaiah envisions as arising in Jerusalem in the aftermath of the approaching disasters is sketched.

These passages are among the more memorable and provocative of his prophetic career. As such they merit careful study. We can do little more here, however, than allude to the way they embellish Isaiah's overall picture of Yahweh's plan.

(a) The Sins of Jerusalem (2:6–5:25)

One senses from 2:12–17 that Isaiah was especially troubled by the arrogant attitudes that prevailed among Jerusalem's leadership elite. In the background of this passage are political developments in Judah just prior to the Assyrian invasions. At that time (as already noted in our study of Amos) there had occurred a sudden (but brief) burst of prosperity in this region (see Is 2:6–8). As happens so often, with this prosperity came greed and loss of respect, and Isaiah saw this only becoming worse and worse.

> People will be ill-treated by one another,
> each by his neighbor;
> the young will insult the aged,
> and the low, the respected (3:5).

Especially grievous to Isaiah was the pomp and arrogance of certain upper class women (3:16–24; 32:9–13) and their domination of equally pompous youths. "I shall give them boys for princes, raw lads to rule over them" (3:4). "O my people, their oppressors pillage them and extortioners [Hebrew: women] rule over them!'' (3:12)—a reference perhaps to Jotham and Ahaz who ruled in Jerusalem after their father Uzziah's tragic contraction of leprosy (a disease that required that he be confined to his bedroom; see 2 Kgs 15:5).

The decadence of Jerusalem is further analyzed in a series of trenchant ''woes,'' in 5:8–24 and 10:1–4. The crimes of an economic elite are singled out in the opening and closing examples. This group, it is charged, adds house to house and field to field (5:8), and does so by totally corrupt means to the detriment of others (5:23; 10:1). It is undoubtedly this same elite, now firmly in control in Jerusalem, that the prophet is addressing in the remaining woes. In 5:11–12, their extravagant parties are mentioned, and, in 5:18–19, their religiously cynical attitude. They lack all moral discretion, calling bad good and good bad (5:20); they are proud (5:21) and prone to ostentatious alcoholism (''whose might lies in wine bibbing, their heroism in mixing strong drinks''—5:22).

This too is the group, no doubt, for whose ears Isaiah crafted his famous allegory of the vineyard, in 5:1–7, for as leaders of the House of Israel and the ''people of Judah'' (5:7) they are the ones from whom Yahweh had expected ''justice'' (*mishpat*) and ''uprightness'' (*tsedekah*), but who had instead become guilty of ''injustice'' (*mispach*) and ''cries of distress'' (*tse'akah*). This is the group whose ''words and deeds affront Yahweh and insult his glorious gaze'' (3:8b). They are the ones responsible for the ruin of Judah and Jerusalem (3:8a). It is they, therefore, who are the target of that invasion that will soon sweep through the land like a flood, purging and cleansing it of its evil (8:7–8).

(b) A New Leadership Elite

Despairing as Isaiah was of the leadership of his time, he did not despair of leadership as such. He was hopeful that the approaching invasion would not only humble and purge the present corrupt elite, but would clear the ground for the advent of a *new* leadership elite, and this too, as he envisioned it, was an integral part of Yahweh's plan—indeed, one of its more important features.

If the somewhat generalized sketch of this new leadership elite, in 32:1–8, is from him (some commentators doubt this), then the essential trait of the leaders Isaiah believed would emerge in the not too distant future would be simply their adherence once again to the ancient norms of ''uprightness'' (*tsedakah*) and ''justice'' (*mishpat*).

However, it is in two other passages that Isaiah's vision in this regard comes to its fullest expression: his justifiably famous sketches of an ideal ruler, in 9:1–7 and 11:1–9. Both are well known to most Christians as "messianic" prophecies foreshadowing the appearance of Jesus of Nazareth some centuries later. Modern interpreters seek to understand them, first of all at least, as having a more immediate relevance for the times and mission of Isaiah himself.

Both sketches have to do with expectations regarding an ideal king on *the throne of David* "and over his kingdom" (9:6; 11:1)—a ruler who would in fact do what it was hoped Davidic kings were meant to do: not just judge by appearances, but judge the wretched with integrity and with fairness give a verdict "for the humblest in the land" (11:3–4; 9:6). It would seem that Isaiah believed such a representative on the throne of David might appear soon (not in some far distant future). This is suggested by the way his portrait of such a king, in 9:2–6, is prefaced, in 9:1, by a reference to the Assyrian invasion of 734 when the northern provinces of Zebulun and Naphtali were taken over and incorporated into the Assyrian empire. But this yoke of the Assyrian oppressor is about to be broken (9:4), he writes, and this quite specifically is the setting for his famous poem about a son born who will embody the finest attributes of the Davidic dynasty (9:6). In other words what Isaiah appears to be hoping for is a "new shoot" from the stock of Jesse (11:1) that would occur in the immediate wake of the Assyrian crisis—that is, the advent of a Davidic king on the throne in Jerusalem who would have all those attributes godly kings were expected to have, and who would bring about that overflowing justice and peace that were heretofore so notably missing (11:5–9; 9:6). Possibly Isaiah's famous "Immanuel" prophecy, in 7:13–17, also relates to this expectation (I will have more to say about this a bit later).

Why then, in summary, is Yahweh bringing the Assyrians to decimate Judah before being crushed itself? It was to humble Judah's proud elite, to purge a remnant in Jerusalem of its sins, to demonstrate that Yahweh is indeed God, and to prepare the way for the advent of a new, more just, more upright leadership and community among those who survive these ordeals.

3. The Political Consequences of this Plan

As earlier indicated, Yahweh's plan, as Isaiah viewed it, had great relevance not only for social and religious affairs, but for public policy. Isaiah believed that those in leadership who really understood what Yahweh was doing would take action (or refrain from acting) along certain quite specific lines. In fact, his attempts at confronting the leadership of his nation with his views in this regard are among the most dramatic episodes of his prophetic career.

What advice did he have in this respect?

From beginning to end Isaiah believed that since Yahweh himself was the ultimate power behind the rise of Assyria and its invasion of Israel, it would be folly to try to prevent this happening by force of arms or alliances. What was called for instead was an inner tranquility and trust toward Yahweh (30:15) that would lead to conversion and faith in Yahweh alone as the One who would bring deliverance (31:4–6). Until then, the Assyrian invasion was inevitable. It simply had to happen, because Assyria was not acting on its own, but as an instrument of Yahweh himself against a "godless nation" (10:5–6). Not to see this, not to recognize what Yahweh was doing in this hour of crisis and to fail to put one's trust in it—not to get ready for the new age that would dawn through these events—this, for Isaiah, was tantamount to apostasy (30:16). National survival and spiritual renewal lay, not in military might, but "in conversion and tranquility" and "serenity and trust" (30:15).

It was thoughts such as these that must have been on Isaiah's mind when, in 734 (in the midst of the Syro-Ephraimitic War), news had arrived in Jerusalem that the combined forces of Syria and Ephraim were poised to the immediate north, ready to invade Judah. It was then (according to a remarkable sequence of passages, beginning at 7:1)—at a moment when panic had swept through the hearts of the citizens of Jerusalem (7:2)—that Isaiah was summoned by Yahweh to go with his son Shear-Jashub to King Ahaz and challenge him with a certain message. As already noted, Shear-Jashub means "a remnant will survive" and powerfully symbolizes Isaiah's belief that in the midst of the approaching invasion a few people would escape death to become the nucleus of a new and better community, headed by a truly upright Davidic leader.

The message he was charged with bringing to the king at this highly tense moment was simply to "keep calm" and not be frightened or demoralized by these "two smoldering sticks of firewood" (Aram and Ephraim) who were threatening to invade Judah and depose him. "The Lord Yahweh says this: 'This [their plot to invade and overthrow] will not happen, it will never occur' " (7:7). And the reason, quite simply, is this: they are merely human and not God (7:8–9; 31:3). *Their* thought is to invade Judah and establish an alliance in opposition to Assyria. But thoughts such as these are futile, in the light of what Yahweh has decreed. What Yahweh has determined is that they shall be swept aside by the floodtide of the Assyrian invasion (7:20; 8:6–7). If the elite in Jerusalem do not believe this, Isaiah implies, they too will be swept away ("If you do take your stand on me [Yahweh], you will not stand firm"—7:9b). This was a challenge to King Ahaz, as reigning Davidic king, to put aside his fear and let the "work" of Yahweh unfold according to plan.

But Ahaz would not hear of it—not even when Isaiah offered him the option of requesting a miraculous sign that would confirm the truth of what he was saying (7:10–12). Then it was that Isaiah uttered his famous promise of a countersign:

The Lord will give you a sign in any case:
It is this: the young woman is with child
and will give birth to a son
whom she will call Immanuel (7:14).

While Christians, not inappropriately, view this passage as a promise pointing to the birth of Jesus of Nazareth, it is clear from its context that *originally* Isaiah had in mind a child *very soon* to be born, for he goes on to say that

before the child knows how to refuse the bad
and choose the good,
the lands whose two kings are frightening you
will be deserted.
Yahweh will bring times for you,
your people and your ancestral House,
such as have not been seen
since Ephraim broke away from Judah . . . (7:16–17).

To whom then might Isaiah be referring? The Hebrew here characterizes the woman who is with child and soon to give birth as a "young woman," not a "virgin," as in the New Testament appropriation of this passage (see Mt 1:23). There is thus no indication in Isaiah that there would be anything unusual or miraculous about the birth itself. Rather the miracle or "sign" has to do with the fact that the son whom the young woman will soon bear will be called "Immanuel," meaning God-with-us. In other words, a child is about to be born whose name symbolizes hope—even though before this child is old enough to know right from wrong Syria and Ephraim will be destroyed, and Judah too will experience troubled times such as have not occurred since Ephraim broke away from Judah (7:16–17).

What "maiden" then and what child might this be? Some have conjectured that the woman in question might have been the queen-mother, Ahaz's wife, and that Isaiah is thereby prophesying that a successor to Ahaz is about to be born who will do what Ahaz has failed to do—namely, embody the presence of God. Another possibility is that Isaiah is here referring to his own wife, since both earlier and later in this section of his book sons of his are mentioned who were given symbolic names (7:3; 8:1–4)—and in the second of these instances (8:1–4), as here, the son's name was announced prior to birth. Furthermore, all of these children symbolize core elements of Isaiah's concept of what Yahweh is doing in and through the Assyrian invasion of this period.

What therefore Isaiah appears to be saying with this pronouncement is that his own wife ("the young woman") is soon going to bear him another son whom she will name Immanuel—an oblique sign (as was the previous son's name, Shear-Jashub) of his conviction that in the midst of the now imminent Assyrian invasion a remnant would survive (Shear-Jashub) with whom God would be manifestly present (Immanuel). That Isaiah did in fact view his children as "signs and portents in Israel" is explicitly stated in 8:18 where these same children are also characterized as having been given him by "Yahweh Sabaoth who dwells on Mount Zion."

"Immanuel" then would be the second of these children, and the one referred to, in 8:1–4, would be the third. This time the name given was a particularly ominous one. In 8:1–2, in his own words and with considerable detail, Isaiah describes how Yahweh instructed him to make public certain words, "Maher-Shalal-Hash-Baz" (8:1). They were gibberish of sorts—intentionally so, no doubt—but also anxiety-producing ("Speedy-spoil-quick-booty"). Their more precise meaning was only fully explained when approximately a year later, they were appropriated as the name of his newborn son—with the further explanation that "before the child knows how to say 'mother' or 'father,' the wealth of Damascus and the booty of Samaria will be carried away while the king of Assyria looks on" (7:4). In other words, like Shear-Jashub and Immanuel, this son's name also had to do with the Assyrian invasion. In this instance, however, the focus was on the *nearness* of that invasion (before the child is old enough to say his first words), with the goal of warning the populace at large of this prospect (not just the king and his retinue, as heretofore).

However, the response of Isaiah's fellow citizens in Jerusalem to this pronouncement was no different than was that of their king. The verses that follow this episode, in 8:5–18, indicate that Isaiah now realized that an unbreachable gulf had opened up between himself and his contemporaries. He did not dread what they feared, nor call conspiracy what they called conspiracy (8:12). They and he had come to a parting of the ways (8:11). For Isaiah the reality of Yahweh Sabaoth was everything (8:13). For them this same God had become "a snare and a trap" (8:14). His message was falling on deaf ears.

It appears therefore that he withdrew at this time from public life and determined to bind up and seal his "testimony" in the "heart" of certain "disciples" (8:16). That done, there was nothing left but to put his trust "in Yahweh who hides his face from the House of Jacob" (8:17). His hope rested now in Yahweh alone who "dwells on Mount Zion" (8:18) and what he would soon accomplish by way of judgment and renewal.

This time of waiting appears to have lasted longer than Isaiah had anticipated. For one thing, the Assyrians did not act to invade this region as quickly or as decisively as he had thought they would. While it is true that they followed up the Syro-Ephraimitic War in 734 with the conquest of Syria and *parts* of Israel, they then withdrew, leaving Ephraim and Judah politically intact. Thirteen years were to pass before the Assyrians returned to wipe out Ephraim as well (721), but even then Judah was spared the devastations Isaiah had predicted would occur in a matter of two or three years at the most.

Nevertheless, seven years later during the Ashdod rebellion in 714 (see historical outline in previous chapter), Isaiah once again appeared on Jerusalem's streets with the very same message he had proclaimed there some twenty years earlier (see ch. 29). To dramatize that his convictions regarding the coming of an Assyrian invasion had not changed, he walked Jerusalem's streets naked for three years. Just so, he declared, would the populations of Cush and Egypt be led away captive by the Assyrians. And if that is to be the fate of these powerful peoples, he added, "how are we [Judeans] going to escape [were we like them to resist the Assyrians]?" (20:6).

Not, however, until a decade later did there transpire what Isaiah had anticipated would happen from the time of his call, now almost forty years earlier! Then it was, in 704, upon the death of Sargon II, that Judah itself took the initiative in the insurgency against Assyria that had broken out in many places. Links may have been forged at this time with an equally rebellious Babylon (see ch. 39). In any event, Assyrian reaction, under a newly crowned and resourceful monarch, Sennacherib, was swift and decisive. The Babylonians were quickly brought under control once again and a campaign mounted against Judah.

What then occurred is graphically recorded in the annals of both the Bible (Is 36–37; 2 Kgs 18:13–19:37) and the Assyrians. All agree in their description of this campaign as an especially catastrophic one. Sennacherib's report specifies that he besieged and conquered forty-six of "Hezekiah the Jew's" strong walled towns and innumerable smaller villages and made to come out from them 200,150 people. Of Hezekiah himself, he wrote, "I shut [him] up like a caged bird within Jerusalem, his royal city." Mysteriously, however (precisely as Isaiah had predicted), Jerusalem was spared and a remnant there did survive. For reasons which are no longer completely clear (note the conflicting reports in Is 37:7; 37:36 and 2 Kgs 18:13–16), before striking the final blow and destroying Judah once and for all as a political entity, the Assyrian forces withdrew, leaving Jerusalem humiliated, but otherwise intact.

With these traumatic events, Isaiah's vision of the "mysterious work" Yahweh was doing in his time had now been remarkably fulfilled, it would seem. The Assyrian invasion had come at last. Its consequences were every bit as devastating as anticipated, and yet Jerusalem had been spared—a remnant had survived. His theo-political insights were thus astonishingly verified beyond all reasonable doubt.

Or were they? What of the renewal that Isaiah thought would result from all this? To complete our study of Isaiah's messages, we must note yet one additional passage in his book where it would seem his thought in this regard was forced to take a new and unexpected turn.

4. The Plan Frustrated

Throughout the ordeal of Sennacherib's catastrophic invasion, in 701, Isaiah's advice came to be valued to an unprecedented degree, it seems (see chs. 36–37). At the same time, it is doubtful that the spiritual consequences of his mission were those he had earlier anticipated. As noted, his expectation had been that this invasion, followed by Assyria's retreat, would bring about a purging and revival in Jerusalem (see again 1:25–28). But of this happening there is no evidence. Indeed, if Isaiah's oracle in 22:1–14 comes from this period (as well it might), then it could be understood as recording a moment of despair on Isaiah's part close to the very end of his forty year mission.

To be more specific, Isaiah 22:11 suggests that in the midst of the Assyrian siege of Jerusalem, instead of looking to the "Creator of these things . . . the One who fashioned them long ago," as Isaiah had hoped they would, the citizens of Jerusalem were thinking only of how they might defend their city (22:8–11), and then, when all seemed lost, cynically ate and drank and amused themselves, saying, "Let us eat and drink, for tomorrow we shall be dead" (22:13).

It was then, Isaiah informs us—faced with this display of entrenched disregard for Yahweh and what he was doing—that he received what might well have been a final revelation:

> Then Yahweh Sabaoth revealed this to my ears,
> "This guilt will never be forgiven you,
> until you are dead" (22:14).

It would appear that in this moment Isaiah came to the same conclusion that a contemporary of his, the prophet Micah of Moresheth, had arrived at, perhaps around this same time: namely, that not just the Judean countryside would be decimated (as it now was), but that Jerusalem itself would have to fall before there could be that new beginning Isaiah so fervently hoped for (see Mi 3).

This then, in summary, is the message of Isaiah of Jerusalem. Because of the pride, the greed, the lawlessness and the socially irresponsible lifestyle of a controlling elite in Jerusalem, Yahweh is bringing a devastating invasion against it. However, this invasion will mark not the end but the beginning of a new era in Jerusalem when a truly righteous king will reign there on the throne of David and justice and faithfulness will be restored—for, he declared, the invader (Assyria) would itself be punished and a remnant would survive this ordeal to begin again the process of building a just and upright city. All this happened, but instead of a flowering of faith and justice in Jerusalem, the pride and cynicism of its leading classes persisted. Isaiah seems to have ended his prophetic career with the intuition that yet additional disasters were still in the offing for his beloved city.

D. Ongoing Relevance

Isaiah's prophecies released a new dynamic into biblical faith: an intensified search for a viable future. His powerful visions of what *might* be clashed with what *was*. His biting criticisms of his society ring as true today as ever, as do his visions of an approaching catastrophe. But he also spoke of a *new* Jerusalem rising gloriously out of the ashes of the old, one where "justice and uprightness" would be established "from this time onward and for ever" (9:6). This did not (and has not yet) happened. As a result eschatological frustration set in, and with it a search for what *in reality* the future might hold for Jerusalem.

This would remain a burning issue for all subsequent prophecy. How could a community that had fallen so low ever be renewed? How might Isaiah's idealistic visions of Jerusalem renewed ever be realized in actual life?

The Book of Isaiah itself testifies to the way its early readers and custodians struggled with this issue. Virtually all of their supplements are efforts at answering these questions—beginning with that amazingly contemporary vision, in 2:1–5, of a world that has found its unity in a Jerusalem now miraculously exalted among the nations. Here, of course, it is not just Jerusalem that is renewed but *"all* the nations" who come on pilgrimage to Zion to have their disputes arbitrated there with the help of Yahweh's law and word (compare Mi 4:1–5) and on this basis begin hammering their swords into ploughshares and their spears into sickles" (2:4). Another supplement of this type, with still another provocative sketch of the future, is in 19:16–25. "That day," it is said there, "Israel, making the third with Egypt and Assyria, will be blessed in the center of the world" (19:24–25).

Other supplements to the book of this type appear to be somewhat more nationalistic in tone. In 11:10–16, for example, the hope is expressed that one day Israel will again become a first-class world power, united and strong, as in the days of David. The cosmic visions of chs. 24–27 also fall into this category, perhaps. In these it is predicted that unheard of devastations and judgments are still to come upon the whole earth because of its many crimes (26:21), but Israel will experience a magnificent restoration at Jerusalem (27:13). "In the days to come, Jacob will put out shoots, Israel will bud and blossom and fill the whole world with fruit" (27:6).

Regardless of how we might feel about the details of these or other sketches of this kind, they do testify to the turn toward a hopeful future that Isaiah's messages inspired in his followers. This prophet's firm conviction that something unimaginably great and beautiful lay ahead for Israel awakened hope in others and they began adding their insights to his. Even more important, Yahweh himself from now on came to be thought of more and more as a God of hope, the guide of a process whose goal is the transformation and peace of the whole world.

To believe this, and to begin to imagine how, concretely, this goal might be attained is a tremendous step forward in human thought. Through Judaism and Christianity, this optimistic prophetic outlook has entered the stream of Western culture and is now widely recognized as one of its more salient and attractive features (see Willis Glover). For encouraging us to think such thoughts and dream such dreams, we will be forever indebted to Isaiah and his disciples.

At the same time it is clear that Isaiah has left us with certain problems as well in this regard. Like Amos and Hosea before him, he saw accurately that judgments must come upon a people as corrupt as his had become, but it would appear that he expected too much of these judgments. Catastrophes as such do not necessarily cleanse and renew, as he had suggested these would.

Hence, the question remains: How *will* such renewal occur? Indeed, what hope is there that our world will *ever* approximate the ideals Isaiah envisioned, *human nature* being what it is? The issue is posed but not answered in the legacy of this prophet. Those who edited and supplemented his book do not answer it either. In fact, it is not apparent that they even sensed the issue, for it is Isaiah's idealism that seems to have caught their imaginations above all.

This issue persists, therefore, as one of our foremost problems, and will keep on engaging us in the remainder of our study. Eric Voegelin has identified it as a core element in prophetic struggle, then and now. "For the first time," he writes (referring quite explicitly to this crisis of frustrated hopes in the time of Isaiah), "men experienced the clash between divinely willed and humanly realized order of history in its stark brutality, and the souls of the prophets were the battlefield in this war of the spirit" (*Order and History,* p. 461). The prophetic movement as a whole can be classified in terms of it, he suggests. There was initially, he says, (1) an *institutional* phase in prophetic thought and expectation, represented by Amos and Hosea (p. 474); (2) then a *metastatic* phase ("metastatic" connoting a supernatural act of cosmic transformation), represented by Isaiah; followed by (3) an *existential* phase represented by Jeremiah (I will have more to say regarding all this in subsequent chapters).

However, even Isaiah may have probed the *existential* dimensions of human renewal further than is generally realized. In his analysis of what was wrong with his community, for example, he clearly views its moral anarchy as the fruit of *inner* dispositions and attitudes: "complacency" (3:9), "human pride" (2:11, 17), and haughtiness (3:16). "I have reared children and brought them up, but they have rebelled against me" (1:2). It is this intransigent human reality that will have to change and be changed, not merely the outward conditions.

But what will bring *such* change about?

It is true that Isaiah may have put too much stock, in answering, on the salvific effect of certain historical events and developments (such as the Assyrian invasion), but are we wrong in sensing a connection as well between the role he foresaw for a new kind of leader in the Jerusalem of his dreams and this problem? His "ideal leader" sketches were obviously of tremendous importance to him and seem to be saying that whatever else might be needed in a better world, leaders of this type are absolutely essential—men whose authority is molded by an inner respect for Yahweh and a compassionate regard for the rights of "the humblest in the land" (11:1–2; 9:5–6). But we might also ask: Are such leaders not necessary as well for bringing about that transformation without which we cannot even *begin* to move in that direction? Indeed, are Christians not fully justified in turning to these texts for help in explaining the transforming excitement they in fact feel in their encounter with Jesus of Nazareth? Do not, in short, our hopes for the future still rise and fall with the advent or absence of people in our midst who approximate this leadership ideal?

The question remains: If such leaders are indeed so important for the world's salvation, how might their numbers be increased—an issue to which we will have reason to return as our study progresses?

Questions for Review

1. Summarize what Isaiah seems to have meant by his references to a "work" Yahweh was doing in the world of his time. Why was Yahweh doing this, according to Isaiah? To what ideal period does he look for a model of what Jerusalem should be like? What has happened that it no longer is this way?

2. How are Isaiah's so-called "messianic prophecies" to be understood within the framework of *his* time and place? What might be the point of reference, specifically, of his famous prophecy regarding Immanuel? How might his "ideal leader" sketches be relevant today?

3. Isaiah appears to have advocated a form of "pacifism" in the face of the Assyrian invasion of Judah. What expectations motivated him in doing so? What did he hope the political leaders of his time in Jerusalem would do? What did they do? Why was Isaiah disappointed in what actually happened when the invasion struck?

4. What is your reaction to the suggestion that Isaiah might have been an idealist, in some sense? What is your reaction to the expectations of a bright future for our world which his prophecies seem to elicit? Is there any sense in which these prophecies and expectations are being realized? Are you an optimist or pessimist when it comes to envisioning the future? What hopes concretely do *you* have?

11

Micah of Moresheth

With Micah of Moresheth, a contemporary of Isaiah's, we come to the last of the great eighth century prophets whose books appear in our Bible. The messages that we can confidently attribute to him, though few in number, are exceptionally forceful. As such, they remind us of Amos and form a fitting conclusion to the half century of prophetic activity that began with him.

A. The Book as a Whole

Despite its smallness the book as a whole poses a number of difficult problems. From the point of view of its content there are three clearly identifiable sections:

(1) chs. 1–3, made up, for the most part, of warnings of disaster and criticisms directed to various groups in the "House of Israel" (1:5a; 3:1, 9), climaxing in a prophecy that Zion-Jerusalem will be totally destroyed (3:12);

(2) chs. 4–5, containing largely oracles of hope for a restoration of Zion-Jerusalem as a political power that one day will be triumphant over all its enemies (4:7; 5:6–14);

(3) chs. 6–7, a mixed collection made up of some additional criticisms and warnings (6:1–16), plus laments (7:1–4), prayers (7:7, 14–20) and oracles of hope for the ultimate vindication of Zion in the sight of the nations (7:8–13).

Editorially the only clue to the book's organization is the admonition to "listen" in 1:2, 6:1, and 6:2. The first "listen" (1:2) summons the *nations* to trial, the second (6:1) summons *Israel,* the third (6:2) summons the *mountains.* The "trial" speeches themselves, in 6:3–8, are in a style reminiscent of Deuteronomy (note especially the references to the exodus, Moses, Aaron and Miriam and the story of the entry into Canaan—6:4–5). Micah 6:8 may be an allusion to the prophetic movement, now a thing of the past: "You have already been told what is right.'' The book's heading is once again of a type we have come to recognize as Deuteronomic (particularly the expression ''word of Yahweh'' and the dating in terms of certain Israelite kings).

From all this the conclusion has been drawn that the Book of Micah already included most of chs. 1–5, at the point its Deuteronomic editors received it, and that they are the ones who appended chs. 6 and 7, as well as the opening passages in 1:2 and 6:1–8 that now head up these two sections.

Mays (*Micah* commentary) thinks these same editors were responsible for adding the supplementary note to the heading that specifies that Micah's oracles had to do with *both* Jerusalem *and* Samaria (1:1b), when in point of fact (as will be noted below) they were more likely directed only to Judah-Jerusalem and should be dated to a time *after* the northern kingdom had already fallen (in 721). For these and other reasons the one passage in the book that predicts the destruction of Samaria (1:5b–7) should very likely also be viewed as an editorial gloss added to make sure that its readers did not overlook the fact that the sins of Jerusalem and the disasters that came upon *it* were not unlike those that befell the north a century earlier (they make this same point in 6:16).

We may summarize our analysis of the book to this point as follows:

''Listen, you peoples'' (1:2)

Section 1	Section 2	Section 3
The crimes and punishment of Jacob (the prophecy against Samaria, 1:5b–7, may be from an editor)	The remnant of Israel becomes a ''mighty nation'' on Mount Zion (4:7) over many nations (4:11–13)	Further reflections on Israel's judgment and vindication (7:15–17)
Chapters 1–3	Chapters 4–5	Chapters 6–7

Which texts in this rather diverse collection come from Micah of Moresheth, the prophet named in the heading (1:1), and which are to be attributed to his disciples or editors? Mays suggests that in answering, the portrait of Micah in Jeremiah 26:16–19 should be kept in mind. There we are told that Micah was remembered by certain of ''the country's elders,'' in the century following his appearance, as a prophet who prophesied of Zion's *destruction*, not of its *restoration*. This would be consistent, furthermore, with Micah's own categorical pronouncement regarding himself and his mission, in Micah 3:8, where he stresses that his calling was "to accuse Jacob of his crime and Israel of his sin."

This would point to the accusations and warnings in chs. 1–3 as the primary collection of Micah's oracles, and raise questions regarding his authorship of the oracles of promise in the remaining chapters. These latter, for the most part, are expectations of a kind that we know from other sources were in vogue among certain Israelite groups in the period *after* the destruction of Jerusalem by the Babylonians, in 586 (see our discussion of Haggai and Zechariah), not the kind of hopes Micah or his contemporaries would have had at a point where Jerusalem-Zion was still intact (note the actual reference to the Babylonian captivity in 4:10).

In our study of Micah we will concentrate therefore on chs. 1–3 only. The messages here (with the exception of 1:2, 5b–7; 2:12-13) are remarkably coherent in style, content and historical background.

B. The Man Behind the Book

However, before turning to these it will be worth our while, once again, to pause and reflect on what can be known about Micah himself. From the few hints regarding him which the editors of his book have provided in its heading, together with a few impressions derived from other sources (including his own words), a remarkably vivid picture of Micah himself begins to take shape.

1. Name

It is of some significance perhaps that he was remembered as Micah of *Moresheth* (literally: Micah the Moreshetite), Moresheth being a reference not to his father or family, but to his *city* (further to this point below). Micah—meaning "Who is like?"—is a shortened form of Micaiah (see 1 Kgs 22:9), meaning "Who is like Yah [or Yahweh]?"

2. Where He Lived

Moresheth is probably the "Moresheth-gath" mentioned in Micah 1:14, a village some twenty-five miles southwest of Jerusalem, on the slopes leading down to the coastal plain. It is also possibly the "Gath" referred to in 2 Chronicles 11:8. This latter was one of six cities of that region which Rehoboam son of Solomon is said to have fortified during his reign (931–913) to secure access to Jerusalem from the coastal road, and defend it against enemy attack (see Wolff, *Micah the Prophet,* p. 20). For this reason soldiers from Jerusalem might well have been stationed in his vicinity, and connections between the two regions must have been close (see 2 Chronicles 11:11–12).

While a Judean then, like his near contemporaries Amos and Isaiah, Micah's background was unique. His world was not that of the sheep-herding bedouin, like Amos, nor was he a resident of Jerusalem, like Isaiah. He lived rather in a heavily fortified region that Jerusalem depended on for its security and well-being.

3. Occupation

We are nowhere told what occupational group Micah might have belonged to, but Wolff has suggested that the fact that Jerusalem elders remembered him a century later not as Micah Son of So-and-so (the traditional way of naming), but as Micah of Moresheth (see Jer 26:17–19) points to the possibility that he too may have been an *elder,* and of that village in particular—perhaps even its chief elder (see Wolff's *Micah the Prophet*).

Such elders and their role in the affairs of the nation are alluded to in a number of biblical passages: notably, Dt 19:12; 21:1–4, 6, 19–20; Ru 4:1–12; 1 Sam 30:26; 1 Kgs 8:1; 2 Kgs 23:1; 2 Chr 19:5–8. One of their chief duties was to see to it that justice was carried out in their respective cities (2 Chr 19:5–11). It is therefore no accident, perhaps, that this was what Micah was supremely concerned about as well.

It is possible then that, like Isaiah, Micah may have played a prominent role in the life of his village as a respected leader, counselor and judge. As an elder of Moresheth, however, his would have been a markedly different background. Theologically, Micah appears to be much closer to Amos in his almost total disregard for those sacral traditions that were unique to Jerusalem (those having to do with temple and kingship especially). From his point of view Yahweh does not dwell on Mount Zion (as Isaiah believed he did; see Is 8:11), but in his cosmic "home" above the earth. It is from there that he "comes down" to tread "the heights of earth" and punish his people for their sins (see Mi 1:3–5a). His prophecies are also devoid of any references to the dynasty of David.

4. Prophetic Call

In 3:5–7 Micah accuses the prophets of his time of being motivated by greed and greed only in speaking or not speaking as they do. He then concludes this accusation with one of the rare self-revelations of his book. "Not so with me," he declares vigorously. That is not what motivated him in his prophetic mission. What motivated him, he asserts is that "I am full of strength (full of Yahweh's spirit) of the sense of right, of energy to accuse Jacob of his crime and Israel of his sin."

This is his only allusion to a prophetic commissioning or call. And yet on this basis alone we may conclude that he too, like the other prophets we have studied, was summoned to his prophetic mission by a quite tangible life-transforming experience. In his case, however, this took the form not of an audition or vision, but quite simply of a sudden tangible infusion of moral energy and courage. This alone is what set him apart from his fellow elders and joined him to the ranks of the prophets: the Yahweh-inspired impulse to remain silent no longer, but "full of strength . . . of the sense of right" to get up and speak what had to be said in this critical moment of his people's history.

5. Historical Setting

What was this moment? The heading of his book (1:1) alludes to a prophetic career that spanned the reigns of three Judean kings: Jotham, Ahaz and Hezekiah. This could be interpreted to mean that he was active as a prophet during some four decades, from as early as 640 to as late as 700. The very brevity of his prophetic legacy contradicts this supposition.

More germane to establishing a date for Micah's mission is the allusion in Jeremiah 26:18 to his being active in the "days of Hezekiah" only. Suggestive also is the vivid, emotional depiction of an invasion that will reach right down to the very "gate" of Jerusalem, in Micah 1:8–16. The cities referred to here as about to suffer humiliation are precisely those that the Assyrian Sennacherib had to conquer (and did destroy) in his devastating invasion of Judah in 701 (see previous chapter). Both the brevity and intensity of the book, together with these quite specific historical allusions, all suggest that Micah's prophetic activity may have been concentrated on this quite specific crisis in Israelite history, following the death of Sargon II in 705, when Judah (under the leadership of King Hezekiah) thought it might escape Assyrian control, but was almost annihilated instead.

The assumption (of the book's editors) that Micah was active as a prophet *earlier* than this (perhaps even as early as the reigns of Jotham and Ahaz) may have arisen as a consequence of the addition to his book of the prophecy against Samaria, in 1:5b–7. This required that Micah be thought of as beginning his prophetic mission prior to Samaria's fall, in 721. But, as already noted (see the discussion of "the book as a whole" above), apart from 1:5b–7, there is not a single additional reference to Samaria in the rest of the book (even the nameless city mentioned in 6:1 is in all likelihood Jerusalem, not Samaria). It seems likely, therefore, that Micah's mission was confined to a relatively short period, just prior to the Assyrian invasion of Judah in 701.

In our study of his messages in the chapter that follows we will assume this to have been the case.

Questions for Review

1. Characterize the Book of Micah in terms of its contents. What features distinguish the opening three chapters from those that follow? Why is it thought that Micah's prophecies are all to be found in these opening chapters? What indications are there of Deuteronomic editing?

2. Why is Micah thought to have been a leading elder of Moresheth? If this were true, how might this distinguish him, so far as background influences are concerned, from Amos or Isaiah who were also Judeans? What were city elders in that time primarily responsible for doing?

3. What evidence is there of how Micah might have become a prophet? What does this tell us regarding the kind of prophet he might have been? During what specific crisis in Judean history was he prophetically active?

12

His Message and Its Relevance

As pointed out in the previous chapter, only the words in chs. 1–3 of Micah can be confidently attributed to the eighth century Micah of Moresheth, and even here there may be a few supplements from the hands of later readers and editors (such as 1:1–2, 5b–7 and possibly 2:12–13). What do we learn from the remaining oracles, laments, woes and reports in this section regarding Micah's message for his contemporaries?

A. Message

1. Disaster Coming!

The basic theme of his prophetic mission is struck in the very first oracle, 1:3–5a. In words reminiscent of the ancient hymn of Deborah, in Judges 5:4–5, Yahweh is here portrayed as coming down from his holy place in the heavens to tread the heights of the earth. In this instance, however, Yahweh's coming is not to rescue his people (as in the days of Deborah), but to strike a "blow" that will reach right into Judah, "on Jerusalem itself" (1:9). "This is why I shall howl and wail," he laments, "why I shall go barefoot and naked, why I shall howl like the jackals, why I shall shriek like the owls . . ." (1:8).

There follows a passionate outpouring of alliterative speech, in 1:10–16, in which twelve cities are summoned to join him in a wailing death-lament (1:16). All lie in the vicinity of Micah's own city. This is the region through which armies traveled that are bent upon capturing Jerusalem (see our discussion of this point in the previous chapter). Indeed, it was precisely this corridor of fortified towns that the Assyrians ravaged in their invasion of Judah, in 701 (as we learn from Sennacherib's Annals). It is possible that this shrill cry of warning was written on the very brink of this catastrophe.

What gives added force and poignancy to the words of this prophet is his astonishing prediction that not even *Jerusalem* will escape the terrors now befalling his people. "For there is no cure for the wounds that Yahweh inflicts: the blow falls on Judah, it falls on the gateway of my people, on Jerusalem itself" (1:9). What is only mysteriously alluded to here is made absolutely clear in the final oracle of his collection, in 3:9–12:

> Zion will become ploughland
> Jerusalem a heap of rubble,
> and the Temple Mount a wooded height.

How shocked his contemporaries were by this message can be gauged by the fact that it was remembered verbatim by the elders of Jerusalem a century later (Jer 26:18–19). This is the first time, so far as we know, that an Israelite prophet unequivocally contradicted the prevailing Jerusalem theology. Davidic kingship and sacred temple are no guarantee against the impending Assyrian invasion, these words imply. A century later another prophet (Jeremiah) will utter the same heresy, and almost lose his life as a result (see Jer 7:1–15; ch. 26). Even *Jerusalem* will not escape the dreadful "wounds" which Yahweh is now inflicting upon the whole of Judah.

2. Why?

Why is this terrible thing happening? "All this is because of the crime of Jacob, the sin of the House of Israel" (1:5). Like Amos, Hosea and Isaiah before him, Micah believes that this massive invasion is Yahweh's response to certain flagrant crimes and sins. What these were, more specifically, is alluded to in the remaining oracles and reports of chs. 2 and 3. *Three distinct groups* are being addressed in these chapters (Wolff's suggestion):
- military officers, in 2:1–11;
- city elders, in 3:1–4, 9–12;
- prophets, in 3:5–8.

The *form* of these passages is reportorial. In them we are informed, at points, not only of what *Micah* had to say, but of the reactions of his audience (2:6–7), and of Micah's reactions to them (3:1, 8). As such they constitute an extraordinarily vivid, first-hand account of a prophet at work.

Let us note briefly the nature of Micah's encounter with each of these groups.

(a) Exploitative Military Officers (2:1–11)

The people to whom Micah was speaking in 2:1–11 are exceptionally powerful, for it is said concerning them that what they plan to do as they lie awake at night, their hands have the strength to execute in the morning (2:1). They can also give orders that Micah be silenced (2:6). Who might they have been?

It was noted above (and in the previous chapter) that Moresheth was a fortified town within a cluster of fortified towns that made up the first line of defense for Jerusalem against invaders from the coast. For this reason it is not unlikely that military troops from Jerusalem (and other regions of the country) would have been garrisoned there on a relatively permanent basis. Are men of this type the ones to whom Micah's words are specifically directed in 2:1–11?

If so, why would these men be coveting fields and seizing them? The climate of Moresheth is exceptionally pleasant, Wolff points out, especially in winter, since it is some 1,200 feet lower than Jerusalem. It must therefore have been tempting for soldiers stationed there from the central highlands to want to buy property in this region, perhaps as a second home for their families. However, property available for purchase would have been scarce, for most of the land was occupied by families who had lived on it for generations. Nor would these families want to sell, for to do so would render them homeless and vulnerable to losing their status as free citizens. Without property a man had no alternative but to hire himself out, or become a slave.

Thus, a class conflict may be simmering in the background of this passage. A relatively well-to-do military elite eager to buy property was stymied in their acquisitive ambitions by a more traditional, relatively poor landholding group who wanted desperately to retain their ancestral heritage.

The famous story of Naboth's vineyard, in 1 Kings 21, is a dramatic example of how such a conflict might be resolved. In this instance it was a king, King Ahab of Israel, who had set his heart on purchasing a vineyard adjoining his winter palace in Jezreel for use as a vegetable garden. Its owner, however, refused to sell, saying, "Yahweh forbid that I should give you the inheritance of my ancestors!" (1 Kgs 21:3). Though greatly disappointed, Ahab was apparently ready to let the matter rest at that point, when his Sidonian born wife, Jezebel, schooled in a different tradition, hit upon a solution. Letters were sent to the city elders instructing them to have Naboth executed on contrived charges. That accomplished, the vineyard was quickly appropriated.

It was this type of criminal behavior, precisely, that Micah must have had in mind when he pronounced "disaster for those who plot evil, who lie in bed planning mischief," and then "no sooner is it dawn than they do it. . . . Seizing the fields that they covet, they take over houses as well, owner and house they seize, the man himself as well as his inheritance" (2:1–2). Actions of this type were explicitly prohibited in Israelite law (see Ex 20:17; Lev 19:13; Prov 14:31; 28:3), but those perpetrating these deeds were apparently unaware of this or totally insensitive to the criminal nature of their deeds. Their punishment would be in kind. What they had seized from others would be "stripped" from them in the approaching invasion (2:4).

The response of the military elite (to whom Micah was speaking) to this fierce criticism and warning is recorded in 2:6–11. From this report of their words we are surprised to learn that they were not only powerful but exceptionally religious. Indignantly they order Micah to stop "driveling" (like a madman), not because of what he has said regarding *them,* but because his words are an offense to their theology and *piety!* "Can the House of Jacob be accursed? Has Yahweh grown short-tempered? Is that his way of going to work? His prophecies can only be favorable for his people Israel!" (2:7). It was not apostates, then, to whom Micah was addressing his sharp words, but loyal Israelites who were confident that because the kindly Yahweh was among them (3:11b) "disgrace will not overtake us!" (2:6b).

In responding to this response (in the verses that follow in 2:8–11), Micah tries to shatter this shell of complacency by trying to make even more specific the crimes he had earlier charged them with:

• you violate and rob innocent pedestrians of their clothing, he declares (2:8);

• you evict women (whose husbands were apparently away in forced-labor brigades in Jerusalem) from their ancestral homes (2:9a) and thereby deprive their children also of the birthright and honor due them as free citizens in Israel (2:9b);

• you impose ruthless fines or collatoral for trifling misdemeanors or debts (2:10).

This passage ends with Micah commenting ironically that the prophet for such an audience would be someone who could preach about wine and whiskey (2:11)—that would really captivate them and win their approval!

(b) Uncaring Elders (3:1–4, 9–12)

The audience addressed in 3:1–4 and 3:9–12 is not the same as the one referred to in 2:1. Here (in 3:1–4, 9–12) Micah is speaking to certain "leaders" of the House of Israel. For Micah, as for Amos and Hosea, Israel was a single people, a single "house," under the leadership of certain "heads" (not "princes" as in the *New Jerusalem Bible*) whose duty it was to meet periodically to see that "justice" (*mishpat*) was done in the various towns and villages (3:1). If Wolff is right in suggesting that Micah was himself such a "head" (or town elder), then in the words of this section he would be addressing *fellow* elders on the occasion, perhaps, of an important assembly of elders in Jerusalem (see our discussion of this possibility in the previous chapter).

Micah's accusations against them were twofold. First, they were, he says, "skinning people alive, pulling the flesh off their bones, eating my people's flesh, stripping off their skin, breaking up their bones, chopping them up small like flesh for the pot, like meat in the stew-pan" (3:2–3). The reference here may be to indignities *his own fellow citizens in Moresheth* were suffering ("my people's flesh") at the hands of taskmasters in the forced labor camps of Jerusalem (Wolff). Forced labor of this kind was a bone of contention in Judah from the time of Solomon onward (see 1 Kgs 9:15–24; 12:6–16). Just prior to Micah's tenure as city elder this practice may have been revived by King Uzziah as a means of refortifying his nation (see 2 Chr 26:1–15). Micah's contemporary, King Hezekiah, might well have resorted to it also—in excavating that famous 1,700 foot water tunnel, for example, that can be still seen in use in Jerusalem today (see 2 Kgs 20:20; 2 Chr 32:2–4, 30).

Seen in this light, the first criticism Micah brought against his fellow elders was that, even though knowing better, they took no leadership in stemming the tide of atrocities those were suffering who were forced against their will to work on these brigades. As a consequence his people were being chopped up like meat in a pot (3:3).

The motive behind this blatant disregard for the welfare of "my people" is the target of a second charge against this group, in 3:9–12. Every level of government, every leadership elite appears to be grasping for one thing, Micah declares: money and more money (3:11). It is this that blinds them to their moral responsibilities and permits them to acquiesce to the building of Zion "with blood" and Jerusalem "with iniquity" (3:10). Their banal confidence that "Yahweh is among us" and therefore "no disaster is going to overtake us" (3:11), he boldly prophesies, will soon be proven tragically mistaken when "Zion will become ploughland, Jerusalem a heap of rubble and the Temple Mount a wooded height" (3:12).

(c) Compromised Prophets

A third group is addressed in 3:5–8: the prophets. Micah's words regarding them are dripping with satire. To those who give them something to eat these prophets cry, "Peace," he says, but "on anyone who puts nothing into their mouths they declare war" (3:5). Just like everyone else they are motivated by money. This is why they are so insensitive to the evils all around, with the result that they "lead my people astray" (3:5).

Once again, their punishment will fit their crime, Micah intimates. Having compromised themselves in this manner, their capacity to hear Yahweh's "answer" to their inquiries will grow weaker and weaker (3:7). From this we can sense how much Micah respected the prophetic office as such. Prophets can be a genuine source of guidance, but only *if* Yahweh truly inspires them, not when they are forsaken by him as these prophets now are, due to their corruption.

It may trouble us to note how scathingly critical were all of Micah's words, and how bleak his expectations. Were conditions in Israel really this bad? If so, it would not be the first or the last time in history when conditions such as these had become predominant in the life of a people. Certainly, the disasters Micah spoke of as Yahweh's response to these conditions were no illusion. Even as he prophesied, the Assyrian armies were on the march, and their invasion of Judah was indeed catastrophic, although not *as* catastrophic as he had predicted. This time Jerusalem itself was spared, not annihilated as he had predicted it would be (see our further comments on this and other unfulfilled prophecies of the eighth century prophets in the following chapter).

Most commentators agree that Micah has left us no hint of what he thought might happen *after* the invasion of Judah had run its course. However, the courage and "energy" (3:8) with which he stood up and accused the leadership groups of his time for their crimes testifies to his love for his people ("my people," as he calls them). It is doubtful that someone would endanger himself in this manner for a people he thought was hopeless. We may assume therefore that Micah too, like several of his contemporaries, did foresee a longer range future for his people, even though it was not *his* task to speak of it.

B. Ongoing Relevance

Precisely that which Micah left unspoken, however, is what concerned those most, it seems, who first edited his book. Zion's future *beyond* judgment, in any case, is the subject of the great majority of the passages that now make up the second half of his book (chs. 4–7). At the head of this supplementary collection, in 4:1–5, is a visionary sketch similar to the one in Isaiah 2:1–5 in which Jerusalem is envisioned not just as restored and renewed, but as a center for international consultation and peace.

Other futuristic sketches in this section appear to be more narrowly nationalistic in tone. In these the hope is expressed that the dynasty of David will be restored and with it a reunited Israel whose greatness and power will extend to "the most distant parts of the country" (3:3). Then Israel will once again be a "mighty nation" (4:7) as in the days of King David (4:8; 7:11–12).

Among these supplements there are a few, however, that restate and reapply the social critique that is such a preeminent feature of *Micah's* legacy. Such, for example, are the warnings directed to a certain city, in 6:9–14, and to Samaria, in 1:6–7 and 6:16. Of these the most insightful is the wonderful summary of prophetic teaching, in 6:1–8. As earlier noted (see previous chapter), this passage may be Deuteronomic in origin. Its authors appear to be looking back on the eighth century prophets as a group. The literary form chosen for their reflections is that of a judgment trial in which Yahweh is portrayed as accusing his people of having forsaken him despite his having so repeatedly helped them (6:1–5).

The people respond by feigning uncertainty as to what Yahweh *really* wants (6:6–7). The trial ends with a voice declaring that such doubts are inexcusable, since "you have already been told what is right," and it is this: "*only* this, to do what is right, to love loyalty and to walk humbly with your God" (6:8). "To do what is right [or act justly]" was the central theme of Amos, "to love loyalty" was a key concept of Hosea, and "to walk humbly with your God" was the very essence of what Isaiah proclaimed.

Micah's own special contribution to the prophetic tradition, perhaps, was the "energy" (3:8) with which he confronted the greed, hypocrisy and cruelty of the leading groups of his society. Though pious to the core and sure of God's presence in their midst, they were like cannibals in cruelty, he declared. This combination of character traits is unfortunately not rare, even today. Religious faith is not necessarily a good thing. When God's grace alone is stressed (see Mi 2:7), it can become an opiate. Then like the people of Micah's time we feel safe on the brink of disaster. Would that within the governing councils of every village, town, city and nation of our world there were at least one elder like Micah, responsible yet bold, wise yet courageous, energized by God to stay awake and help us see what the consequences of *our* most blatant sins and hypocrisies might be.

Questions for Review

1. Compare and contrast Micah's view of the approaching judgment through Assyria with that of Isaiah's. In what sense might his prophecies of what was about to happen be regarded as a heresy by those who espoused Jerusalem theology?

2. What groups in Judah did Micah see to be primarily responsible for the devastation about to take place? What kinds of crimes does he accuse them of? How would you characterize these people religiously? Were they apostate? Did they adhere to one or another of the prevailing Yahwistic theologies? What does he regard as the root problem of his time?

3. Characterize the supplements to the Book of Micah in chs. 4–7. In what sense might Micah 6:1–8 be regarded as a summary of the messages of the eighth century prophets we have been studying? What impresses you as the chief relevance of Micah's messages for today?

SECTION THREE

THE PROPHETS OF THE BABYLONIAN AND PERSIAN PERIODS

When you search for me
you shall find me;
when you search
wholeheartedly for me,
I shall let you find me.
        Jer 29:13–14a

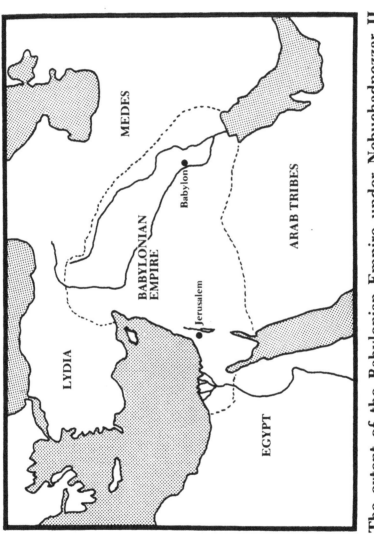

The extent of the Babylonian Empire under Nebuchadnezzar II (605–562 B.C.)

13

Between the Times:
Zephaniah, Nahum, Habakkuk, Obadiah

A. Looking Back: What Have We Learned?

Having surveyed the four eighth century prophets, it may be useful to pause briefly and reflect on what we have learned—on the impressions we have gained from this initial phase of our study.

How would you describe the *books* we have just studied? No doubt, their compositional analysis has been one of the more tedious aspects of our study so far. Yet, if you have not avoided this step, you will no doubt feel a little more confident by now in approaching a book of this nature. At least you will realize that not just the prophet whose name the book bears has had a hand in its composition, but others as well who lovingly preserved, edited and supplemented it through the centuries.

What impressions do you have at this point of the *prophets themselves* whom we encounter in these books? What manner of men were they? You are possibly more aware at this point than you were of the *diversity* of their biographical, theological and cultural backgrounds. All were Yahwists, of course, but one was a sheep-breeder from southeast of Jerusalem (Amos), another a farmer from the Levitical groups in the north (Hosea), still another a seer or teacher who moved easily among the elite of Jerusalem (Isaiah), yet another a leading elder of one of Judah's more strategic fortified cities (Micah). Theologically, it seems, some were more "at home" in traditions stemming from the exodus from Egypt and the Sinai covenant (notably Hosea), others in "Jerusalem theology" (notably Isaiah). Still others (Micah and Amos) reflect yet alternative emphases: the paramount importance of Yahweh's gift of a sacral homeland, and of living there justly and caringly.

Diverse too were the ways each of these men seems to have become a prophet. One was called through a series of visions (Amos), another through his marriage to a woman compromised by her association with Canaanite worship practices (Hosea), another while worshiping at the Jerusalem temple (Isaiah), and still another by a surge of energy and of courage (Micah).

The messages of these prophets were also diverse in certain respects. While each came to believe that a devastating invasion of their region was imminent, some spoke of it as being destructive of Samaria primarily, others as sweeping into Judah as well, with only Jerusalem being spared; others said that Jerusalem too would be destroyed.

They were also different in what they foresaw happening in the *aftermath* of this catastrophe. Amos was not even certain that Yahweh would be gracious to those who would break with the prevailing amorality and work for justice at the village "gates." Hosea was far more hopeful. His visions of the future picture Yahweh reuniting his people to himself in the wilderness (as of old), and then resettling them once again, forever now, in a land miraculously transformed. Isaiah saw this wonderful new beginning taking place through a remnant that would turn to Yahweh in the midst of Jerusalem's punishment and miraculous redemption. To this remnant an ideal king would be given (on the throne of David) whom God would empower to bring justice and peace to the fullest degree, forever.

One has the distinct impression that these prophets were no mere conduits of God's word to them, as sometimes imagined. Rather, it was as unique, thoughtful, existentially engaged individuals that Yahweh's "word" rose up so compellingly within them. And while admittedly different in many respects, was there not also an impressive unity to what they had to say to the people of their time? On three points at least, I suggest, they were at one in their messages: (1) all were utterly certain of the *imminence* of a catastrophic invasion of their region—the Assyrians were coming and nothing could be done to prevent it; (2) they were also united in believing that this invasion was no historical accident, but related somehow to a "decision" Yahweh had made—their God *Yahweh* was bringing all this to pass; (3) he was doing this, they were equally convinced, because of intolerable religious and social conditions now prevailing in Israelite society.

Additionally, on a further point, two of these prophets were also in agreement (and the others were certainly not in contradiction of this): according to Hosea and Isaiah the approaching invasion would not mark an end to Israel's story—indeed, in its aftermath a *new* Israel would emerge better by far than anything that had existed heretofore.

As the call accounts of these prophets indicate (those of Amos and Isaiah especially), in coming to these convictions they were compelled to experience a conversion of sorts. Each prophet in his own way had to realize that Yahweh's patience was not endless. Yahweh is a God of grace, but of righteousness as well. This means that there comes a point when even *his* patience comes to an end and he can no longer overlook the sins and cruelties of his people (see Am 7:8–9).

Indeed, to these prophets the truth dawned with pristine force that nothing matters so much with God as basic decency, fundamental goodness—*not* endless sacrifices, *not* pious pilgrimages to sacred shrines, *not* even sacred theologies (like those of Jerusalem). What matters most with God, and this only, is "to do what is right, to love loyalty (to the basics of the Yahweh covenant), and to walk humbly with God" (Mi 6:8).

These then are the prophets of the eighth century, and this is their message. But what then did in fact happen in the aftermath of their prophetic missions? And what was the fate of their messages? A brief attempt at answering these questions may serve as a bridge to the next and final group of prophetic writings we will be surveying in this study: the prophets of the seventh and sixth centuries.

B. What Happened Next?

Regarding what happened next, it should be noted first of all that while remarkably accurate in predicting the *invasion* of their region by Assyria, the prophets of the eighth century were much less so in their intimations of what would happen in the *aftermath* of this invasion. While Hosea, for example, does not say exactly *when* the restoration and renewal of his people will occur which he predicted would follow this invasion, his words imply that it would be soon afterward. Isaiah was more explicit. According to him Assyria would not only be stopped short of destroying Jerusalem, but would be humiliated at the point of doing so, and this would be followed by a new era of righteousness and peace in Jerusalem such as had not existed there since its earliest days.

We have already noted that Isaiah's expectations regarding Jerusalem's survival during the Assyrian invasion were remarkably fulfilled (Micah, on the other hand, was wrong—at least wrong about Jerusalem being destroyed during the *Assyrian* invasion). But in other respects Isaiah's prophecies, it seems, were *not* fulfilled. Not only was there no repentance movement in Jerusalem, as anticipated (and hence nothing like the restoration of justice and peace there, as prophesied), but Assyria, far from being defeated and humiliated (ch. 10), remained the dominant power in the ancient Near East for another eighty years.

More specifically, after the Assyrian invasion of 701, Judah-Jerusalem, while surviving, became a client state of the now firmly established Assyrian empire. This fact is graphically reflected in the religious policies that seemingly prevailed there at this time during the long forty-five year reign of Manasseh (687–642). In this period, according to 2 Kings 21, not only were various Assyrian astral deities worshiped in the courtyard of the Yahweh temple there, but in the temple itself was placed an image of the Canaanite mother goddess Asherah (2 Kgs 21:7). In short, instead of there being a revival of faith in Jerusalem at this time, with these developments Jerusalem became an essentially pagan city little different from other cities of the Assyrian realm.

Those in Judah who remained loyal to Yahweh *alone* during these Judaean Dark Ages (those, for example, who would have treasured the messages of the prophets we have just studied—and there must have been many such, even in the midst of all this unfaithfulness) must have been greatly perplexed by this turn of events. We can imagine them struggling with at least three issues: (1) If what Hosea and Isaiah implied about Assyria were at all true—that Assyria too would one day be punished and defeated—why is it that this day of reckoning has been so long postponed? (2) Furthermore, if what these same prophets had said about the spiritual renewal of Israel was *also* correct, when was *this* going to take place? And *how?* (3) Finally, what of Micah's unnerving prophecy that *Jerusalem too* might one day be totally destroyed? Was he wrong about this? Or is this an event *still* to happen?

We must imagine that many of the *prophets* of the next decades and centuries were *also* engaged with questions of this nature, in one way or another. It will not be possible in this introductory survey to study all of them as thoroughly as we would like. Many are of lesser importance than others, in any case. By far the most substantial of the prophetic responses to the ongoing crisis of Israel's existence during the next two centuries were those of Jeremiah, Ezekiel and Second Isaiah (Is 40–55). In the remainder of our study it is these three prophetic books in particular on which we will be concentrating.

Before turning to them, however, I do want to at least summarize the messages of several other minor prophets who spoke during the *opening* phase of what might be called the "second wave" of prophecy in Israel, during the seventh century. These are Zephaniah, Nahum,

Habakkuk and Obadiah. We know virtually nothing about them as individuals except their names and where they lived. All appear to have been prophets of Jerusalem, sharing in the general theological outlook of that city (as earlier described in our discussion of Isaiah). The extreme brevity of their books also makes it especially difficult to know how to distinguish *their* words from those of the circles who edited them.

In the following comments I will focus primarily on their messages as these relate to their historical circumstances and to the legacy of hopes and prophecies of their eighth century prophetic predecessors.

C. Minor Prophets of the Seventh Century

1. Zephaniah

The prophecies of Zephaniah reflect the deplorably apostate conditions in Jerusalem that prevailed there during the long reign of Manasseh (see the references to the worship of pagan deities in Jerusalem, in 2 Kings 21 and Zephaniah 1:4–5), even though the editors of his book dated it to the reign of Josiah, Manasseh's successor in Jerusalem. According to 2 Chronicles 34:3, Josiah began purging Jerusalem of its alien deities in his twelfth regal year. Hence, Zephaniah's prophetic activity must have occurred prior to this, although it is not impossible that he was one of those who prepared the way for these reforms.

A key feature of Zephaniah's prophecies is his prediction of the demise of Assyria (2:13–15). With this he was saying in effect that what *Isaiah* had already foretold (Assyria's eventual humiliation) is *now* soon to take place, and with a vengeance appropriate to Assyria's criminal behavior. However, Zephaniah does not share Isaiah's earlier optimism that this would be followed by a spectacular renascence in Jerusalem of righteousness and peace. In fact, *his* conviction is that yet another purging judgment will be necessary before this can happen. He appears to have been influenced by Amos in this regard. In any case, like Amos (see Am 5:18–28), Zephaniah announced a fearful "day of Yahweh" (1:7) that will sweep across the face of the whole earth (1:2, 14–18) and purge it of its evil. Only when this fire-storm of Yahweh's jealousy (1:18) has run its course will the "humble of the earth" in Jerusalem finally be purged of their sin and cynicism (1:4–13; 2:3; 3:12). Either Zephaniah or his editors came to believe that then too this "remnant of the House of Judah" (2:7) would become *militarily* powerful once again (see 2:4–10)—a people of "praise and renown among all the peoples of the earth" (3:20).

In Zephaniah the aspirations of the Yahweh loyalists in Jerusalem during the waning years of the Assyrian Dark Ages found a voice. Despite the apostasy that surrounded them, and the doubts they themselves might have had about Assyrian control and influence in their region, they were still confident that Yahweh was God and the words of his prophets were true. Assyria's demise, though delayed, was certain, just as Isaiah had predicted. However, fresh insight was needed regarding what would follow that demise. Yet additional terrors would have to befall his city, Zephaniah came to believe, before that new age of righteousness Isaiah had also spoken of would actually dawn.

2. Nahum

Another who represented the Yahweh believing circles of Jerusalem during the fading away of the Assyrian Dark Ages was the prophet Nahum. His oracles also reflect (as did Zephaniah's) a familiarity with those of Isaiah, especially his words regarding the demise of Assyria. Isaiah, it will be remembered, had spoken of this as of a yoke that would be lifted one day from Judean shoulders (9:4). Nahum repeated this prophecy in almost identical terms: ". . . for now I shall break his yoke which presses hard on you, and snap your chains" (1:13). For him, as for Isaiah, this stupendous event will usher in a new era of peace and righteousness. So real were his expectations in this regard that he could already "see on the mountains the feet of the herald" hurrying to bring news of it:

"Peace!" he proclaims.
Judah, celebrate your feasts,
carry out your vows,
for Beliel [Assyria] will never pass through you again;
he has been utterly destroyed (2:1).

He is certain that with this event Yahweh's purposes for Israel will have been achieved. Having once been made to suffer, Judah will be made to suffer no more (1:12). The utter annihilation of Assyria, which Nahum spends the greater part of his book describing (2:2–3:19), was thus for him more than a demonstration of the truth that though slow to anger Yahweh is "great in power" and will not let evil go unpunished (1:2–3). It will also mark a new stage in salvation history. With Assyria's demise a new age will dawn for Judah (2:1). Unlike Zephaniah he did not think that further punishments or judgments would be necessary.

3. Habakkuk

Habakkuk, who prophesied somewhat later than either Nahum or Zephaniah—at a time when the *Babylonians* were already threatening to replace the Assyrians as the major power of the ancient Near East (1:6; perhaps as late as the fall of Assyria, in 612, or the death of Josiah, in 609)—speaks to these same issues in a somewhat more philosophical manner. He is a prophet, of course (not a philosopher), and is identified as such in the heading to his book (1:1). It has been conjectured, in fact, that he may have been a prophet by profession—one, even, who was attached to the *Jerusalem* temple for the purpose of receiving or "incubating" oracles there, as his words in 2:1 seem to imply:

> I will stand at my post,
> I shall station myself on my watch-tower,
> watching to see what he will say to me,
> what answer he will make to my complaints.

The problem that perturbs him is the divine rationale behind the raising up of a people as fierce and amoral as the Babylonians (see his critique of them in 2:5–20) as an instrument of punishment and justice against a people better than they (1:12–13). This alerts us to the fact that already in this period the prophetic slant on history as the arena of divine action in judgment was beginning to pose problems. Later on intellectuals in Israel would grapple with such questions more and more (see Job and Ecclesiastes, for example).

It appears that Habakkuk could not find an *intellectually* satisfying solution to the issue he posed, but concluded, nevertheless, that the "upright" need not lose faith, but should persevere and wait patiently for the outworking of Yahweh's purposes (2:1–4). However, apart from a continuing belief that evil *would* be judged and righteousness vindicated for all nations, including the Babylonians (see 2:5–20 and ch. 3, absent from the Commentary on Habakkuk discovered at Qumran), his book has very little *concretely* to say about what that "outworking" might look like eventually. In this regard, one might say, Habakkuk appears to have been much more tentative about the future than were Nahum and Zephaniah.

4. Obadiah

The message of Obadiah, the shortest book in the Hebrew Bible, is again more in line with Isaiah and Nahum in that he believed fervently in the survival of a righteous remnant in Jerusalem—one that would become the nucleus of a new and powerful people in a restored Zion (vv. 17–18). The historical context of this prophecy appears to have been the aftermath of Jerusalem's destruction by Babylon, in 586 (see v. 11), when the Edomites to the south took advantage of the plight of their "brother Jacob" and mistreated him (vv. 10–14). Obadiah is vehement about the ruin that will befall the Edomites because of this (vv. 16, 18), and envisions the triumph of the "House of Jacob" (and hence the triumph of Yahweh from Mount Zion—v. 21) as a reconquest of the land of Canaan as far as Zarephath, in the north (between Tyre and Sidon) and the towns of the Negeb, in the south (vv. 19–21).

D. Ongoing Relevance

These more or less minor prophetic voices give testimony to the seriousness with which certain circles in Jerusalem were attending to the words of the eighth century prophets a century later (and to the words of Isaiah in particular). At the same time they also indicate the extent to which that legacy had proven to be problematical. All shared Isaiah's certainty of Assyria's eventual demise and of the promise of a new era beyond that demise. But precisely *when* this would occur and *what*, exactly, would then happen—regarding this there appears to have been considerable confusion.

Some (notably Habakkuk) were frankly perplexed at the way events were unfolding. They were sure that Yahweh was still working things out, but that was about all. Others (notably Zephaniah) appear to be anxious and frightened. They foresee yet additional catastrophes of cosmic proportions coming upon Judah, before a brighter future will dawn for the inhabitants of Judah-Jerusalem. The thoughts of still others (notably Nahum and Obadiah) are much more hopeful. They believe that a new Davidic state will soon arise (in the wake of the Assyrian and Babylonian invasions), and when it does, Yahweh's sovereignty and peace will be manifest in history as never before.

These more nationalistic sketches of the future have played an especially influential role in the thinking of subsequent generations. Even today there are Jews *and* Christians who believe that these prophecies are being fulfilled right before our eyes in the advent of the modern Jewish state and its recovery of territory once belonging to David's empire. Might these developments not signal the dawning of the Messianic era? they ask. Can the advent of the Messiah himself be far off?

Another view would be that while these expectations may be valid as a first tentative expression of the belief that there is indeed a good future in store for Israel (and the world), additional insights would be needed as to *how* this might occur, if the new beginning was not to be just a repetition of what had already happened. In short, a better understanding of the road ahead awaited the appearance of yet other prophets who might go deeper into the problem of frustrated hopes posed by the non-fulfillment of the too idealistic predictions of certain eighth century prophets.

In summary, with these prophets we can sense that a decisive turn toward the future has now occurred in the thought of many among Israel's Yahweh loyalists. The problem was now posed: "What of the future? Will there be a future?" It was also agreed: "Yes! This is *not* the end! There *will* be a future—and a *good* one!" Simply by declaring this as forthrightly as they do, these prophets have made a permanent contribution to the life of the world. They have helped *us* turn toward the future. They have encouraged us to think *positively* about this future and face it with *hope,* not just in fear or in dread, as we are often prone to do.

However, regarding the precise shape of that future there was still much to be thought about and discerned.

Questions for Review

1. How would you describe the books we have just studied now that you have had an opportunity to read and think about them yourself? Also, what impressions do you now have of the prophets themselves? Are they the way you thought they might be, or different? In what ways? Summarize the points where they agree with each other in their messages.

2. What happened historically to Israel-Judah in the aftermath of these prophets? In what respects were their expectations of the future of their people fulfilled? In what respects were they unfulfilled? What questions might their messages have awakened among those of the following generation who read them?

3. Compare the prophecies of Zephaniah and Nahum concerning Assyria. Did they foresee the same thing happening after Assyria's fall? What is it that was so puzzling about the events of his time for the prophet Habakkuk? How does he go about finding a solution and what

is it? How would you characterize the hopes that Obadiah expresses for the future of his people?

4. What explanation do you have for the fact that the hopes of many of these prophets for a restored Davidic kingdom have not yet been fulfilled? Do you see them as still coming to fulfillment one day? How do you feel about the suggestion that they were valid in part, but that further insight would be needed?

14

Jeremiah, Son of Hilkiah

This is the largest of the prophetic volumes we have studied so far. Unfortunately, it is also one of the most disorganized. In addition, it is not as easy in this instance to distinguish the person from his message. An unusually large number of stories *about* Jeremiah turn up in this volume, with the consequence that man and message gradually become inextricably linked in our minds. It is as though with this prophet, to some special degree, the word was becoming flesh.

A. The Book as a Whole

A *Greek* translation of Jeremiah dating from the third century B.C. (commonly called the Septuagint) is not only differently organized but an eighth shorter than the Hebrew text on which most English translations are based. This suggests that quite differing versions of this book came into existence in the aftermath of Jeremiah's prophetic career.

Why this was so is not difficult to surmise. Jeremiah prophesied in the midst of tumultous events culminating in the invasion and destruction of his country. At the end of his life he was taken to Egypt by a band of refugees who fled there for safety (Jer 44). Most of his contemporaries had already been deported to Babylon (Jer 52). The Jewish people were now becoming a scattered community living in various parts of the world. One marvels that under these circumstances anything at all has survived, much less a book the size of this one. Understandably, the versions of this book that were eventually assembled in different places might vary from one another.

That his book is somewhat disorganized is also understandable in this light. Nor is it surprising that scholars disagree regarding the details of its compositional history. Controversy centers especially on the numerous, quite distinctive personal reports scattered throughout the book (see chart below). Are these from Jeremiah himself, or did others have a hand in composing them? Since their style is reminiscent of the prose

sermons in the Book of Deuteronomy (and elsewhere), many are sus-
picious that certain "Deuteronomists" might once again have played a
role in the editing and supplementing of this book—in this instance,
they suggest, an exceptionally large role.

What follows is only one response among many to these and other
issues. My hope is that as a "working hypothesis" it might help clear
up at least some of the organizational confusion that confronts us as we
begin reading this book.

1. The Heading (1:1-3)

A first hint of the way this book originated is to be found in its
heading, in 1:1-3. There seem to be here (as in the case of Amos) *two*
headings which were at one time independent of each other, but are now
spliced together—the first, in 1:1-2; the second, in 1:3.

The first of these headings (again like Amos) begins with a title
that characterizes the contents of what follows, not as words of *Yahweh*, but as "the words of *Jeremiah* son of Hilkiah, one of the priests
living at Anathoth in the territory of Benjamin" (1:1). This is followed by what appears to be the opening sentence of the collection
so headed: "The word of Yahweh came to him in the days of Josiah
son of Amon, king of Judah, in the thirteenth year of his reign . . ."
(1:2). One would expect as a sequel to this a collection of messages
from this *opening phase* of Jeremiah's prophetic career, such as we
in fact have in 1:4-9. Other reports of a similar type, one is led to
imagine, would have followed in a more or less chronological sequence, perhaps.

However, this initial collection must not have included *all* of Jeremiah's prophecies—not initially at least—for when the book in its
present form was assembled, the original heading had to be enlarged,
it seems (1:3): "then [also, the heading continues, the word of Yahweh came to him as well] in the days of Jehoiakim son of Josiah,
king of Judah, until the end of the eleventh year of Zedekiah son of
Josiah, king of Judah, until the deportation of Jerusalem, in the fifth
month" (1:3).

We can guess at who it was who expanded the heading (and the
book) in this manner. It might have been the same group that appended
chapter 52 (after the sentence, "Here end the words of Jeremiah"—
51:64b), for there (in ch. 52) a detailed report is given of the very deportation alluded to in 1:3—a report that is almost identical to one we
find at the end of the Deuteronomic history, in 2 Kings 24-25. This
would suggest that the same Deuteronomic circles that compiled the

Book of Kings had a hand in shaping the final edition of Jeremiah as well (even as they contributed to the editorial form of Amos, Hosea, Isaiah and Micah, as previously noted).

In summary, the heading of this book hints at a *two-stage* process in its development. An original collection was entitled "Words of Jeremiah . . ." (1:1). This collection began with a record of the oracles that came to him from the thirteenth year of Josiah onward (1:2). However, this first collection was incomplete and eventually had to be enlarged to include as well his messages from the days of Jehoiakim until the Judean deportation (1:3).

Is there any evidence elsewhere in the book of such a two-stage development?

2. Jeremiah 25:1–13a

Jer 25:1–13a may have a bearing on this issue in that it obviously served as a conclusion of some sort to some initial document or collection. This is clearest in the Septuagint version of Jeremiah referred to above, where the final words of this passage are: ". . . all that is written in *this book*" (25:13a). This is followed (in the Septuagint) by a series of appendices, beginning with Jeremiah's foreign nation oracles in Jeremiah 46–51 (located here in the Septuagint, rather than where they are in the Hebrew text). Note too that these verses contain a *first person* report, in 25:3–13a (stylistically very similar to the one, in 1:4–19), in which Jeremiah relates how "for twenty-three years, from the *thirteenth year of Josiah* son of Amon, king of Judah, until *today*," the word of Yahweh had been addressed to him and he had persistently spoken it (25:3).

From this it is apparent that this passage is the ending to a document prepared for a quite specific moment—one in which Jeremiah summarized his messages of the previous twenty-three years for a certain occasion identified, in the chapter's opening verse, as the "fourth year of Jehoiakim son of Josiah, king of Judah" (25:1). Since the period being summarized is one that began in "the thirteenth year of Josiah" (25:3)—exactly as specified in 1:2—and since the style of this summary is identical to that of 1:4–19 (*first-person* report, ostensibly therefore, Jeremiah's *own* account) these verses appear to be the *conclusion* to a document that had its beginning there.

In summary, an original collection of Jeremiah's words may have begun with the heading in 1:1–2 and the opening personal report of early prophetic experiences, in 1:4–19, and ended with the personal summation of his prophetic mission to that point, in 25:3–13a. This document was prepared in the fourth year of Jehoiakim (25:1). It recapitulated what he had been saying to his people for a period of some "twenty-three years" (25:3). From its opening and closing verses we would gather that one of its major purposes was to warn of an imminent invasion by "families of the north" (1:15; 25:8—direct references to Nebuchadnezzar and Babylon are missing from the Septuagint version of this passage).

Thus 25:1–13a may mark the conclusion to *stage one* in the development of this book. However, were this the case and were it also true that Jeremiah *himself* had a hand in assembling this "book" of his messages in Jehoiakim's "fourth year" (as the first-person style implies), might we not expect some confirmation of this elsewhere in his book? As every student of Jeremiah knows, this confirmation is not lacking. In Jeremiah 36 we have a remarkably detailed report that relates how Jeremiah did in fact prepare just such a collection of his messages, on a scroll, and at precisely this time of his life.

3. Jeremiah 36

Jeremiah 36 is one of an unusually large number of biographical narratives scattered throughout this book (see chart below). Their author might well have been Baruch, the young scribe who is mentioned here and elsewhere as Jeremiah's friend and confidant (see especially ch. 45). If so, they are eyewitness reports of unusual value in reconstructing the life and times of this prophet.

What this particular chapter tells us is that Jeremiah did in fact do the very thing alluded to in 25:1–13a. In Jehoiakim's "fourth year," it is said here, he felt constrained (by Yahweh) to write down the messages that had come to him from "the time of Josiah, until today" (36:2). This was accomplished by dictation to Baruch, who then took the scroll he had written and read it at the temple on a certain "fast" day, in Jehoiakim's fifth year. So impressed were those who first heard it that it was read a second time to certain "chief men" (36:12), and then a third time to the king (36:21). The king's response, however, was far from positive. As the scroll was being read to him, he cut it to pieces and threw it into the fire, and then gave orders for the arrest of Jeremiah and Baruch. The account closes with the information that "Yahweh had hidden them" (36:26b), but that while in hiding another scroll was prepared like the one the king had burned, to which additional words were added (36:32).

If we add the information given here to that previously derived from our analysis of the book's heading (1:1–3) and ending (25:1–13a), two conclusions regarding the compositional history of Jeremiah can now be drawn:

(a) Jeremiah himself, after having been active as a prophet for some twenty-three years, in the fourth year of Jehoiakim prepared a written summary of his messages for reading at the temple;

(b) the *beginning* of this written summary is most likely to be found in 1:1–2 and the oracles that follow, in 1:4–19; its *conclusion* is the summarizing report in 25:1–13a ("everything written in this book").

If then, as it seems, 1:1–2, 4–19 and 25:1–13a are the opening and closing passages of this scroll, is it possible that the intervening chapters (chs. 2–24) were also once a part of it? The very size and diversity of the materials assembled here would suggest otherwise. According to Jeremiah 36 the scroll Jeremiah prepared in Jehoiakim's fourth year was designed for *public* reading on a certain fast day at the temple. It summarized *past* messages and warned of an invasion (see 36:29–30). Clearly, not nearly everything in these chapters would be suitable for such a document. From chapter 11 onward, for example, there are some exceptionally intimate prayers from a time of persecution and despair in Jeremiah's life (see chart below for specifics); other *poetic* passages in this section (see especially chs. 2–6 and 8–9) have a similarly intimate, *private* feel about them (4:19; 9:1)—much like the journal type entries we observed in Hosea 4–14. There are also a number of specifically *thematic* collections here: words spoken in connection with a drought, in ch. 14; aphorisms in ch. 17; words concerning kings and prophets in 21:11–23:8 and 23:9–40. Contained in 21:1–10 and ch. 24 are reports of events occurring in the very *last* period of Jeremiah's career (during the reign of Zedekiah, not the reigns of Josiah or Jehoiakim).

From this it is evident that chs. 2–24 are a composite collection of different types of materials from a great variety of times, experiences and sources. Even so, we might ask, were not at least some of the passages assembled here once part of the scroll referred to in Jeremiah 36? If so, which ones?

4. The Personal Prose Reports

One possible answer to this question arises from an analysis of the *personal reports* referred to earlier which are scattered throughout this collection (for a listing see the chart below). Stylistically, they are quite similar to the prose reports that, we conjectured above, opened and closed this scroll—those in 1:4–19 and 25:1–13a. That the remainder of the scroll would be written in a comparable style is only to be expected, so this, in and of itself, would seem to mark these passages as the ones most likely to have been part of this original scroll.

Yet, as previously noted, it is these prose reports that are also most under suspicion today among scholars so far as their Jeremiah authorship is concerned, and precisely because of certain stylistic features which are regarded as "Deuteronomic." Some imagine this to mean that "Deuteronomists" were their authors, not Jeremiah, others that they were simply shapers and molders of the Jeremiah tradition. However, as will be noted below, Jeremiah *himself* may have been a "Deuteronomist" of sorts in that he grew up in a Levitical community north of Jerusalem in which this tradition was rooted (as was noted in our introduction to Hosea; see chapter 7). If then, when dictating his messages for reading at the temple, he did so in a Deuteronomic style, it would not be surprising. That was the style he grew up with, perhaps one characteristic of Judean prose generally in the seventh and early sixth centuries.

Furthermore, it is often overlooked that, while similar to other prose forms, these personal reports of Jeremiah's are also unique in ways that might be expected of a document prepared for public reading and for summarizing a prophet's messages of previous years.

What I have in mind at this point can best be made clear through an illustration, perhaps. A good example of the narratives we are talking about is the one in 13:1–11. It will be observed that it opens with Jeremiah personally explaining how on one occasion Yahweh addressed him ("Yahweh said this to me") and told him to "go and buy a linen waistcloth and put it around your waist. But do not dip it in water" (13:1). Later he was told to put it in water. A report is then given of how he responded to these instructions and how as he did so Yahweh's word came to him: "Then the word of Yahweh was addressed to me as follows, 'Yahweh says this . . .' " (13:8). There follows as the limax of this report, in 13:9–11, a recitation of the oracle he received *on this particular occasion.*

What we have here, then, are not simply prose reports, but *summaries* of *prior* revelations (and the concrete circumstances in which they were received and transmitted) recorded in this way, ostensibly, so that they could become effective and understandable for a *new* audience—precisely what, we are told in Jeremiah 36, the scroll prepared at that time was intended to do. In several instances, in fact, these past events are even dated (1:2; 3:6; 25:3); in other instances, quite specific events are alluded to that were undoubtedly of relevance to the new audience for which these reports were prepared (11:2, 9; 14:13).

In short, these unique texts represent Jeremiah doing what Jeremiah 36 suggests it was his intention to do in preparing his famous scroll: that is, make the oracles of the previous twenty-three years real and effective once again at a critical moment in the life of his nation, in the fourth year of Jehoiakim.

It seems not unreasonable to conclude from all this (as indeed a number of scholars do) that the scroll which Jeremiah himself is said to have prepared (and which subsequently must have become the core of his literary legacy and eventually the present book) was originally made up exclusively of reports of this nature.

5. From Original Scroll to Present Book

How then, if the earliest collection of Jeremiah's oracles was such a scroll, made up exclusively of prose reports of this kind, did the present form of the book emerge? A very tentative proposal would be that this scroll, as defined above, provided the *basic framework* for the first major division of the book and that the prose reports in Jeremiah 1–25 are even now, for the most part, in the order that they appeared in the original scroll. This means that we can begin to make some sense of the bewildering array of materials in these chapters if we imagine this to have actually been the case and that other materials in this section of the book (chs. 1–25) were at different points *spliced in*, so to speak. I have attempted to illustrate this (and at the same time convey an impression of the contents of these chapters) in the following chart (see page 156).

I would also hypothesize that to this initial collection (chs. 1–25:13a) *appendices* were then subsequently attached illustrative of Jeremiah's activity during the latter part of the reign of Jehoiakim on through the destruction of Jerusalem (these appendices corresponding to the addendum to the heading in 1:3, as noted earlier). The total structure of the book with these appendices attached can again be best conveyed by a chart, as follows (see page 157).

The chief gain from this, as it might seem, tedious analysis of the book as a whole, apart from the clarity it might bring as to the growth and present organization of the book itself, is, I suggest, to highlight the importance of the personal prose reports and of Jeremiah's action in preparing a scroll made up of these for reading at the temple in the fourth year of Jehoiakim. If these reports were in fact dictated by Jeremiah himself—and at a crucial juncture of his prophetic mission—

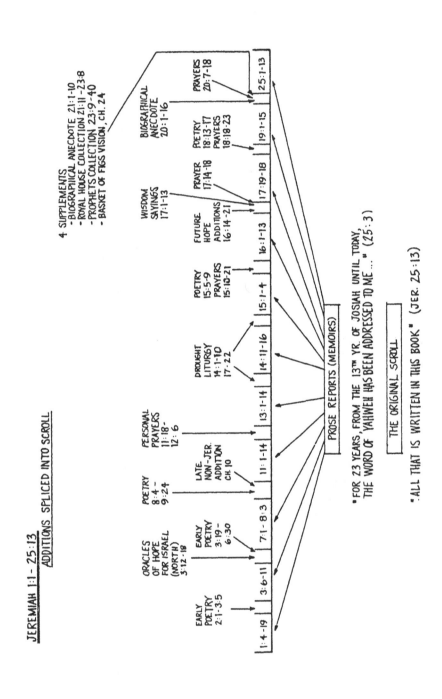

JEREMIAH 1:1 - 25:13

ADDITIONS SPLICED INTO SCROLL

4 SUPPLEMENTS
- BIOGRAPHICAL ANECDOTE 21:1-10
- ROYAL HOUSE COLLECTION 21:11 - 23:8
- PROPHETS COLLECTION 23:9 - 40
- BASKET OF FIGS VISION, CH. 24

EARLY POETRY 2:1 - 3:5 | 1:4-19

ORACLES OF HOPE FOR ISRAEL (NORTH) 3:12-18 | EARLY POETRY 3:19 - 6:30 | 3:6-11 | 7:1 - 8:3

POETRY 8:4 - 9:24 | LATE NON-JER. ADDITION CH. 10

PERSONAL PRAYERS 11:18 - 12:6 | 11:1-14 | 13:1-14

DROUGHT LITURGY 14:1-10 17:22 | 14:11-16 | 15:1-4

POETRY 15:5-9 PRAYERS 15:10-21 | 16:1-13

WISDOM SAYINGS 17:1-13 | FUTURE HOPE ADDITIONS 16:14-21 | PRAYER 17:14-18 | 17:19-18

POETRY 18:13-17 PRAYERS 18:18-23 | 19:1-15

BIOGRAPHICAL ANECDOTE 20:1-16 | PRAYERS 20:7-18 | 25:1-13

PROSE REPORTS (MEMOIRS)

" FOR 23 YEARS, FROM THE 13TH YR. OF JOSIAH UNTIL TODAY, THE WORD OF YAHWEH HAS BEEN ADDRESSED TO ME ... " (25 : 3)

THE ORIGINAL SCROLL

" ALL THAT IS WRITTEN IN THIS BOOK " (JER. 25 : 13)

THE WORDS OF JEREMIAH ... (JER, 1:1)

THE INITIAL COLLECTION (CHS 1:2 - 25:13)
("THE WORD OF YAHWEH WAS ADDRESSED TO HIM
IN THE DAYS OF JOSIAH ... IN THE 13th YR. OF HIS
REIGN" 1:2)

APPENDICES TO THE INITIAL COLLECTION (CHS 25:14 - CH 52)
("... THEN IN THE DAYS OF JEHOIAKIM ... UNTIL THE
DEPORTATION WHICH OCCURRED IN THE 5th MO." 1:3)

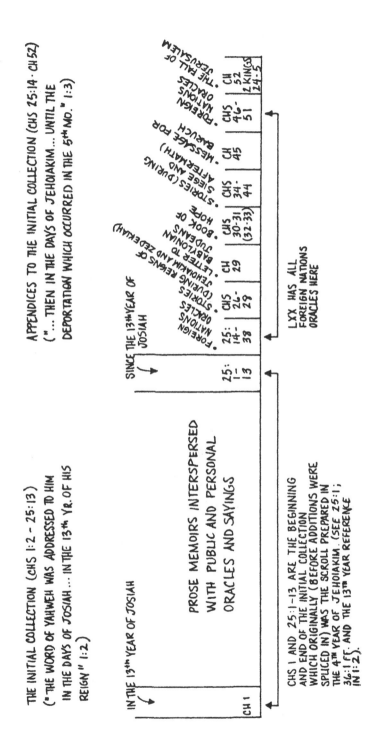

SINCE THE 13th YEAR OF JOSIAH

IN THE 13th YEAR OF JOSIAH

PROSE MEMOIRS INTERSPERSED
WITH PUBLIC AND PERSONAL
ORACLES AND SAYINGS

CH 1

• FOREIGN NATIONS ORACLES — 25: 1-13

• FOREIGN NATIONS ORACLES — CHS 25: 14-38

• STORIES OF (DURING REIGNS OF JEHOIAKIM AND ZEDEKIAH) — CHS 26-29

• LETTER TO BABYLONIAN JUDEANS — CH 29

• BOOK OF HOPE — CHS 30-31 (32:33)

• STORIES (DURING SIEGE AND AFTERMATH) — CHS 34-44

• MESSAGE FOR BARUCH — CH 45

• FOREIGN NATIONS ORACLES — CHS 46-51

• THE FALL OF JERUSALEM — CH 52 2 KINGS 24-5

LYX HAS ALL FOREIGN NATIONS ORACLES HERE

CHS 1 AND 25:1-13 ARE THE BEGINNING
AND END OF THE INITIAL COLLECTION
WHICH ORIGINALLY (BEFORE ADDITIONS WERE
SPLICED IN) WAS THE SCROLL PREPARED IN
THE 4th YEAR OF JEHOIAKIM. (SEE 25:1;
36:1 FF. AND THE 13th YEAR REFERENCE
IN 1:2).

they will obviously merit our closest attention as we seek to give an account of his life and message.

B. The Man Behind the Book

But before turning to his message we want again to pause and get acquainted, in a preliminary way at least, with Jeremiah himself, the man behind the book.

1. Name

His name is a compound of Yah (Yahweh) and a verb (*yarum*) meaning possibly "exalted" (hence: Yahweh is exalted). That he should bear such a name is consistent with the reference in the heading of his book to his being "the son of Hilkiah of the *priests* living at Anathoth" (1:1). It would appear that he came from a home where Yahweh was exalted to a unique degree.

Who, more precisely, *were* these priests of Anathoth?

2. Religious Background

Anathoth was a Levitical village (Jos 21:18) three miles north of Jerusalem to which Abiathar, one of the two chief priests under David, was banished by David's son and successor, Solomon (see 1 Kgs 2:26–27). This information is important. It tells us that Jeremiah grew up in a village where priests lived who once officiated at the temple in Jerusalem. But even more significant is the fact that at least some among these priests could trace their ancestry, through Abiathar, to the priestly house of Eli that once officiated at the pre-Jerusalem worship center at Shiloh in the days of Samuel (see 1 Sam 1–3). This genealogy is spelled out in 1 Samuel 14:3; 22:20; 1 Kings 2:27. The house of Eli in turn knew itself to be in a tradition stretching back to the founding families of the Yahwistic movement in Egypt under Moses (1 Sam 2:27; Ex 32:29). This rich spiritual heritage is reflected in Jeremiah 15:1 and 7:12 where Jeremiah refers to Moses and Samuel as spiritual models and to the pre-Jerusalem shrine at Shiloh as the place where Yahweh had once given his name a home.

The significance of all this is that even though Jeremiah lived only three miles north of Jerusalem, his roots were not in the traditions of that city (as were Isaiah's for example), but rather in the all-Israelite traditions that we have already learned through our study of Hosea were nurtured and preserved in the Levitical communities to the north of Jerusalem (note too how the book's heading, in 1:1, underlines the fact that Anathoth is "in the territory of Benjamin" and that he was not, therefore, a Judean).

However, Jerusalem is not for Jeremiah just another city, either, as it seems to have been for Hosea (or even Amos and Micah). Rather, a temple bearing Yahweh's name (7:10–11) is there, one where this name now has a "home" as it previously did at Shiloh (7:12). This concept of Yahweh putting his name at a certain place and of it dwelling there and of that place becoming thereby the supreme place of worship is Deuteronomic (see Dt 12:2–7) and Jeremiah seems to share it. Furthermore, he believes (as do the Deuteronomic editors of Kings) that since the destruction of Shiloh the place so chosen by God for his name to dwell is the temple in Jerusalem.

However, in Deuteronomic theology, this presence of Yahweh's "name" at a given shrine is *conditional* on the people's obedience to the covenantal laws. Deuteronomic theology differs in this regard from Jerusalem theology, where it is declared that Yahweh has chosen Zion to be his home unconditionally *forever* (Ps 132:13). If the citizens of Jerusalem are apostate, temple and city will be destroyed, Jeremiah declares, just as earlier the Yahweh shrine at Shiloh was destroyed (Jer 7:12–15). As already noted, in this and other matters Jeremiah reflects the language and theology of the Deuteronomists, whose roots, like Jeremiah's, were among the northern Levites (see also our discussion of these issues in chapter 7).

It was Jeremiah's fate, therefore, to have been called to speak *to* Jerusalem, but from a spiritual and theological background *outside* of Jerusalem. When this point is kept in mind, the reasons for the opposition and hardships he experienced in his mission are greatly clarified.

3. Historical Setting

The heading to his book (1:1–3) informs us, right off, that Jeremiah was a prophet for an exceptionally long period of time—some forty years, it is implied there—from Josiah's thirteenth regal year (626 by our reckoning) until the time of the destruction of Jerusalem and the deportation of its surviving population to Babylon in 586. The materials assembled in his book amply confirm this, and to understand them properly we must look now, in a summary way, at what was happening during this tumultuous final period of Judean national existence.

Three major developments form the backdrop to Jeremiah's prophetic career: the *Dark Ages of Manasseh* that immediately preceded it; the *reforms* of Josiah; the *tragic aftermath* of Josiah's death, along with the subsequent destruction of the Judean state by Babylon.

(a) Spiritual Apostasy

Our survey of Jeremiah's times must begin by referring once again to the spiritual Dark Ages that descended on Judah-Jerusalem during the middle part of the seventh century, after the Sennacherib invasion of 701 (see our discussion of this in the previous chapter). At that time Hezekiah's son and successor, Manasseh, unlike his father, opened wide the doors in Jerusalem to Assyrian cultural influence, even to the point of permitting altars of Assyrian gods to be placed in the courts of the temple (2 Kgs 21). Also, of Manasseh's son Amon it was said that he "abandoned Yahweh" (2 Kgs 21:22). In short, in the immediate background of Jeremiah's mission was an approximately seventy-five year period of almost unprecedented religious apostasy, especially among the elite in Jerusalem.

(b) Attempted Reforms

But then, two years into Amon's reign, there occurred a dramatic sequence of events pointing, it seemed, in a new and more hopeful direction. When (according to 2 Kings 21:23) Amon was assassinated, in the second year of his reign (640), it was not his assassins who took charge, but certain "people of the country," as they are called, for they are the ones who are said to have succeeded in placing on the throne at this time an eight year old boy-king named Josiah (2 Kgs 22:1).

That more than power politics was involved in this move is indicated by 2 Chronicles 34:3 where we are told that already in the eighth year of Josiah's reign (when he was still only a youth of sixteen) he began seeking the God of his ancestor David, and in his twelfth year began to purge the land of idolatry. Then in his eighteenth year, in the course of repairing the temple, a book of the law was discovered that, after some uncertainty as to how seriously to take it, was prophetically authenticated as from Yahweh (2 Kgs 22:14–20).

With this settled, Josiah undertook to do a remarkable thing. He summoned the elders of the entire Judean community to Jerusalem and there had this book read to them, after which an agreement was reached by those assembled that they would pledge their allegiance to Yahweh on the terms of the covenant spelled out in this book (2 Kgs 23:1–3). Subsequently, we read, sweeping reforms were enacted which involved the destruction of all outlying sanctuaries (both pagan and Yahwistic) and the designation of the Yahweh temple in Jerusalem as the one exclusive place of Yahweh worship for the whole land. In line with this even the Passover was celebrated there for the first time "since the days when the judges ruled Israel" (2 Kgs 23:21–23).

Most agree that the book referred to in this account of Josiah's reforms was some version of the biblical book of Deuteronomy, for only there (among the law codes of the Pentateuch) is it said that worship of Yahweh should be confined to a single shrine (see Dt 12), and only there is it specified that even the Passover should be celebrated at this place (see Dt 16:1–8; elsewhere the Passover is assumed to be held in each locality; see Ex 12–13). It is interesting to note that in 2 Kings 23:15–20 this sweeping reform was implemented not only in Judah, but *north* of Judah in Samaria as well—territory once belonging to the now non-existent northern kingdom (since its fall to Assyria a century earlier). This in itself is evidence of the degree to which Assyrian control of this region had now already weakened.

In short, for many Yahweh loyalists in Judah at this juncture (that is, in 621, with these reforms in place and the now evident waning of Assyrian power) it must have seemed that a new era in Judean life was now dawning. Seldom before had such sweeping changes for the better occurred in the life of this nation. Not since the days of Solomon had a Davidic king in Jerusalem ruled over *all* Israel. Were these perhaps the days of rebirth and renewal to which the earlier prophets had so exuberantly pointed? Many must have been tempted to think so.

(c) The Tragic End

However, as events transpired, such hopes were sadly mistaken. To be sure, Assyria was by now in rapid decline, but other nations stood ready in the wings to take its place. Chief among the contenders were Egypt and Babylon. In 612, just nine years after the reforms referred to above, Nineveh (Assyria's capital city) fell before the combined forces of Babylon and Media. Three years later (609) Egyptian armies entered the fray in support of the retreating Assyrians, hoping thereby, it seems, to create a buffer between themselves and the now increasingly powerful Babylonians—but to no avail.

While doing so, however, a bizarre thing happened. When moving their forces northward, the Egyptians sought passage through Israelite territory at the pass of Megiddo. They had no wish for a fight with little Judah, but Josiah, overly confident perhaps in his belief that Yahweh was with him because of his reforms, may have seen this as an opportune moment for the assertion of Judean autonomy. However, the poorly prepared and equipped Israelite forces were routed "in the first encounter," we are told, and Josiah himself was killed (2 Kgs 23:29). His son Jehoahaz occupied the throne only briefly in his stead when the Egyptian armies returned from their unsuccessful northern foray and put him in chains, took him to Egypt and installed another son of Josiah on the throne in his place—one more to their liking. This was Jehoiakim, who, it seems, quickly lifted the ban on foreign gods in Jerusalem imposed by his father and adopted a life-style befitting a king in league with an Egyptian pharaoh (note what Jeremiah has to say about this proud young man in Jeremiah 22:13–19).

But if Egypt thought it was thereby gaining power in this region on a permanent basis, these hopes were shattered in 605 when the armies of Egypt and Babylon met in the upper Euphrates at Carchemish and there fought a decisive battle in which the Egyptian armies were routed. A year later these same Babylonian forces, under the leadership of Nebuchadnezzar (the famous founder of this new Babylonian insurgency), marched southward to the border of Egypt, effectively laying claim to this whole region.

However, released thereby from *Egyptian* control, Judah, under Jehoiakim, was not about to capitulate to *Babylon*. As a consequence, shortly thereafter he began openly defying this newly established Babylonian hegemony. The Babylonian response was swift. Troops were sent and Jerusalem put under siege, with Nebuchadnezzar himself directing the attack in its final phase (2 Kgs 24:1–10).

In the midst of these traumatic events, Jehoiakim died and his eighteen year old son, Jehoiachin, reigned in his stead. In the third month of his reign he had the good sense to surrender, with the surprising consequence that instead of destroying the city, Nebuchadnezzar merely sacked it of its treasures, and then, to secure its allegiance, deported ten thousand of its craftsmen and ruling elite to Babylon (2 Kgs 24:13–17). As a further indication of his intentions of preserving the city, were it to submit to his authority, when withdrawing from Jerusalem he installed yet another of Josiah's sons on the throne there, changing his name as he did so from Mattaniah (meaning "gift of Yah") to Zedekiah (meaning "Yah has integrity").

But even this was of no avail. Nine years later Zedekiah, under the influence of religious fanatics (the prophets of hope—see Jer 28), once again, like his predecessor Jehoiakim, defied the Babylonian hegemony. This time, in 589, when the armies of Babylon again swept into this region, it was Judah alone that was the target of their attack. After devastating city after city, they reached Jerusalem in December 589 and put it to siege. A year and a half later the city was on the verge of starvation when its walls were breached and its inhabitants either slaughtered or force-marched to Babylon. A month later Nebuchadnezzar gave the order that the city should be put to the torch and its houses, walls and temple leveled to the ground. The end had come to this holy city.

Miraculously, Jeremiah himself survived this ordeal and was permitted to remain in the vicinity of the ruined city with a small contingent of people left there to till the fields (see 2 Kgs 25:22–24; Jer 40–44). But once again tragedy struck. The leader of this community, Gedaliah, was brutally murdered and the tiny group that remained took flight to Egypt for refuge, compelling Jeremiah to accompany them. There, so far as we know, he died.

4. Jeremiah's Prophetic Call

It was at the dawn of these tumultuous events, four years before the Josiah reforms (at a time, therefore, when the apostasy of the Manasseh era was still predominant), that Jeremiah was called, as a young lad, to be a prophet. The personal report of this call, in 1:4–10, reflects Jeremiah's Levitical (Deuteronomic) heritage. From Deuteronomy 18:13–20 we learn that among the Levitical communities to which he belonged there was the belief that in every generation a man would appear who would be, for that generation, a prophet like Moses (Dt 18:14–15). Yahweh would put his words in his mouth and by virtue of this he would be Yahweh's messenger for that particular time (Dt 18:18–19).

In the account of his call Jeremiah informs us how he was singled out as a child to be such a Moses-like prophet for *his* generation. Indeed, Yahweh impressed upon him, we are told, that already in the *womb* of his mother he was being shaped to this end, and not just for being a messenger to Israel, but to the *nations* (1:5, 10). Confirmation of this came when he experienced a "touch" sensation about his mouth, while Yahweh assured him of his having put "my words into your mouth" (1:9).

5. The Man and His Message

From this moment on Jeremiah's life was totally at the disposal of Yahweh. So far as we know, he had no other vocation or work during his entire life than that of a prophet. Yahweh even forbade him to marry and have children, we learn in 16:1–2. It is this astonishing fact that dictates a somewhat different approach for our study of his book than the one we have been following thus far.

In acquainting ourselves with a given prophet it can be useful, as we have seen, to distinguish the man from his message, and focus initially on what can be known about the prophet himself. However, in

Jeremiah's case, *his role as messenger was his life,* his life the mission to which Yahweh commissioned him. To survey them separately would be repetitious. In this instance, therefore, we are going to turn (in the chapter that follows) to a review of *both* life and message together.

Questions for Review

1. How might we explain the wide variations in the Septuagint version of Jeremiah from the Hebrew version that we have? What factors might have entered into making this book as disorganized as it appears to be?

2. What evidence is there that Jeremiah himself may have had certain of his messages written down on a scroll? Why has it been suggested that this scroll was composed of the personal reports now scattered throughout chs. 1–25? For what occasion was this scroll prepared? How might we in general imagine the book as we now have it to have developed from this original scroll?

3. How significant for an understanding of Jeremiah is the reference in his book's heading to his having grown up among the "priests living at Anathoth"? Who were these priests? Why were they living at Anathoth? What theological outlook did they have? How does this compare to the theological outlook of the other prophets we have studied? What attitude did these priests have toward Jerusalem and the theological outlook of those living there?

4. Through what major historical upheavals did Jeremiah live and prophesy? What was happening to Assyria during his lifetime? What nations were contending for Assyria's place in that region? What developments gave rise to the Josiah reforms? What were these reforms intended to accomplish? Why are they often referred to as Deuteronomic reforms? Why were they so quickly abandoned? What state policies led to the destruction of Jerusalem?

5. How is Jeremiah's Deuteronomic background reflected in the account of his prophetic call? Why might it be no exaggeration to say that when accepting this call he understood himself to be stepping into the shoes of Moses? Why in his case is it especially difficult to separate the man from his message?

15

His Message and Its Relevance

A. His Life and Message

The long forty year mission of Jeremiah was marked by periods of intense activity, followed, it seems, by times of withdrawal and waiting. These can be related to the major historical developments of his time outlined in the previous chapter. He was very active, for example, both before and after the famous Josiah reforms, and then again during the first four critical years of Jehoiakim, when Babylon was on the rise. Then, due to the incident with the scroll, he was forced to go into hiding, but returned to the streets of Jerusalem as the Babylonian forces asserted their control of this region during the final months of Jehoiakim's reign and the reign of Zedekiah.

These rather distinct phases of Jeremiah's prophetic career (five in all) may be charted as follows:

Assyrian decline			Babylonian ascendency		
640 Josiah's reign			609 Jehoiakim's reign	598 Zedekiah's 586 reign	
Jeremiah's call 626	Josiah's reform 621	Fall of Nineveh 612	Battle of Carchemish 605 (4th yr.)		Jerusalem destroyed
(1) Before the reform	(2) After the reform		(3) First four years	(4) Personal crisis	(5) Final period

I will try now to review briefly what Jeremiah did and said during each of these five periods of his life, in chronological sequence, turning first to the opening phase of his mission in the thirteenth year of Josiah (1:2).

165

1. Before the Josiah Reform (626–621)

Because the oracles, memoirs and notes assembled in chs. 1–6 reflect so clearly the rank religious apostasy that prevailed in Judah *prior* to the Josiah reforms, they are generally dated to the earliest period of Jeremiah's prophetic career. Jeremiah himself informs us, in 1:11–19, that the essence of what he had to say during this phase of his mission was revealed to him shortly after his call, during two visionary experiences.

The first of these (1:11–12) conveyed the simple assurance that Yahweh would be "watching" over his word (to Jeremiah) to "perform it" (fulfill it). This conviction dawned, Jeremiah informs us, while he was gazing at the branch of an almond tree (called a "wake" or "watchful" tree in Hebrew). Shortly thereafter he saw a "cooking pot on the boil," its contents "tilting from the north" (1:13) and was suddenly seized by the thought that *from the "north"* invaders would shortly sweep down upon his people and bring *Jerusalem itself* to judgment ("They will come, and each will set his throne in front of the gates of Jerusalem"). It is noteworthy that at this point he seemingly did not know *who* precisely these invaders might be—only that disaster *would* be coming from *the north* because of the apostasy (1:14–16), and that Jerusalem too would suffer because of it.

This may strike us at first as very much like the warnings of disaster that the prophets of the previous century had brought. It must be kept in mind, however, that *their* warnings had already been fulfilled during the Assyrian invasions and that now in fact Assyria was in decline. Furthermore, none of them, with the exception of Micah, had singled out *Jerusalem* in this way as the target of these disasters, and even he (Micah), so far as we know, was not told to bring his warnings right to Jerusalem itself as Jeremiah now felt compelled to do (see 1:17–19). Small wonder he was forewarned to expect that "they will fight against you" (1:19).

The words that follow, in chs. 2–6, remind us of Hosea and may in fact reflect his influence. In the first of his messages there, 2:1–13, Jeremiah, like him, places the blame for the sorry state of affairs into which the "House of Israel" has fallen on certain priests who neither "know" nor care about Yahweh (2:8). Also like Hosea he looks back on the wilderness period of his people (prior to their entry into Canaan) as the ideal time (2:1–3). Then "Israel was sacred to Yahweh, the first-fruits of his harvest . . ." (2:3). Israel's fall came when it entered the sphere of Canaanite influence and began exchanging its God for "cracked water-tanks that hold no water" (2:13; compare 2:28; 3:2). This is why Yahweh is bringing disaster from the north (4:6), a prospect that the highly personal poems of this section reveal brought Jeremiah to the brink of emotional collapse (4:19).

Several passages in this section articulate an urgent appeal for a change of heart, implying that were this to happen, the disaster might be averted (3:12–13; 3:21–25; 4:1–4). So at this stage of his mission, it would seem, Jeremiah was not altogether without hope. This raises the question whether he might have been one of those who prepared the way for the Josiah-Deuteronomic reforms of 621.

2. *After the Josiah Reform* (621–609)

2 Kings 23 describes the revolutionary reforms that were enacted in Judah after a book was discovered in the temple—one which we think was some version of the Book of Deuteronomy (see our discussion of this point in the previous chapter). Under the leadership of their king, Josiah, all pagan shrines were destroyed and the men of Judah agreed to worship Yahweh and Yahweh only at his temple in Jerusalem. Suddenly, all the false religion that Jeremiah had been criticizing was swept away. Suddenly and surprisingly, all that he had been calling for in his prophetic mission to this point had been heeded and implemented, or so it seemed.

What was Jeremiah's reaction to this astonishing turn of events? One of those personal summary reports I identified in the previous chapter as having been prepared for reading at the temple in the fourth year of Jehoiakim—the one in 11:1–12—appears to be relevant to this question. There certain "terms" of a "covenant" are mentioned which Jeremiah was then told (by Yahweh) to proclaim "in the towns of Judah and in the streets of Jerusalem" (11:6). This would suggest that *initially* Jeremiah actively supported these reforms, even to the point of preaching and teaching on their behalf. Consistent with this would be the high regard he expresses, in 22:15–17, for the king who inaugurated these reforms, King Josiah, as well as his buoyant oracles of hope for the renewal of Ephraim, in chs. 30–31 (many believe these were written during this period when the territory of the northern kingdom was being liberated and brought back under Judean control; see 2 Kgs 23:15–20, and also his appeal to the "north" to "come back," in 3:11–13). Furthermore, it should be observed that in 11:9–12 a "conspiracy" among the people of Judah is mentioned, and their reversion to "the sins of their ancestors who refused to listen to my words" (11:10). This could be a reference to developments under Jehoiakim, *after* Josiah's tragic death, when, it seems, these Deuteronomic reforms of the previous generation were abandoned.

However, Jeremiah 3:6–11 indicates that *even earlier* than that (Jehoiakim's reign), already during Josiah's reign, Jeremiah had come to recognize that something was seriously amiss in this regard. In spite of the reforms, Jeremiah says there, Judah "has come back to me' [Yahweh] *not in sincerity, but only in pretense*" (3:10). A similar point is made in 5:1–5, where we are told that after searching high and low in Jerusalem for a single man who does right, Jeremiah was forced to conclude that there were none, even though its citizens professed loyalty to Yahweh with their lips (5:2). Likewise, in 6:20 the costly sacrifice cult is alluded to that was then in vogue at the temple (following the Josiah temple reforms), but what good was this, the prophet asks (6:20), if little or no attention is being paid to Yahweh's "law" (6:19b)—the "good way" that brings "rest" (6:16).

In short, already during *Josiah's* reign Jeremiah seems to have realized that the Deuteronomic reforms which he himself at first so vigorously supported were superficial, in that they had only succeeded in centralizing worship, not in reinstating a truly Yahwistic way of life (justice and uprightness). It had now become clear to him, no doubt, that even a well intentioned king fostering sweeping changes in the religious life of his people may not be able to effect a really genuine transformation of their character!

An especially graphic illustration of the religious mentality in Jerusalem he may have had in mind in making the criticisms he did at this time is set forth in Jeremiah 34:8–22. Here an incident is reported that occurred during the siege of Jerusalem, in 588. During that time of crisis, we are told, the elite of the city, wishing perhaps to placate Yahweh and win his approval (and their deliverance), decided, in obedience to Israelite law (see Ex 21:1–10; Dt 15:12–17), to release their Hebrew slaves. The ploy seems to have worked, for no sooner had they done so than the siege was lifted (34:21). But then, the report continues, they "changed their minds" and re-enslaved the men and women they had just set free (34:11)!

With the awareness that the Josiah reforms had failed, Jeremiah's earlier premonitions of a devastating invasion "from the north" in punishment for the sins of his people must have become very real again. There is no indication, however, that at this point yet he had become clear regarding who, precisely, the invader might be.

3. The First Four Years of Jehoiakim's Reign (609–604)

A new chapter in Jeremiah's prophetic career began in the wake of Josiah's tragic death (see 22:10) and the succession to the Judean throne of the Egyptian puppet king, Jehoiakim (regarding him, see 22:13–19). We have already noted Jeremiah's action in Jehoiakim's fourth year, when a report of the messages of his twenty-three year mission as prophet was transcribed on a scroll and read at the Jerusalem temple (see Jer 36, and our discussion of this in the previous chapter). Right at that moment armies were massing on the upper Euphrates at Carchemish for a battle to determine whether Egypt or Babylon would replace Assyria as the dominant power. For Jeremiah, who since the time of his call had had a premonition that disaster would be coming upon Judah *from the north,* the outcome of this battle was not in doubt. Not Egypt (to the south), but Babylon would gain the upper hand. If we are correct in thinking that Jeremiah 25:1–13 is the concluding passage of the scroll prepared and read at the temple at this time, then it is clear that *at this juncture* of his life he was doing everything he possibly could to warn his people of the terrible catastrophe that he believed was now soon to come upon them from that region.

But the remaining passages in this scroll are also testimony to the fact that Jeremiah had not waited until Jehoiakim's *fourth year* to do this. They clearly imply that he was already doing so in the earlier years of this period. Jeremiah 26:1, for example, indicates that the famous temple sermon synopsized in Jeremiah 7:1–15 (which I earlier suggested was a part of this scroll) was preached at the very *beginning* of Jehoiakim's reign. If, as we conjecture, the prose reports that follow (scattered through chs. 7–20) were also part of this scroll (for a list of these see chart in previous chapter), then all of them would refer to actions and messages of Jeremiah from this same time period, or earlier (a fact that can be independently verified in the case of 3:6–10 and 20:1–6).

Looking at these reports with this in mind, it will be noted that they all relate either how Jeremiah himself became certain (see 7:16; 11:14; 14:11), or was told to tell others of the catastrophe from the north which he now believed was imminent (7:15, 20, 29, 34; 8:2–3; 13:10, 13–14; 14:16; 15:2; 16:4, 13; 18:11; 19:11, 14–15; 20:4–6). For example, 7:1–15 informs us that on one occasion he was commissioned to stand at the very gates of the Jerusalem temple itself and warn those who entered and exited of the futility of trusting in *it* as a guarantee against this disaster.

Seldom were covenantal and Jerusalem theology more sharply juxtaposed. Those to whom Jeremiah spoke were convinced that this was "*Yahweh's* temple" (7:4), the very place Yahweh himself had chosen for his home, *forever*—hence, a place of security, never to be destroyed. For Jeremiah such thinking was "delusive" (7:8)—Jerusalem was not a whit more sacred than Shiloh (now in ruins), nor was Judah more sacrosanct than Ephraim (now deported—7:15). With Yahweh one thing is important—fidelity to covenant law: no murder, no adultery, no perjury, no alien gods, and the like (7:5–7; compare 6:16–21). Where these laws are violated, as they now were, disaster must follow.

This in substance was the message that Jeremiah sought to bring to the people of Judah-Jerusalem, during the *opening* years of Jehoiakim—in every possible way with every possible means at his disposal. Earlier prophets had also resorted to peculiar actions, signs and symbols as a means of getting public attention and conveying their messages. None matches the audacity, passion or novelty of Jeremiah in this regard, during this period of his mission. At Yahweh's command he neither married, nor mourned, nor made merry (see 16:1–9). A bright new linen cloth around his loins was later ruined as a symbol of disaster (13:1–11). A visit to a potter's house served to dramatize how Yahweh was "shaping" evil against his people (18:1–12). On still another provocative occasion an earthenware jug was smashed before startled witnesses at the Jerusalem dump (19:1–11)—again a sign that just so this people and city would be smashed.

In the aftermath of this latter action Jeremiah was placed in the stocks for the night (see 20:1–3), and then prohibited altogether, it appears, from ever again entering the temple precincts (36:5). It was this restriction that prompted his plan to prepare a scroll and have someone else read it there (ch. 36). This in turn led to the order being given that he be arrested (36:26), with the consequence that he and Baruch were now forced to go into hiding. With these traumatic developments this most intense period of prophesying came to an abrupt end.

4. *After the Scroll Incident* (604–598)

The story of what happened next must be pieced together from a number of scattered texts. Many conjecture that it was at this time, in the wake of the scroll incident (while in hiding), that both Jeremiah and Baruch went through the spiritual crisis alluded to in Jeremiah 45 and 15:15b–21. Soon thereafter, with Baruch's help, Jeremiah may have rewritten not only his scroll (as indicated in Jer 36:32), but some of his foreign nation oracles as well (see 46:2). Then, toward the latter part of Jehoiakim's reign, when Babylonian forces were already beginning to invade this region (and Jehoiakim's credibility as king was severely shaken), Jeremiah once again, it seems, returned to public life. In any case, this is the setting for a most remarkable piece of street theater which Jeremiah staged at this time with the help of a venerable Yahwistic clan (the Rekabites) who had fled to Jerusalem for refuge (see ch. 35). By calling attention to their fidelity to the traditions of their forebears, he sought to highlight (by contrast) the fickleness of the Jerusalem elite and make dramatically clear why it was that the city was about to fall (35:16–17).

Of these several developments during this stage of his life the most noteworthy, perhaps (from the point of view of new insights into Jeremiah's experience as a prophet), was the spiritual crisis through which he and Baruch went at this juncture. Baruch's crisis was a deep depression resulting from his acute consciousness of how bleak his personal prospects were in the light of the picture generally of the future Jeremiah was presenting (see ch. 45). Jeremiah is reported to have counseled him not to seek great things (or special treatment) for himself in such a troubled time, but to be content rather with the simple promise that Yahweh *would* protect him in the midst of the approaching ordeals (45:5).

Evidence of *Jeremiah's* spiritual crisis is to be found in a series of prayers scattered throughout chs. 11–20 (for the list of these see the chart in the previous chapter). We are amazed, on reading them, at his capacity for self-understanding and candor. Indeed, the self-revelations here are such that one wonders what motivated him to write them down. Among these is the astonishing fact that at one point in his prophetic career he had abandoned both it (see 20:9) and his faith (see 15:18). In fact, so despairing was he at one juncture, we are told, that he cursed the day he was born and the man who brought news of his birth to his father for not having aborted him instead (20:14–17).

What brought *him* to such depths of despair was not (as for Baruch) the bleak future, or even (as we might imagine) the severe opposition he encountered among the elite of Jerusalem (*that* was something he had anticipated from the very beginning of his prophetic career). It was rather, he informs us, the discovery that the people of his *own village,* Anathoth—yes, even of his *own family*—were plotting to kill him (11:18–21; 12:6)! Never in his wildest imagination had he anticipated such a thing happening, for it was they afterall (the elders of Anathoth together with his family) who had taught him to believe as he did, and who up to this point had undoubtedly been his most loyal supporters.

The revelation that even *they* had now turned against him and wished him dead (11:21) must have come as a crushing blow.

In the midst of his despair, however, something remarkable began happening. Yahweh began speaking to him again—*not* now about others, however, but about *his own* spiritual condition. First, his self-pity was challenged (12:5), and then his apostasy (15:19). On condition that he "repent" and be more careful from now on to distinguish the "precious" from the "base" within himself (15:19), it was promised that he would be "restored" to his prophetic vocation and be Yahweh's "mouth" once again—a forceful reminder of the inner work required of those who were true to this calling (unlike those false prophets Jeremiah refers to, in 23:9–32, who just say whatever pops into their minds).

5. *The Final Fifteen Years* (600–585)

The next fifteen years of Jeremiah's life (from the final years of Jehoiakim, through Zedekiah's reign, to the year after the siege and fall of Jerusalem) are chronicled with a fullness unparalleled in prophetic literature (see chs. 27–44). Throughout this period he was amazingly steadfast, tough and forthright. Clearly, the earlier doubts had been surmounted and he was content now to be what he had been called to be: simply a prophet of Yahweh, in season and out, come what may.

His message in the *immediate* aftermath of Nebuchadnezzar's conquest of Jerusalem, in 598, was not merely a repetition of earlier thoughts, nor could it be. After all, Jerusalem had *not* at this time been smashed like a jar (19:11) as he had predicted it would be. Rather, when the city surrendered, it was sacked of its wealth and weakened by deporting the king and ten thousand of its leading citizens to Babylon (2 Kgs 24:10–17), but otherwise left intact. This unexpected development confronted Jeremiah with two new questions: (a) Now that the city had been spared, what *would* be happening to it? Was it *still* fated for destruction at some future date, or was it being given a second chance? (b) Furthermore, what would be the fate of those who were deported to Babylon? Was this the end for them? Would they simply disappear as had the Israelites to the north deported by Assyria a century earlier? Or would they survive and return home again to Judah, perhaps soon?

To the first of these questions (the fate of Jerusalem) Jeremiah's initial answer was a surprising one. For some thirty years he had warned of Jerusalem's imminent destruction. Now, suddenly, he began saying that if Judah and the other nations of this region would only humble themselves and *submit* to Babylonian rule, they might live, and not be destroyed after all (see ch. 27). This prospect of survival was so real and urgent for him that he resorted to one of his more audacious actions in publicizing it. Donning a massive ox yoke, he marched to each of the foreign embassies in Jerusalem, and then to his own leaders and people, with this simple message: Bend your necks to the yoke of the king of Babylon and survive (27:12)! This radical shift from doom to hope in his message is arresting. He was able, it seems, to approach each new crisis open to receiving Yahweh's special "word" for that unique moment (see Jer 18:7–10 for the theology undergirding this remarkable flexibility).

Regarding the second question confronting Jeremiah at this point (what was to become of those who were deported to Babylon), he was less certain at first, apparently—at least that is the impression we get from his silence when confronted on this issue by a certain Hananiah son of Azzur (see 28:11). However, it could not have been long thereafter that his thoughts on this matter were significantly clarified through a vision of two baskets of figs, one full of excellent figs, the other with figs so bad they could not be eaten (see ch. 24). The excellent figs were symbolic of those who were deported, for it was they, he was told, over whom Yahweh is watching "for their good" to give them a heart to acknowledge him and to return them again to this land—whereas the uneatable figs were symbolic of those who remained behind in Judea and would be destroyed.

At this point, obviously, the hopes that Jeremiah had for saving Jerusalem were abandoned. Once again it had become clear to him how "rotten" conditions really were in Jerusalem and that only those *in Babylon* had any hope at all for a better future (24:9–10), for only *there* was there the prospect of a genuine revival of faith—of a return to Yahweh "with all their heart" (24:7). Jeremiah felt that he could now envision the basic shape of the future: Jerusalem would be destroyed; only those in Babylon had anything to look forward to. But they *did* have something to look forward to, for a time was coming when they would return to the land spiritually renewed.

But *when* would *this* happen? Jeremiah's audacious answer is put forth in that famous letter of his which he wrote to his fellow countrymen who had been deported to Babylon in 597 (see ch. 29, especially 29:1–14). In it he advises them to settle down, plant gardens, marry, have children and seek the welfare of the place to which they had been sent, for they will be there, he wrote, some *seventy* years (a lifetime), *not* merely two years as some of his contemporaries were predicting (see ch. 28). Only then—*but then*—will there occur a restoration, one accompanied (he repeats) by a remarkable quickening of faith. "When you search for me, you will find me; when you search wholeheartedly for me, I shall let you find me . . ." (29:13).

In another equally famous oracle Jeremiah would refer to this revival and inner transformation of his people as the advent of a "new covenant" in which the law of God would be written deep "within them" (31:33; see also 32:37–41). *Where* and *when* this miracle would occur is clear: in Babylon, in about seventy years. As to *how* it would happen, he appears to be less certain. The implication is, however, that *time* will be needed: time for detaching from Jerusalem, time for settling down and having families, time for broadening their horizons and getting back to basics, time for heartfelt prayer. It is those who prepare for the future by building houses, planting gardens, forming families, praying and working for the good of the country to which Yahweh has exiled them (29:4–7) who will experience "the plans I have in mind for you, Yahweh declares, plans for peace, not for disaster" (29:11).

Jeremiah had yet many other things to say about the future (see his oracles in chs. 30–33), about prophets (23:9–33), about kings, past, present and future (21:11–23:6). The essence of it all, however, was his insight that something was deeply wrong in the *heart* of his people (17:1, 9) that would have to be changed, and which would be changed among those of his contemporaries who were deported but would surely return again one day to their homeland.

During the siege that would lead to Jerusalem's destruction Jeremiah advised surrender, if not by the city as a whole, then by individuals who, he said, could save their lives by leaving the city for the Babylonian side (38:2). Bitterly resented for doing so by those still seeking to defend the city, he was once beaten and imprisoned (37:15–16), another time thrown into a cistern where he almost perished (38:4–6). Yet, Yahweh's promise held true (see 38:7–13).

> They will fight against you
> but will not overcome you
> because I am with you
> to save you and rescue you,
> Yahweh declares (15:20).

Paradoxically, through all this suffering his confidence in Yahweh grew stronger (see 17:5–8, 12–13), as did his belief that good times lay ahead. "Houses, fields and vineyards will again be bought in this country," he proclaimed at the height of the siege (32:15), and still later, when the disaster had struck: "I shall plant you and not uproot you" (42:10).

Jeremiah's prophetic mission began with a vision of a disastrous invasion boiling forth over his people "from the north." Its middle years were taken up with fruitless reforms. Then it was, no doubt, that he came to realize that "the heart is more devious than any other thing, and is depraved; who can pierce its secrets?" (17:9). Small wonder that in the end, more than any earlier prophet (or few since), his thoughts were taken up with the prospects for a healing for this inner depravity. Was *his own* spiritual renewal the key perhaps to his optimism in this regard? If when lost *he* had been able to find Yahweh again (and be found by him), maybe others could too. In any case, the last we hear of him he was still testifying boldly for his God in a foreign land to which he had been dragged against his will (see ch. 44).

B. Ongoing Relevance

Despite its disorganization the legacy of Jeremiah has come down to us remarkably intact. For a book this large there are few readily identifiable editorial supplements or additions that digress significantly from Jeremiah's own orientation (one exception being Jer 33: 14-26). Furthermore, the many first-hand personal and biographical reports in this collection, together with his personal poems and private prayers, put us in touch (as do few other books of the Bible) with a recognizable personality—an authentic man of God.

How might we summarize what we experience of him in this regard? His heroes were Moses and Samuel (15:1), he informs us. But how different *they* were from him! Their sternness was proverbial. Jeremiah by contrast appears to have been a gentler, more sensitive, more self-aware individual. He is sometimes portrayed as the "weeping" prophet and there is truth in this. There were times when the plight of his people overwhelmed him to the breaking point (4:19; 9:1). Of course, in time he too became more steadfast and bold, but he was never violent. From beginning to end he devoted himself to saving others, often at great personal cost.

His insights were uncanny, but he probably never realized the degree to which *he himself* would one day be a factor in the better future he envisioned. And yet with him (and not just his words) something new was being born—a new image of what a redemptive individual might look like: not a king, not even a prophet in the traditional mold, but someone who can look inward, sort out the "base" from the "pre-

cious'' (15:19), speak truth (in season and out) in a simple, straight-
forward, compelling manner, and take the consequences, trusting the
One who inspired him in the face of all the indignities he suffered.
Small wonder that later on as people groped for a way of identifying
who Jesus of Nazareth was, some thought of Jeremiah and imagined it
was he come to life again (Mt 16:14)! We call such men martyrs, witnesses. Without at least a few of them in every generation, an ancient
Jewish legend states, the world would collapse.

Jeremiah belongs to the second wave of prophecy. Like the prophets who preceded him he believed that Yahweh was "shaping evil"
(18:1–11) in punishment of his people's sin. This would be followed,
he said, by new beginnings. One senses, however, that he did not share
Isaiah's vision of a new Jerusalem emerging quickly or easily from the
ashes of the old. Nor did he pin his hopes on the advent of yet another
king on the throne of David. While Davidic kings would indeed reign
again in Jerusalem and contribute to its welfare, he believed (see 23:5–
6; 30:21), "the sin of Judah was written with an iron pen, engraved with
a diamond point on the tablet of their heart . . ." (17:1). How could
even a king deal with that condition? Long before Freud, Jeremiah had
come to realize that only an inner transformation of his people's col-
lective "unconscious" could bring about any real or lasting renewal.

But how might this come about? As noted, the answer he gives
centers not so much on "how" but on "where" and "when." Jeremiah
was the first of the prophets to recognize that certain quite specific conditions would be needed for the inner changes to occur which he foresaw as so essential for his people's future. Such conditions, he
insightfully came to see, were being afforded his people by precisely
those circumstances in which those of them were now living who had
been deported to Babylon. There, he wrote them, they would remain
for some seventy years, and during this time what was needed was to
settle down into saner patterns of living: planting gardens, marrying,
having children, caring for their children and working "for the good of
the city to which I have exiled you" (29:6–8). Were they to do that, he
promised them, they would become more "wholehearted" toward
Yahweh once again as well (in time), and have a future full of hope,
when Yahweh restored them to their homeland.

This advice is remarkably congruent with modern insights into
how we mature, gain inner values and find God. Without sensible patterns of work and leisure, family living and community involvement—
without parents with time for each other and their children, without fathers and mothers with regard for their offspring and a hopeful eye on

the future—there can be no wholehearted love and respect for others and for God. Even today, disasters may be necessary to rid us of false cultures, but they alone will not bring us to a "future full of hope" (29:11). Is it not still true that *this* happens only where people get back to basics, "plant gardens" and take time to have families and care for them in hopeful, supportive, loving ways? Is not this still the way Yahweh writes his law deep within us, in our hearts (31:33)?

Questions for Review

1. What was the earliest premonition Jeremiah had regarding his people's future? Why, in the light of this, might it be thought that the Josiah reforms came as something of a surprise for him? How, in summary, does he seem to have responded to these reforms? It has often been noted that Jeremiah's message during the early part of his mission was much like Hosea's. What is the evidence of this and why might this have been so?

2. Why were the beginning years of Jehoiakim's reign especially traumatic ones for the people of Judah? What evidence do we have of Jeremiah's activity during this period? What about his messages at this time was so offensive to the authorities in Jerusalem that they wanted to have him executed? Summarize the nature of the spiritual crisis through which he and his disciple Baruch went when forced to go into hiding. What enabled Jeremiah to recover from this crisis?

3. After Jerusalem was spared, in 598, many of Jeremiah's contemporaries were deported to Babylon. At this time Jeremiah had to come to a fresh understanding of what Yahweh was doing. What conclusions did he arrive at? Why eventually did he feel as hopeful as he did about the future of those who had been deported? How might what he had to say to these deportees relate to his famous vision of a new covenant written on the heart?

4. Characterize Jeremiah as a person. What qualities are reflected in the portrait of him in the personal and biographical prayers and reports that are scattered throughout his book? How especially did he conduct himself during the siege of Jerusalem and its aftermath? How would you compare him and his message to the other prophets we have studied so far? Write down your own thoughts regarding the relevance of his life and message for today.

16

Ezekiel, Son of Buzi

Ezekiel was among the ten thousand elite of Jerusalem who were deported to Babylon in 598, some twelve years before Jerusalem's final fall and destruction. That makes him a contemporary of Jeremiah. It was not in Jerusalem, however, that he received his prophetic call, but on the banks of the Chebar in Babylon (1:1). There he began a mission among his fellow deportees strikingly similar in certain respects to that of Jeremiah. But again, before turning to the man and his message we want to look at his book.

A. The Book as a Whole

None of the prophetic books we have looked at so far prepares us for what we encounter when we turn to Ezekiel. From our previous study we would expect a somewhat loosely organized compilation of messages, anecdotes and first-person memoirs, touched up and supplemented here and there by the notes and additions of later editors and readers. What we discover instead, when opening this book, is one first-person report after another, and this *only*—with one minor exception: the brief editorial note regarding the prophet in 1:2–3. In other words from verse 1, ch. 1 (beginning with the words, "In the thirtieth year, on the fifth day of the fourth month, as I was among the exiles on the bank of the river Chebar, heaven opened and I saw visions from God") to the final temple vision that begins in ch. 40 ("In the twenty-fifth year of our captivity . . . the hand of Yahweh was on me") the Book of Ezekiel, with the sole exception of verse 1:2–3, is made up entirely of prophetic first-person reports and nothing else!

Personal reports of this kind are of course, as such, no novelty in prophetic literature. Amos recorded his visions in this manner (see 7:1–8), as did Hosea when relating how he restored his wife (3:1–3) and Isaiah when reporting his call (ch. 6). Jeremiah especially made frequent use of this form. Indeed, his famous scroll may have been dictated in this manner throughout (see chapter 14 above). That an entire prophetic collection of the size and scope of this one should be made up exclusively of such memoirs is nevertheless quite surprising.

Perhaps the circumstances under which Ezekiel lived and prophesied in Babylon during the early settlement there may have had something to do with this. Very likely there would not have been at that time and place a forum for *public* gatherings. As a result the prophet's *own house,* it seems, became the place where his oracles were shared with whomever came to listen (see for example the scene portrayed in Ezekiel 33:30–33). Under these circumstances, if his oracles were going to be preserved in writing, *he* would have to do it. In assuming this responsibility he may have followed Jeremiah's example. Just as Jeremiah had his messages of previous years written out in the form of personal reports (at a certain juncture of his mission), so would he. In any case, Jeremiah's scroll might well have been known to Ezekiel from his having been at the temple, perhaps, on the day it was read there (see Jer 36; also our comments below on Ezekiel's call).

But the first-person memoir style is not the only peculiarity of this book. Another unique feature is the careful manner in which its contents are *dated* and *arranged.* A quick review of these dates can serve to clarify facets of its compositional history as well as introduce us to the book as a whole.

Two of these dates pose problems that should be dealt with right off, however, if misunderstandings are not to arise. The book's very first date, in 1:1 ("in the thirtieth year, on the fifth day of the fourth month"), is obviously out of synch with the dates that follow. This in fact is one of the reasons for the editorial note that has been added right at this point, in 1:2–3. This note seeks to clarify that this "thirtieth year" reference, whatever else it might mean (and I will return to this below), is identical with "the fifth year of exile for King Jehoiachin"— the point of reference for all subsequent dates in the book.

A second date that is puzzling is the one in 33:21 where it is said that a refugee from Jerusalem had arrived in Babylon with the news that the city had fallen. The date of his arrival is given as the *twelfth* year of the captivity, fifth day of the tenth month. Jeremiah 39:2 states that Jerusalem fell in the *eleventh* year of Zedekiah, the fourth month. This would suggest that it took this messenger almost *a year and a half* to get to Babylon, a journey that can be made by caravan in about four months. The Septuagint version of this text has here instead, "*eleventh* year, tenth month." This is generally regarded as the more accurate reading.

With these corrections and clarifications the dates in the book can be outlined as follows (see page 181).

It will be noted that apart from the foreign nation oracles (chs. 25–32) there are *six dates*, plus a seventh reference to passage of time ("After seven days . . ."—3:16). Each of these is progressively later than the others, spanning the time from the prophet's call (in the fifth year of the captivity) to a point some twenty years later. Another seven dates occur among the foreign nation oracles, but several of these are chronologically out of phase. This suggests that this section of the book was once an independent collection. The summarizing conclusion in 28:24–26 hints at the possibility that chs. 25–28 were once the core of this collection, to which chs. 29–32 were added at a later stage.

Turning again to the book as a whole and observing its various dates, it becomes evident that Ezekiel's mission had *three* chronologically distinct phases: (1) from the time of his call in the fifth year of the captivity (593) to the beginning of the siege of Jerusalem four and a half years later (chs. 1–24); (2) from the beginning of the siege (24:1) to the day a messenger arrived in Babylon announcing that Jerusalem had been destroyed (33:21–22)—a period of two years; (3) a final period after this (chs. 33–48), extending to at least 571 (the twenty-seventh year referred to in 29:17).

In each of these periods certain themes or activities were predominant:

● in the first period, prior to the siege, Ezekiel was primarily intent upon *warning* his fellow Israelites in Babylon of Jerusalem's approaching fall;

● his wife died on the day the siege began (24:15–16)—from then until the news arrived that the city had fallen he was apparently withdrawn and silent (see the references to this "dumbness" in 24:17, 25–27; 29:21; 33:22), although he might have done some writing (several of the foreign nation oracles are dated to this period).

● once everyone knew Jerusalem was no more, Ezekiel began speaking of a wonderful future for his people—this is the content of the third and last section of his book.

This unique chronological and thematic arrangement of his book can be charted as follows:

Before the siege chs. 1–24	During the siege chs. 25–32	After the siege chs. 33–48
Warnings of destruction	Foreign nation oracles	Messages of hope

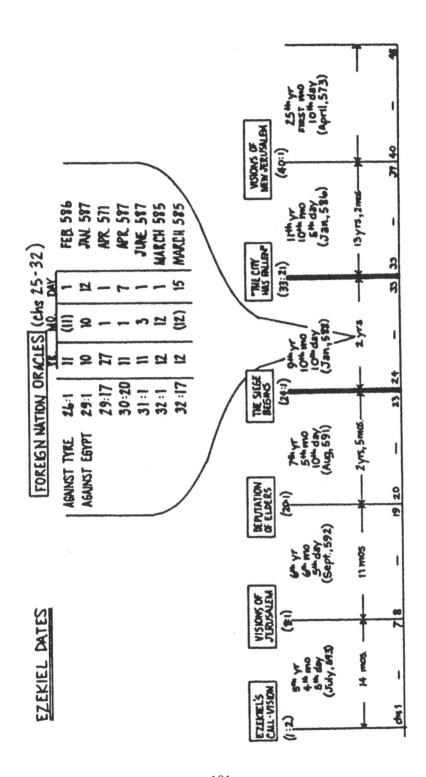

EZEKIEL DATES

FOREIGN NATION ORACLES (chs 25-32)

		YR	MO	DAY	
AGAINST TYRE	26:1	11	(11)	1	FEB 586
AGAINST EGYPT	29:1	10	10	12	JAN. 587
	29:17	27	1	1	APR. 571
	30:20	11	1	7	APR. 587
	31:1	11	3	1	JUNE 587
	32:1	12	12	1	MARCH 585
	32:17	12	(12)	15	MARCH 585

EZEKIEL'S CALL-VISION (1:2)
chs 1

5th yr
4th mo
5th day
(July, 593)

14 mos

VISIONS OF JERUSALEM (8:1)
7, 8

6th yr
6th mo
5th day
(Sept., 592)

11 mos

DEPUTATION OF ELDERS (20:1)
19, 20

7th yr
5th mo
10th day
(Aug, 591)

2 yrs, 5 mos.

THE SIEGE BEGINS (24:1)
23, 24

9th yr
10th mo
10th day
(Jan, 588)

2 yrs

"THE CITY HAS FALLEN!" (33:21)
33

11th yr
10th mo
5th day
(Jan, 586)

13 yrs, 2 mos

VISIONS OF NEW JERUSALEM (40:1)
37, 40

25th yr
FIRST mo
10th day
(April, 573)

48

Who gave this book this carefully crafted, architectonic structure? Again, it is not hard to imagine that Ezekiel himself might have had a hand in this, even as he must have been the one who wrote down the individual units (virtually all of which, as noted above, are first-person reports). However, there is ample evidence that others also may have supplemented and shaped its contents somewhat, here and there (Zimmerli speaks of an Ezekiel "school"). An example would be the famous Gog-Magog prophecies in chs. 38 and 39. These not only break the continuity between the reference to a "sanctuary" at the end of 37 and its further description in chs. 40:1–43:1–4), but picture the future in quite different terms than does Ezekiel, in ch. 34 for example. In ch. 34 it is stated that when Israel is once again restored to its land, "no one will disturb them again" (34:28), while the Gog-Magog prophecies predict that after "many days" (38:8) nations from the north will rise up and attack it.

Supplements of this kind can also be identified in chs. 40–48. The description of the temple and its personnel in 43:10–46:24, for example, is far more literal and down-to-earth than is Ezekiel's visionary temple in chs. 40:1–43:4 and 47 (note the awesome return of Yahweh, in 43:1–4, and the miraculous waters originating there, in ch. 47).

There are two additional features of the book which are also likely the result of editorial tampering and which might cause some confusion if not understood properly. One is the "sentry" commission in 3:17–21 in which Ezekiel is told to be a warner of *individuals* to save them from the consequence of their sins. This commission is strange and unexpected coming at this point just "seven days" after having *already been* commissioned to be a prophet of *doom* to the *entire* House of Israel *even though* they will "not listen" (see 2:3–7; 3:1–5). However, this same "sentry" commission also occurs in 33:7–9 (see also ch. 18). Here it is in the setting of the new era Ezekiel saw opening up for his people now that Jerusalem had been destroyed. This, as we shall see, was the far more likely occasion for this redefinition of his prophetic role. It was the book's editors, not Ezekiel, who introduced it at 3:16–21 (also ch. 18 may be chronologically misplaced). Their reasons for doing so were no doubt to alert the book's readers right off to this important facet of the prophet's activity. Nevertheless, in rearranging the book in this manner they have caused a certain amount of confusion.

Even more confusing is the command in 3:25 that Ezekiel shut himself up in his house where he will be dumb and no longer able to warn the people at all (see also 4:4–8), when at this point yet his mission had not even begun! The experience alluded to here (like the sentry commission) fits much better to a later phase of Ezekiel's career. As already noted, there are several texts elsewhere in the book that refer to just such an experience of dumbness and confinement, but they all have to do with the time of the Jerusalem siege (note again 24:17, 27; 29:21; 33:21f), not this earlier period when his mission had not even started.

Finally I would call attention to one additional organizational feature of the book, this one attributable perhaps to Ezekiel. Each of the dated visions, which prior to the fall of Jerusalem conveyed to Ezekiel the certainty of its approaching destruction, is followed, first, by reports of symbolic actions (or "signs") and then by oracles or messages. After Jerusalem's fall, when Ezekiel's thought turned toward a more hopeful future, this same arrangement recurs (vision, signs, oracles). The pattern I am referring to may be graphed as follows (see page 184).

It can be said in summary that the Book of Ezekiel is unique among the prophetic books of the Bible in the plenitude of its first-person reports, in the careful way it is organized and in its chronological notations. Nevertheless it too shows signs of having been edited by later readers who adapted it in various ways to make it more relevant to their needs.

B. The Man Behind the Book

Who is the prophet who has given us this unique book? What manner of man was he? What were his beliefs? How did he become a prophet? It is again appropriate to consider questions such as these, before turning to a consideration of his message, even though here too (as with Jeremiah) man and message are closely intertwined.

1. Name

In 3:3 we learn that his name was Ezekiel son of Buzi. "Ezekiel" is a compound of the Hebrew verb "to strengthen" (*hazak*) and "God" (*'el*), signifying "God strengthens." His father (Buzi) is otherwise unknown to us. In 24:24 we read that "thus Ezekiel is a sign for you." That is the only other time this name occurs either in this book or elsewhere in the Bible.

2. Occupation

Ezekiel 3:3 informs us that either he or his father was a priest. The text reads (in Hebrew) ". . . Ezekiel son of Buzi the priest." A priest trained for this position through an apprenticeship during his twenties

EZEKIEL

PATTERN OF VISIONS, SIGNS, ORACLES

VISIONS OF GOD (SCROLL) 1-3	SIGNS BRICK FOOD SWORD TURN CLAP 4-6	ORACLES CH.7	VISIONS OF TEMPLE DESTROYED 8-11	SIGNS EXILE TREMBLING 12:1-20	ORACLES 12:21- CH.19	REVIEW OF DECADENT HISTORY CH.20	SIGNS TURN CURSE DROWNING 21:1-12	ORACLES 21:13- CH.23	RESOLUTION OF SIEGE 24:1-14	SIGNS DUMB EZEKIEL A SIGN 24:15-27	ORACLES CHS. 25-32, 33-36	VISION OF DRY BONES COME ALIVE 37:1-14	SIGNS TWO STICKS UNITED 37:1-14	ORACLES 38-39	VISIONS OF NEW TEMPLE 40-48

184

(1 Chr 23:24; Num 8:24). He did not become a full-fledged priest until he was thirty (Num 4:3). It is this that has led to the suggestion that the reference in 1:1 to "the thirtieth year" ("In the thirtieth year . . . as I was among the exiles . . .") may allude to *Ezekiel's* thirtieth year. At precisely that moment of his life when he would have been ordained to the priesthood, were he still in Jerusalem, he was called instead to be a prophet, as he sat on the bank of the river Chebar in Babylon.

3. His Background

According to 1:2 Ezekiel was among those in Jerusalem who were taken captive and brought to Babylon during the exile of King Jehoiachin. At the time of his prophetic call this was "the fifth year" of this captivity. This means that only five years earlier Ezekiel had been among "all the nobles and all the notables" of Jerusalem (2 Kgs 24:14)—or more specifically, as just noted, among the *priestly* elite of that city.

Nothing is more important for understanding Ezekiel than this fact. His message, as we shall soon see, was similar to that of Jeremiah's, but the traditions that shaped him were vastly different. In some respects he was much closer to Isaiah (also a Jerusalemite), although Isaiah was more at home, it seems, in the educational and political institutions of that city, whereas Ezekiel's habitat was the temple.

What this meant, more concretely, can be sensed by reading the priestly codes in vogue there (such as the famous Holiness Code in Leviticus 17–26) and noting how many similarities there are between his thought and language and theirs (regarding this see Zimmerli). A concrete, vivid reminder of how powerfully Ezekiel was shaped by traditions such as these is his highly emotional reaction, in 4:14, to the suggestion that he use human dung for fuel. He cries out, "Lord Yahweh, my soul is not defiled. *From my childhood until now*, I have never eaten an animal that has died a natural death or been savaged, no tainted meat has ever entered my mouth" (for the priestly tradition in this regard, see Lev 17:15–16). If such matters as this were this important to him, how much more those basics of Jerusalem theology earlier referred to (see Isaiah): God's choice of Zion to be his home forever (Ps 132:13–14), God's covenant with the House of David (2 Sam 7; Ps 89), along with the already mentioned sacral codes regulating the life of the temple and those who worshiped there (Num 17–26).

Moreover, as a background to Ezekiel's visions in chs. 1–3 and 8–11 (where he sees the "glory of Yahweh" departing from the temple and being revealed to him in the skies over Babylon) one needs to pay special attention to the priestly concept of "glory" (*kavod*). As the priestly circles in Jerusalem understood it, not just Yahweh's "name" dwelt in the temple (this was the way the Deuteronomists thought of it), but Yahweh's "glory" (see Ex 40:34–35; 1 Kgs 8:11)—a divine radiance or essence.

Only when we have begun to realize how deeply rooted Ezekiel was in the priestly traditions of Jerusalem can we begin to appreciate what it must have meant for him to be uprooted from the temple there and taken a thousand miles away to the banks of the Chebar on the outskirts of Babylon. Psalm 137 testifies to the despair of his contemporaries there in the period after the destruction of Jerusalem in 586. However, at the time of Ezekiel's call, in the fifth year of his captivity (593), Jerusalem had not yet fallen. What was the mood then?

4. Historical Setting

Numerous bits and pieces of evidence point to this as being a time of great confusion, with various groups holding at least three conflicting opinions regarding what would be happening next. From Jeremiah we learn there were those, first of all, who believed that the defeats and humiliations Jerusalem had recently experienced were temporary, and that even those deported to Babylon would be returning soon—"in exactly two years," some even said (see Jer 28:1–4). With this in mind many of Ezekiel's contemporaries might well have thought that their stay in Babylon would be a short one and that they would be returning home soon to a Jerusalem whose future was bright.

A second opinion was that those who had been deported to Babylon were the only ones who had been singled out by God for judgment and punishment. Therefore they would remain in captivity there, and their vacated property in Jerusalem could be rightfully taken over by those who escaped this fate and remained behind. According to Ezekiel 11:14 this group was now declaring, "This country has now been made over to us!"

But there was still another opinion regarding the future in circulation among at least a few of Ezekiel's contemporaries in Babylon (or at least Ezekiel himself might well have been pondering it), and that was the prospect so vigorously advocated by Jeremiah that Jerusalem would yet be destroyed in spite of having so often escaped this fate (and now once again just recently). Ezekiel nowhere mentions Jeremiah, but the numerous striking similarities in the form and content of their messages suggest that he knew of him and, indeed, may have been among the temple priests who tried to silence him when he prophesied there just prior to the deportation in 598 (see Jer 7; 26; 36).

5. *His Prophetic Call*

In any case, this latter possibility (that Ezekiel knew of Jeremiah) is worth remembering as we turn to Ezekiel's vivid account of his prophetic call, in 1:1–3:15. Note the reference here to "visions from God" (1:1). What he is attempting to describe for us in this text is not something he actually saw, although an all too real thunderstorm (1:4) may have been a factor. Also bear in mind that originally the account of these visions may have been somewhat shorter and simpler than it now is (1:7–11, 14–21, 23–25 may come from the hand of later readers intent upon amplifying the visual features of this epiphany).

The "four living creatures" he saw in this vision (1:5) are described from below upward, with their wings bearing aloft a cosmic dome representing the sky (1:22), upon which there was the form of a sapphire throne, and seated on it one "having the appearance of a human being" (1:26). The whole sight, Ezekiel summarizes, struck him "as like the glory of Yahweh" (1:28). In other words, in this awe-inspiring vision he was made aware of the presence of that very same divine reality that he as priest had believed was uniquely present at the temple in Jerusalem. However, what must have caused him to fall to the ground (1:28b) was not just the vision itself but that Yahweh was thus revealing himself in the skies over Babylon. In that moment he must have begun to realize that Yahweh's "glory" was no longer resident at Jerusalem but had departed from there (a point made explicit in a later vision; see chs. 8–11).

But even with this his visionary experience was not over. While still prostrate from the impact of what he had just seen, he informs us, a voice addressed him as "Son of man" and told him to get to his feet so that he could be spoken to (2:1). He was then commissioned as a prophet to his fellow Israelites in Babylon, not to change them (for it is emphasized that they are rebellious people), but simply that they might know that a prophet of God had been in their midst when the things he predicts will have come to pass.

Right at this point, then, he was told to eat something Yahweh was giving him, and upon looking to see what it was, he saw a hand reaching down from the sky with a scroll that when unrolled was observed to be written all over with "lamentations, dirges and cries of grief" (2:10). When he ate this scroll, the commission to be a prophet to the rebellious House of Israel ("whether they listen or not"—3:11) was repeated.

Ezekiel concludes his report of this vision by telling us that in its aftermath he was like a man ''in a stupor'' for a full seven days (3:15). A line drawing by one of my students may help us envision some of its details and capture something of its awesome impact upon him.

One thing this drawing makes visually clear is how centrally important the *scroll* was that Ezekiel was commanded to eat on this occasion. With this in mind note too how in the description of this phase of his vision this command is repeated and how forcefully he must be told not to be stubborn, but to listen and open his mouth and really *eat* this scroll (3:1–3). Note also how just prior to eating the scroll it was unrolled in front of him so that he might verify that it was indeed written all over (on both sides) with words of lamentation and *nothing* else (no message of hope here). It is furthermore implied that this scroll contains the message that *he*, Ezekiel, must now bring to the people, for in 3:1 he is told: ''Son of man, eat what you see; eat this scroll, then go and speak to the House of Israel.'' In other words, it was precisely in this way, through this concrete visionary experience, that Ezekiel the priest was compelled to become a prophet of disaster.

But why, we might ask, would this be so? Why in this instance would a ''scroll'' need to play such a prominent role in a prophet becoming a messenger of judgment? The answer may lie in an event that occurred in Jerusalem a decade earlier, at a time when Ezekiel might have been a priest in training at the temple there. It will be remembered that in Jehoiakim's fifth year Jeremiah had had just such a scroll (written all over with dire predictions of Jerusalem's destruction) read at this temple, and that on *that* occasion this scroll, when read to the king, was callously cut to pieces and burned (Jer 36). Even prior to that Jeremiah had been almost killed by the temple hierarchy for proclaiming this very same message in person (Jer 26).

It is difficult to imagine that Ezekiel, at the time himself a member of the Jerusalem temple hierarchy, would not have been present on these occasions and perhaps even participated in the persecution of this prophet. If so, a comparison could be drawn between him and the apostle Paul, who after fiercely rejecting Jesus and persecuting his followers became one himself through a vision of Jesus on the Damascus road. By ''eating'' the scroll let down from heaven (in his vision) Ezekiel like Paul underwent a traumatic conversion and joined the ranks of those who now believed (as Jeremiah did) that Jerusalem was not indestructible after all.

This meant as well (and this for Ezekiel may have been the most traumatic point of all) that Jerusalem was also, therefore, not what all

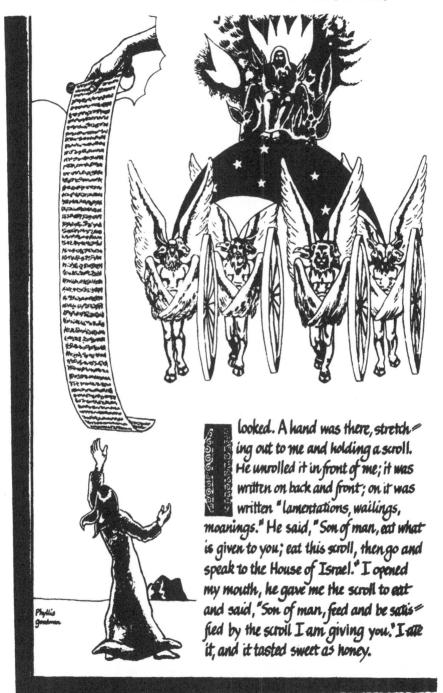

Phyllis
Gendman

looked. A hand was there, stretch⸗ing out to me and holding a scroll. He unrolled it in front of me; it was written on back and front; on it was written "lamentations, wailings, moanings." He said, "Son of man, eat what is given to you; eat this scroll, then go and speak to the House of Israel." I opened my mouth, he gave me the scroll to eat and said, "Son of man, feed and be satis⸗fied by the scroll I am giving you." I ate it, and it tasted sweet as honey.

his life he had been taught to believe it was: the place chosen by Yahweh to be his home *forever* (Ps 132:13–14). In fact, Yahweh's "glory" (as already noted), appearing as it did (in his vision) in the skies over Babylon, had seemingly already left from there. Later (as also noted) this point was made absolutely clear to him. In the visions described in chs. 8–11 he was taken back to Jerusalem and shown the sins being practiced there; simultaneously he witnessed Yahweh's "glory" departing the city like a great bird in flight (Ez 10:18–22; 11:22–23) while the terrors of judgment began falling (9:7).

With these visions Ezekiel the priest was wrenched loose from his old ways of thinking and became a prophet of disaster, like Jeremiah, but with a commission to speak Yahweh's word, not to Jerusalem, but to his fellow refugees in Babylon.

Questions for Review

1. How is the Book of Ezekiel different, so far as its literary form is concerned, from the other prophetic books we have studied? How might one account for these differences? Indicate how the divisions of this book relate to the major periods of Ezekiel's mission.

2. Why is it thought that the sentry commission in 3:17–21 is out of place there? Also explain why it is believed that the reference to his confinement and dumbness in 3:25 is better understood as belonging to a later period of his mission. What other well-known portions of his book appear to be later additions, rather than from Ezekiel himself? What evidence would suggest this?

3. What indications are there that Ezekiel's background was that of a priest at the Jerusalem temple? What implications might this have had for the way he lived and thought prior to his prophetic call? What differing opinions regarding the Judean future were being debated at this time?

4. How does Ezekiel summarize what he saw, essentially, in his visions from God at the time he was called to be a prophet? By what means was he compelled to take on the role of a prophet of impending disaster for Jerusalem? Why might this have been an especially traumatic experience for him? What part might Jeremiah have played in his conversion to this role?

17

His Message and Its Relevance

A. Message

The analysis of the Book of Ezekiel, in the previous chapter, has already alerted us to the fact that his prophetic mission unfolded in two very distinct phases: one occurring *before* the siege began that led to the fall of Jerusalem in 586 (chs. 1–23; see ch. 24), and the other *after* news had arrived in Babylon that Jerusalem had actually been destroyed (33:21–22). What Ezekiel felt he was to do and say in the *second* phase of his mission was quite different from what he had to say in the *first* one. These two phases were marked off from one another by two traumatic events: the death of his wife on the evening of the day the siege of Jerusalem had begun (24:1, 15–17), followed by a period of some two years of dumbness (24:27; 33:22), during which he was seemingly confined to his house (some scholars would also assign the episodes described in Ezekiel 4:4–8 to this period).

In our review of Ezekiel's messages we will keep these clearly demarked stages in mind, looking first at what he had to say prior to the siege.

1. Before the Siege of Jerusalem (593–589)

Ezekiel's messages from the fifth year, fifth month of his captivity (1:2) to the very day the siege of Jerusalem began, in the ninth year, tenth month (24:1), are assembled in chs. 1–24 of his book. These were determined and shaped to some considerable degree by two awesome visionary experiences he had at the beginning and middle of this four and a half year period.

The first of these in chs. 1–3, with their revelations of the glory of Yahweh in the skies over Babylon and of a scroll written all over with lamentations (as already noted in the previous chapter), persuaded him that contrary to what many of his contemporaries believed, Jerusalem was now destined for total destruction. The second set of visions fourteen months later, in which he was taken on a tour of his beloved city (see chs. 8–11), deepened his sense of the necessity of this happening due to the rank apostasy now in vogue there (see 8:3–18 especially). Indeed, during these visionary experiences he was witness to the awful reality of judgment and destruction actually beginning (9:7).

It should be noted, however, that the focus of this second set of visionary experiences was not exclusively on Jerusalem's sin and impending destruction, but on the future of his people *beyond* judgment as well—a theme which completely preoccupies him later on in his mission. "Ah, Lord Yahweh, are you going to annihilate *all* that is left of Israel by venting your fury on Jerusalem?" he asks (9:8; 11:13). The answer he received at this time was quite similar to one Jeremiah arrived at during this same period, and concerning which he had written his famous letter to Babylon (see Jer 29). "No," Jeremiah had said in effect, "not all will be destroyed; some *will* escape—some have *already* escaped—those now in Babylon!" To Ezekiel the same message was now given. Yahweh has been and will be a "sanctuary" to the Babylonian deportees, he was told, and will eventually see to it that they are brought back again to the land of Israel, purged of their "horrors and loathsome practices"—with a new heart and spirit within them (11:18–21).

With this clarification an element of *hope* was introduced into Ezekiel's outlook at this point, so that the messages of this opening section may be said to touch on not merely one or two, but at least three themes: the approaching destruction of Jerusalem, an analysis of why this was happening, and thoughts regarding what will happen next (the bright future beyond judgment). A fourth theme is also recurrent, as we shall see: Yahweh's sovereign purpose in all this (expressed in the repeated phrase: "that you [or they] may know that I am Yahweh"). Because the records of his mission are so full for this opening period especially, it will not be possible to do more than briefly illustrate what he has to say on each of these four subjects.

a. Danger Ahead!

The oracles of chs. 1–24 are framed by two dramatic pantomimes or "signs" in 4:1–3 and 24:15–24. Both illustrate the intensity with which Ezekiel set about being the prophet he was called to be and warning of danger ahead "whether they listen or not" (3:11).

Ezekiel 4:1–3 describes the first in a series of symbolic actions by means of which Ezekiel tried to bring home to his contemporaries in

Babylon the reality of the approaching destruction of Jerusalem a thousand miles away. In this particular instance he was told to take a clay brick, scratch a map-like drawing of Jerusalem on it and then, very much as a child playing in a sandbox might do, enact a silent pantomime. First, the brick was placed on the ground and a trench dug around it. Then earth-works were built, camps pitched, and tiny battering-rams moved into position for besieging the toy-sized city. Having done all this, an iron pan was taken and positioned between Ezekiel and the mock siege (4:3). This, it seems, was to dramatize his conviction that Yahweh (represented by himself) was now cut off and removed from his own city and hence could not be counted on to rescue it (as it was believed he had done on previous occasions).

Then came the climactic moment of his pantomime, when he was urgently commanded to "fix your gaze on it; it is being besieged and you are besieging it" (4:3). Ezekiel now visually enacted before the unbelieving eyes of those who had gathered to witness all this how the city was destroyed, proclaiming as he did so that "this is a sign for the House of Israel" (4:3).

We are familiar by now with the fact that other prophets also resorted to symbolic gestures to bring home the point of their messages (Jeremiah especially)—none of them, however, with as much flair or attention to detail as Ezekiel. His one purpose in doing so was to make forcefully clear to an unbelieving people the fate that awaited them. Their beloved city Jerusalem was going to be destroyed and Yahweh himself was doing this!

A final sign of this kind, at the end of this period, reveals the degree to which Ezekiel was himself *personally* involved in this tragedy. In 24:1 we learn that even though in Babylon a thousand miles from home, he knew intuitively the precise day when the armies of Babylon began their siege of Jerusalem, and wrote it down for subsequent confirmation: it was "the ninth year, on the tenth day of the tenth month" (see Jer 39:1).

On that very same day, he informs us in 24:15–16, he had a premonition that his wife would die, and that when this happened, he was to forego the usual rituals of mourning and "groan in silence" (24:17). "I told this to the people in the morning," he reports, "and my wife died in the evening, and the next morning I did as I had been ordered" (24:18). When the people asked him why he was behaving so strangely, he replied in effect that *her* death was symbolic of *Jerusalem's* death. In the face of such tragedies the normal rituals of sorrowing had become obsolete. By the depth of his depression ("groaning in silence") Ezekiel had himself, at this juncture of his life, become a potent "sign" to his people of the depth of the tragedy about to befall them (see 24:24).

In these and other ways Ezekiel sought to prepare his people for the approaching catastrophe. By thus predicting it as persistently and dramatically as he did he not only demonstrated that a prophet was among them (2:5), but that the event itself, when it transpired, was no accident but an "act of Yahweh" their God.

b. Why?

Like his prophetic predecessors Ezekiel sought to explain not only *that* disaster was coming, but why. What he says, in summary, is that the Israelite people are and have been in the grip of an irrational apostasy. They have flagrantly and repeatedly violated the laws of their God. These violations are listed with unsparing detail and fullness in 22:6–12:

> Look! In you the princes of Israel, one and all, have furthered their own interests at the cost of bloodshed; in you people have despised their fathers and mothers; in you they have ill-treated the settler; in you they have oppressed the widow and orphan. You have treated my sanctuary with contempt, you have profaned my Sabbaths. In you informers incite to bloodshed; in you people eat on the mountains and act licentiously; in you they have sexual intercourse with their fathers; in you they force themselves on women in their periods; in you one man engages in loathsome practices with his neighbor's wife, another lewdly defiles his daughter-in-law, another violates his sister, his own father's daughter. In you people take bribes for shedding blood; you lend for profit and charge interest, you profit from your fellow by extortion and have forgotten about me—declares the Lord Yahweh.

The level of behavior in Jerusalem has fallen below that of the surrounding nations, he declares in 5:5.

Ezekiel is unique among the prophets in stressing that this bent toward apostasy was a characteristic of his people from the time of its origins. It will be remembered that Hosea and Jeremiah looked back to an ideal time "in the wilderness" prior to Israel's entry into Canaan (Hos 9:10; Jer 2:7). For Isaiah too there was an earlier period when Zion was "full of fair judgment" and "saving justice used to dwell" there

(1:21). But this was not Ezekiel's point of view. In his sweeping historical overviews in chs. 20 and 23 he traces his people's bent toward rebellion right back to its origins in Egypt (see 23:1–3; 20:8) and then goes on to say that nothing since then has changed very much. Of Jerusalem itself he writes, in 16:8, that while Yahweh has truly chosen her and thereby forged a quite special "covenant" between himself and this city (as Jerusalem theology implied), its flagrant political, social and religious "whoring" requires that she too be treated as those are judged who commit adultery and murder (16:38). So even *that* covenant is now worthless.

c. Hope

And yet Ezekiel is not without hope—even during this opening phase of his mission. This is the third theme touched on by him in chs. 1–24. It is one that dominates his messages later on when the news arrives that Jerusalem has in fact fallen (ch. 33), but it is also introduced as a sub-theme already in this section, in the midst of the visionary experiences described in chs. 8–11.

There, as previously noted, in reply to his twice repeated cry: "Ah, Lord Yahweh, are you going to annihilate all that is left of Israel by venting your fury on Jerusalem?" (9:9; 11:13), he was granted a quite similar vision of the future *beyond* judgment to that which Jeremiah had received while contemplating two baskets of figs (see Jer 24). The future lies, he came to see, not with those still in Jerusalem, but with the Judean refugees in Babylon—not, however, because they are better than those in Jerusalem, but because Yahweh has promised to be a "sanctuary" to them "for a while" (11:16) and will one day bring them back to their homeland again from the lands to which they have been scattered (11:17).

In this connection Yahweh also intends to put a new spirit within them (11:19), he writes, removing their heart of stone and replacing it with a heart of flesh, so that "they can keep my laws and respect my judgments and put them into practice"—a vision of things to come that also corresponds exactly to Jeremiah's vision of an Israel upon whose inward being the divine law would one day be written (Jer 32:31–34).

However, both here and in 20:34–44 there are aspects of his vision of the future which are unique as well—two in particular. (a) Prior to the restoration, Ezekiel writes, another judgment of sorts will occur in which those who persist in clinging to their older lawless ways will be purged from the community (11:21). In 20:35 it is stated that this purging will take place in the "desert of the Nations" (Syrian desert) on the journey back to Israel from Babylon, but prior to the re-entry into the homeland. Then in 20:36–38 he writes:

> As I judged your fathers in the desert of Egypt, so will I judge you—declares the Lord Yahweh. I shall make you pass under the crook, bring you to respect the covenant and rid you of the rebels who have revolted against me; I shall bring them out of the country where they are staying, but they will not enter the country of Israel, and you will know that I am Yahweh.

(b) A second supplementary insight unique to Ezekiel is the expectation that once the restoration occurs, it will be in such a manner that the surrounding nations will come to recognize the splendor of the God who has accomplished all this. "Through you," he writes, "I shall display my holiness for all the nations to see . . ." (20:42). It will have, in short, revelatory significance for the whole world.

d. Yahweh's Sovereign Purpose

This latter point introduces yet another theme running through these oracles (and not only those of the opening section, but throughout the whole book). This is Ezekiel's concept of Yahweh's sovereign purpose in history, expressed in the phrase (occurring some seventy-two times in all): "that you (or they) might know that I am Yahweh" (6:7; 7:4, 9, 27; etc.). This leitmotif of the book, as we might call it, expresses the core conviction of this prophet that Yahweh's action in Israel's history is simply an outworking of his desire to make himself known—and not only to Israel, but to the whole world. Were this not the case, he writes in ch. 20, Israel itself would have perished long ago. It is only the fact that Yahweh's "name" has become associated with Israel that Yahweh is thereby compelled to spare her time and again, for were Israel to perish, Yahweh's name would perish with her and be profaned in the sight of the nations (20:9, 14). Thus, everything Yahweh has done in the past, is doing in the present, or will do in the future, as far as his people Israel is concerned, is designed to overcome this liability and see to it that ultimately he *will be known* worldwide.

2. The Final Phase (585–572)

It is to this theme of Yahweh's future actions to vindicate his name and reveal himself in and through Israel that Ezekiel turns in the final phase of his prophetic career (chs. 25–32 and 33–48). While the siege of Jerusalem was in progress (and he was dumb), his thoughts turned (it seems) to the fate of Israel's neighbors: Ammon, Moab, Edom, Philistia, and especially Tyre and Egypt (see chs. 25–32). In powerful, often erudite oracles he puts into writing his conviction that they too will be humiliated or destroyed by the Babylonians—this as a prelude to Israel's restoration to her homeland (28:25–26).

But it was at the point that news arrived in Babylon that Jerusalem had fallen (33:21–22) that Ezekiel's mission took an especially radical new turn toward the future. Then it was that the interlude of withdrawal and dumbness (about which I earlier wrote) came to an end and a whole new era began for him and his people (as he came to view it). Up until this point he had been a prophet of doom, primarily, addressing his people *collectively,* whether or not they would listen. Now, he believed, a hope-filled future lay ahead. In the not too distant future his people would be liberated from Babylon and able to return once again to their homeland. However, as already noted, a peculiarity of this future would be (as he envisioned it) a judgment and sorting out of rebels on the journey homeward, so that *only those* would be able to complete this journey and finally return home who were truly qualified (see Ez 20:35–38).

His task now was, therefore, a twofold one: first and foremost, to convince his contemporaries in Babylon that they do in fact stand before such a hope-filled future; but, second, to be a *watchman* among them preparing them for this homeward journey (33:7–20; also ch. 18; 3:16–21; regarding the chronological issues involved, see the previous chapter).

In this latter role (that of watchman) he was now given to see that his responsibilities as prophet would be significantly altered from what they had been. Up until this point he had been primarily a prophet of doom to the whole nation. Now he was being summoned to function as a *hope-filled* caretaker of *individuals.* In the past judgment had fallen on the nation as a whole (the good and the bad), but now a future full of hope lay ahead, but only for those who were worthy of it—only for those who in actuality live by Yahweh's laws and are thereby declared to be upright (see ch. 18). Only *they* shall live. But it is Yahweh's desire that they *shall* live—every last one among them. This is Ezekiel's new, burning conviction. And this is why he now begins to address his community with a pastoral fervor and passion unprecedented in prophetic tradition.

> So in future, House of Israel, I shall judge each of you by what that person does—declares the Lord Yahweh. Repent, renounce all your crimes, avoid all occasions for guilt. Shake off all the crimes you have committed, and make yourselves a new heart and a new spirit! Why die, House of Israel? I take no pleasure in the death of anyone—declares the Lord Yahweh—so repent and live! (18:30–32).

> As I live—declares the Lord Yahweh—I do not take pleasure in the death of the wicked but in the conversion of the wicked who changes his ways and saves his life. Repent, turn back from your evil ways. Why die, House of Israel? (33:11).

As just noted, this passionate, evangelical regard for individual souls and their welfare is something new in prophecy. Until now the Israelite prophets had to be concerned primarily with an approaching catastrophe and its meaning for the community as a whole. Now that that catastrophe had struck and the "House of Israel" lay in ruins, a totally new situation prevailed. Earlier prophets (Jeremiah in particular) had foreseen that an opportunity for beginning over again would be afforded Israel right at this time, but it was Ezekiel's unique insight that the *prophetic role itself* would need to be significantly changed for this to happen. Its mode and style would need to be different. The prophet would need to become more pastoral, more attentive to each individual and his or her personal disposition. He would need to become an evangelist: an awakener of hope, an arouser of the will to goodness and to life for each individual.

But what more specifically is it that Ezekiel saw ahead for those who would be awakened in this manner? What, concretely, would be happening to them in future years? If they were going to return to their homeland, when would this happen, and under what circumstances? In this last phase of Ezekiel's mission many of his earlier seminal ideas in this regard were enlarged upon and embellished. According to Ezekiel 4:6 he seems to have even earlier anticipated a period of some forty years as the time allotted for Judah's punishment and stay in Babylon— or about a generation. As to what would happen then, one thing Ezekiel stresses in ch. 34 is that however the liberation and restoration from

Babylon will come about, it will be (as it were) *Yahweh himself* who will accomplish this, not Israelite actions or leaders (see especially 34:11–22). Therefore, only *after* the restoration had been accomplished, he goes on to say in 34:23 and 37:24, will the Davidic dynasty be restored over a now *united* Israel (37:22). Thus here as in Jeremiah's vision of things to come the role of the Davidic dynasty is quite modestly portrayed. Yahweh's own actions will be the paramount factor in the actual liberation and restoration.

Of course, before this can occur the hostile nations occupying and surrounding the homeland will have to be dealt with. It is their fate that is discussed in chs. 35 and 36 where it is promised that they will be so decisively humiliated that they will never again taunt or rob the restored community (36:15). Indeed, those who are left among the surrounding nations will be amazed to see how wonderfully Israel's now ruined homeland is restored and in this way come to recognize that what has happened is truly Yahweh's doing (36:33–36).

However, at the very center of these futuristic visions (again as in the case of Jeremiah) is not this triumph of Israel over the surrounding nations so much as the miracle of *inner* renewal that will occur at this time in the community itself. Jeremiah had prophesied of this under the aspect of a new covenant with the law written upon the heart. In a very similar vein Ezekiel speaks of inner cleansing, spiritual renewal, and a heart transplant.

> I shall give you a new heart,
> and put a new spirit in you;
> I shall remove the heart
> of stone from your bodies
> and give you a heart of flesh instead.
> I shall put my spirit in you,
> and make you keep my laws
> and respect and practice my judgments (36:26–27).

A final feature of Ezekiel's futuristic visions (and being a priest one would expect this) is his detailed sketch in chs. 40–43:6 of a majestic new temple to which Yahweh is envisioned as returning in "glory" forever (43:1–6). From this citadel of worship at the center of the restoration community a wonderful stream will originate, Ezekiel writes in 47:1–12, which flowing eastward will become a mighty river filled with fish and bringing life to this heretofore barren region.

But realistically how is all this going to come to pass? How, in the first place, will the Israelites now resident in Babylon ever become convinced that such a future really awaits them?

A similar question seems to have haunted Ezekiel at this point in his mission, when (as he describes it) he had another of his life-transforming visions—this time of a valley strewn with dead men's bones all dried up (ch. 37). To the question that came to him as he gazed upon this scene: "Son of man, can these bones live?" he could only reply, "You know, Lord Yahweh [not I]." The twice repeated summons to "prophesy" (37:4, 9) and the amazing consequences of his doing so (the bones coming to life before his very eyes) must have been a stupendous confirmation of the importance of his own role as prophet (as he had so recently come to understand it) in preparing his people for their hope-filled future. Just as it was prophecy that had been essential in preparing Israel for the advent of judgment, so, it was now revealed, prophecy would also be essential in awakening a hopeless people and preparing them for the advent of the new spirit (37:11–14).

Unique in these visions of the future is the way Ezekiel unites the best of both Jerusalem theology and the older all-Israelite traditions reflected in Deuteronomy. At the very center of his picture of the future is the Deuteronomic vision of a people *inwardly* renewed by prophecy, the law of God written on their hearts (36:25–28; 37:14). But he has combined this with the Jerusalemite vision of a people united under Davidic rule, worshiping at the Jerusalem temple and situated in a land so richly blessed that even the surrounding nations will come to know that Yahweh is truly God (34:27–31; 36:7, 36). In all this he is clearly heir to the visionary legacy of his prophetic predecessors: Hosea, Isaiah and Jeremiah especially.

B. Ongoing Relevance

Those who first transmitted the Book of Ezekiel were especially awed by the grandeur of his futuristic visions. It is in any case at those points in particular in his book that their notes, comments and embellishments multiply. His visionary blueprint for a new temple, for example, was obviously of great interest to those who returned to the Judean homeland in 537 intent upon rebuilding their now ruined temple, even though the hard realities called for many an addition and modification (see their supplements in 43:7–ch. 46). Likewise, when the new age Ezekiel had anticipated did not dawn as expected, yet additional end-time scenarios had to be fashioned. Among the earliest of their kind are the famous sketches in chs. 38 and 39 of yet another invasion of this region from the north, but this time of such a magnitude and with an outcome so spectacular that now there would *really* happen what Ezekiel had predicted was to have happened earlier: the display of Yahweh's glory among the nations (39:21).

Such expansions as these are testimony to the kinds of thoughts the non-fulfillment of some of Ezekiel's more spectacular expectations aroused in subsequent generations. These have in turn unleashed a train of speculations regarding *their* eventual fulfillment. Even today many regard Ezekiel 38 and 39 as a vivid, literal picture of what may yet transpire in the Middle East in the period leading up to the consummation of history. However, in our quest for relevance instead of focusing on prophecies in this book that have obviously not come to pass (and which we have no way of knowing whether they ever will), would it not be better to pay more attention to those of Ezekiel's insights which *have* borne fruit?

One of these, I suggest, was his recognition that the *inner* renewal of his people would be central to their destiny, and his uncanny insight that for that to happen a prophet would be needed who would become intimately involved in the leadership of this people as a "watchman" or guardian of individuals. With this was born the image of the prophet as a pastor of souls: a man for others who desired passionately that not one of those under his care should die.

Can it not be said that at least Ezekiel was right regarding this: that since his time the awakening of his people from the dead has in fact been largely the result of precisely this kind of leader functioning in their midst? And is it not also true that through the influence of the prophets and wise men in Israel, and then through Jesus of Nazareth, pastoral figures of this type have become increasingly important to the life and mission of both Jews and Christians worldwide? And even today do we not realize more and more (and this partly as a consequence of witnesses like Ezekiel) that God's kingdom comes not so much by might or by power as by caring, hope-filled words on the lips of precisely such leaders?

We will have reason to consider these matters further, both in our discussion of Second Isaiah (in the following chapter), and also (as mentioned) when reflecting on the relevance of the prophets overall in our concluding chapter.

Questions for Review

1. Outline the main themes of Ezekiel's first period of prophetic activity. What was he *mainly* intent upon accomplishing during this period? How do his views regarding his people's past differ from those of

other prophets we have studied? What fresh ideas regarding the future came to him already at this time? What overall did he see God accomplishing through Israel in history?

2. How did Ezekiel's perception of his task as prophet change when news had arrived in Babylon of Jerusalem's fall? In what way did this change of roles relate to his vision of the future? Prepare a summary of the several facets of Ezekiel's portrait of Israel's future. Why might his thought in this respect be characterized as a blending of both Deuteronomic and Jerusalemite streams of thought? Relate Ezekiel's visionary experience of the valley of dry bones to his mission at this point of his career.

3. How do you regard the "unfulfilled prophecies" of Ezekiel? Are there aspects of his futuristic visions that *have* been fulfilled? Are some still *being* fulfilled? Might there be some that will be fulfilled in the future? What for you is the biggest impediment to this world becoming a better place? How do you see this impediment ever being overcome? What are for you the most significant points of relevance of this prophet and his message?

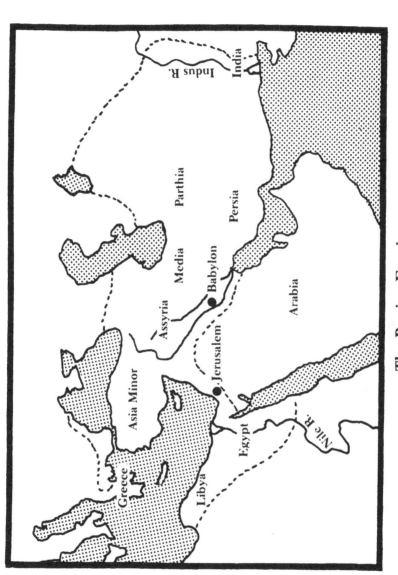

The Persian Empire

18

Second Isaiah

From a discussion of Ezekiel we turn now to another prophet who lived among those who were deported to Babylon, one whose name is unknown to us. Since his words were preserved as a supplement to those of Isaiah of Jerusalem (the First Isaiah), he has come to be called the Second Isaiah. Ezekiel's mission occurred at the *beginning* of the Babylonian captivity, his at its conclusion some thirty years later.

A. The Book as a Whole

As noted in our discussion of Isaiah of Jerusalem (see Chapter 9), internal evidence points to Isaiah 40–55 being a distinct unit or collection of prophetic messages from someone living not in Jerusalem in the middle of the eighth century (as did the First Isaiah), but in Babylon in the middle of the sixth century (see references to the conquests of Cyrus in Is 44:28; 45:1). We will not repeat here what was already said there regarding this issue. Nor is there much to be said as to *why* these anonymous messages were attached as they are to the messages of Isaiah of Jerusalem (1–39), rather than being assembled as a book in their own right (with the name and date of the prophet clearly specified as in the case of the other prophetic writings). Perhaps their author thought of himself (or was so regarded by *his* disciples) as a disciple and interpreter of the "Isaian tradition" rather than as an autonomous prophet.

Regardless, a closer look at the collection itself does yield certain clues to its compositional history.

1. Literary Character

An initial reading of Second Isaiah comes as a bit of a shock to someone coming to it from just having studied Ezekiel. There we encountered a carefully arranged series of personal reports, each easily separated from the other and often dated. While personal memoirs of this kind are not altogether missing in Second Isaiah, they are few in number (see 40:6; 49:1–6; 50:4–9). What then *do* we find here?

As before, there are divine messenger speeches (where the prophet speaks in Yahweh's name as though Yahweh himself were speaking through him; see for example 40:25; 41:1; 45:1–6; 45:14). But there are also many examples of the prophet expressing his *own* thoughts in his own unique way (40:12–24, for example, is not an oracle *from* God, but a homily *about* God). What further study of both the prophet's oracles and personal reflections has revealed is the *variety* of forms used in both instances and the peculiar manner in which they are woven together in a flow of speech whose boundaries, in many instances, are difficult to establish. In other words, what we seem to have here is a much greater variety of literary forms assembled in longer units than is usually the case in prophetic collections.

A few examples of the *forms* of speech here are the following (for additional examples see Mays, *Ezekiel, Second Isaiah*):

Salvation Oracles
This form is drawn from worship practices in which prayers of lament were responded to by words of assurance (". . . do not be afraid, for I am with you; do not be alarmed, for I am your God"; see Is 41:8–11; compare Lam 3:55–57; 1 Sam 1:17).

Trial Speeches
These are oracles which draw on legal terminology and proceedings to create an imaginary setting like that of a judicial court (". . . let us assemble for judgment"; see 41:1–5; 43:8–15, 22–28; 50:1–3).

Dispute or Controversy Speeches
In these the prophet himself speaks in his own right and advances an argument against a mood or opinion held by his audience ("How can you say, Jacob, how can you repeat, Israel, 'My way is hidden from Yahweh . . .' "; see 40:12–31; 42:18–25; 45:9–13; 49:14–26; 51:17–23).

Short Hymns
These anticipate the future salvation and summon Israel to celebration ("Sing a new song to Yahweh"; see 42:10–13; 44:23; 45:8; 48:20f; 49:13; 52:9f; 54:1f). The frequency of such hymns suggests that Second Isaiah may have belonged to a circle of people in Babylon who cultivated hymns and prayers as a way of keeping faith alive during the exile there (Mays' suggestion).

2. Organization

But what can be said about the way this collage of literary units has been assembled? While it is true, as stated, that the literary units flow together, there is evidence that these chapters, overall, are more meaningfully arranged than is often recognized.

To begin with, this collection appears to have an introduction (40:1–8) and a conclusion (55:6–13). In the introductory unit (40:1–8) we not only observe allusions to a prophetic call, but themes are announced which recur throughout the book. There is also a correspondence between the climactic line of the introductory oracle, regarding the "word of our God" which "remains for ever" (40:8), and the "word" that will "not return to me unfulfilled" in the concluding oracle (55:11). So, the opening and closing units of this collection appear to be deliberately placed and thematically related.

Also, one notices a decisive break in the middle of this collection, at the end of ch. 48. A number of characteristics distinguish these two major divisions (chs. 40–48 and 49–55). The audience addressed in 40–48 is consistently identified as Jacob/Israel (the one exception being 40:1–2), whereas in chs. 49–55 the audience is Zion/Jerusalem. Furthermore, in chs. 40–48, the prophet appears to be preoccupied with the approaching fall of Babylon and the role of Cyrus, and engaged in a dispute with Jacob/Israel regarding these matters (see especially ch. 45), while in 49–55 there is no reference to these events or this dispute at all. Here, instead, he appears to be relating to problems of a smaller group of his followers (those who "pursue saving justice" and "seek Yahweh"; see 51:1–3, 7), as well as to a personal crisis of some sort that he is facing (more regarding this later).

These initial observations of the book's organizational profile may be charted as follows:

Prologue	Audience: Jacob/Israel	Audience: Zion/Jerusalem	Epilogue
	Theme: fall of Babylon	Theme: personal crisis/disciples	
40:1–8	40:9–ch. 48	Ch. 49–55:5	55:6–13

These are not, however, the only observations that can be made regarding the arrangement of units in these chapters. The following features should also be noted:

• An ecstatic summons to leave Babylon at the end of ch. 48 (48:20; followed by call to bear witness to the great things that are now about to occur, in 48:20b–22), indicating perhaps that with this a decisive moment had arrived in the prophet's mission (the time for getting ready to leave Babylon had come).

• Another such summons at the end of Isaiah 52 (vv. 11–12, again followed by a testimony to the greatness of what is about to happen; compare 48:20b–22)—then in ch. 53 one of the most surprising and unique passages of the book. Here a plurality of voices breaks into the flow of these chapters ("Who has given credence to what *we* have heard?") and bears testimony to what they had recently experienced in relation to one whom they had initially despised, but have now come to regard as having suffered vicariously on their behalf (Is 53:4).

• Chs. 54–55, which look back on chs. 49–52 and assure Zion a final time that she will soon be heir to a magnificent salvation.

• The complex of units in 44:24–47:15, at the *center* of the first section (chs. 40–48), in which Cyrus, Babylon and the gods of Babylon are expressly named, after having been spoken of in the previous chapters in a rather general and indefinite manner—an arrangement which seems to have been deliberately designed.

• Finally, an obviously important first-person memoir standing at the head of the second section, 49:1–6, followed by a second memoir of a similar kind, in 50:4–9. It has long been thought that there is some connection between these and the commissioning oracle in 42:1–4, as well as the communal testimony in ch. 53. Together they are sometimes referred to as the Songs of the Suffering Servant (a misnomer, as I will be suggesting in the next chapter).

Adding these observations to those previously made heightens the impression that Second Isaiah is meaningfully organized. More precisely, with this last group of observations in hand, it would appear that Second Isaiah has not just two (as previously suggested), but three main parts: the first two, chs. 40–48 and chs. 49–52, each concluded by a summons to get ready to leave Babylon; the final section, chs. 53–55, having the appearance of an appendix.

This may be charted as follows:

Prologue	Jacob/Israel (Babylon/Cyrus, 44:24–47:15)	Zion/Jerusalem	Communal testimony	Concluding oracles (Appendix)	Epilogue
40:1–8	40:9–ch. 48	chs. 49–52	53	54–55:5	55:6–11

Leave Babylon   (Servant Songs: 42:1–5; 49:1–6; 50:4–9; ch. 53)

It is possible that this seemingly meaningful arrangement is due in part at least (as in the case of Ezekiel) to the literary activity of Second Isaiah himself.

B. The Man Behind the Book

From what has already been said about the anonymity of Second Isaiah, it might be thought that it would be futile in this instance to say much at all about the prophet himself before proceeding to a discussion of his message. However, as already intimated, the book of this prophet is by no means completely devoid of personal references. Indeed, one of the more important of these confronts us right off, in 40:1–8, at the very beginning of his writings, and may have been put here by the prophet himself. The references to "voices" speaking in this passage (see vv. 3 and 6), rather than God (but note v. 1), impart a rather mysterious atmosphere to this account, but in all other respects it appears to be the personal report of a prophetic call—very much, for example, like the report in Isaiah 6 of the prophetic call of the First Isaiah. As such we may expect it to tell us something of importance regarding both the prophet himself and his sense of mission.

1. Prophetic Call (40:1–8)

There appear to be three distinct auditions reported on here, the first two in 40:1–2 and 40:3–5, the third beginning at verse 6 with the reference there to a "voice" that commanded the prophet to "cry aloud" (or preach), to which he responded: "What shall I cry?—All humanity is grass and all its beauty like the wild flower's. The grass withers, the flower fades when the breath of Yahweh blows on them" (40:6–7). This reaction suggests that he initially resisted his call, as had other prophets before him (Jeremiah, for example). Something within him had to be changed or overcome before he could accept this calling to preach. What might this have been?

It will be remembered that in the case of the *First* Isaiah it was his uncleanness and guilt that had to be purged before *he* could become a prophet (Is 6:5). Jeremiah, on the other hand (it appears), was very young and quite timid by nature—this, he tells us, is why *he* resisted his calling (Jer 1:7). By contrast, for *Second* Isaiah the inner problem that prompted his hesitancy would seem to have been an oppressive sense of the transiency of life. "All humanity is grass." We are all like the flowers of the field which blossom beautifully for a moment, but then are gone when the "breath of Yahweh" blows them away (see

Ecclesiastes 1:4–8 for an example of a similar fatalistic mood). It is an attitude that we can imagine was pervasive in Babylon at that time among Second Isaiah's contemporaries, living as they did so long now (since the deportations of 598 and 586) in such a far-off pagan environment.

In summary, in the personal report of his prophetic call, in 40:1–8, Second Isaiah alludes to the fact that at the time of his call he was in a mood of despair. He was still a "Yahwist" (he speaks of the "breath of Yahweh"), but he was beginning to think of his God as a somewhat abstract, distant figure who rules the world in a blind, impersonal way.

But then, he tells us, in response to his lament "What shall I cry?" an astonishing message was given him—an insight that overcame his despair and established him in his prophetic role: Yes, "The grass withers, the flower fades, *but* the word of our God remains for ever!" (40:8). Yahweh's *word* is true and enduring! It will be fulfilled! That is the promise that fired his imagination and moved him to act.

But what "word" is this that is being referred to here? The answer is intimated in the previous two oracles that he reports were given him at this time—those summarized in 40:1–5.

In the first of these, 40:1–2, he is summoned to console Jerusalem and announce to her that "her period of service is ended, her guilt has been atoned for" and that "she has received [from the hand of Yahweh] double punishment for all her sins." In the second, 40:3–5, he is told to prepare in the desert "a straight highway for our God," for "the glory of Yahweh" is about to be "revealed and all humanity will see it together . . ." (40:5).

But what, more concretely, is the meaning of these exuberant oracles? The answer may be found in the references to quite specific historical events already transpiring or soon to occur, which the prophet refers to again and again in his subsequent oracles. To understand these we must note the outlines, at least, of the specific historical context in which this prophet is now living.

2. *Historical Setting*

In the opening oracles of Second Isaiah there is great excitement over something that is about to happen, but it is not until 43:14 that we are informed of the details of what this might be. There it is written:

Thus says Yahweh,
your redeemer, the Holy One of Israel:
For your sake I have sent to Babylon,

> I shall knock down all the prison bars,
> and the Chaldaeans' shouts of joy
> will change to lamentations.

This is the first explicit reference to Babylon and it declares in no uncertain terms that it will soon be invaded and conquered. The identity of the army that will do this is then specifically referred to in 44:24–47:15. Twice in this section Second Isaiah mentions the name of the great founder of the Persian Empire, Cyrus (44:28; 45:1). Furthermore, the references are such that we can identify the exact historical moment in which this prophet was living and speaking. It was a time when Cyrus had *not yet* conquered Babylon or set the Judeans there free. But he had *already* subdued nations and disarmed kings (45:1). From extra-biblical records we know that Cyrus conquered the Median empire to the north and northeast of Babylon in 550. Four years later (546) he defeated Croesus king of Lydia and took over his capital at Sardis. Then he waited for the right moment to move south and finish his conquests of this region by defeating Babylon also. This he did, without a battle, seven years later, in 539.

The prophecies of Second Isaiah may thus all be dated to the decade of waiting between Cyrus' sweeping victories over Media and Lydia in 550 and his conquest of Babylon in 539. Needless to say this was a time of enormous uncertainty for the peoples of this region, and most especially for those living in Babylon. Cyrus' advent had been so swift and unanticipated. Why then did he now wait before striking a blow against Babylon? Would he even do so? Dare he do so? Had he not already bitten off too much, perhaps? And what might happen if he did? Would Babylon fall as had Media and Lydia? And if that were to happen, what would become of the deported peoples there, including the Judeans? Would he allow them to return to their homelands? Would they *want* to return if he did? These must have been some of the thoughts going through the minds of the Judeans who were residents of Babylon and its vicinity at this critical juncture.

3. Life Situation

There is more that might be said regarding the personal life situation of this prophet—a good bit more, if the personal reports in 49:1–6 and 50:4–8 are reflective of his own experiences, and the lament in ch. 53 also refers to him. I will be exploring this possibility in the following chapter. Here, yet, I want simply to take note of the fact that he was quite obviously a member of that Judean Israelite community just referred to (that had been deported to this region some sixty years earlier) and reflect briefly on what that might have meant in his case.

Where did these Judean deportees live when they arrived in Babylon, and what did they do there, precisely? There is very little known regarding this, but from Ezekiel's reference to their being settled at Tel Aviv by the river Chebar (3:15), one of the tributary canals of the Euphrates River southeast of Babylon, the conclusion has been drawn that some of them, at least, were put to work on the canal systems of that city. That, however, was at the beginning of their sojourn there. By the time of Second Isaiah many might well have found employment in Babylon itself and become quite well adapted to life in this region.

Already in our discussion of Second Isaiah's prophetic call the impact that living here so far from their homeland might have had on their faith was alluded to. The impression we get from Second Isaiah's writings is that those whom he addresses were still (like himself) Yahwists. They still believed in the God of their fathers—in some respects more so than ever, perhaps (note the satire in 44:9–20 on Babylonian image-worship). Furthermore, they were still *Jerusalem* Yahwists. Memories of the temple there (44:28) and of the dynastic promises to David (55:3b) were still living realities for them. In addition, as we shall see shortly, prophetic writings of the kind we have been studying may have been circulating among them (as well as other sacred writings). Hence, scriptures were being studied; a form of public worship may have been fashioned (as noted, the wealth of liturgical forms in Second Isaiah's writings testifies of this)—the synagogue may have had its origins in this period. New ways were being forged at this time already to keep faith alive in an alien land.

However, there appears to have been a pervasive sense of despair and God-forsakenness as well. "How can you say, Jacob, how can you repeat, Israel," Second Isaiah queries his audience, " 'My way is hidden from Yahweh, my rights are ignored by my God?' " (40:27). It was as though in this place, so far from the Judean homeland, on the outskirts of Babylon (one of the great cities of the ancient world), Yahweh had forgotten his people. Were they even his people any longer? Clearly, some had begun to wonder about this, including (as we have seen) Second Isaiah himself.

It was to speak to this issue that this prophet was called, converted and commissioned.

Questions for Review

1. Summarize the evidence for thinking that Isaiah 40–55 is not a record of the words of Isaiah of Jerusalem, but of a prophet living some two hundred years later. How would you compare this collection with the other prophetic books you have studied? Identify its major organizational features.

2. What justifies our regarding the opening unit of this collection (40:1–8) as a prophetic call account? What do we learn from this passage concerning the theological and existential dilemma of this prophet at the time of his call? What was revealed to him that helped him to overcome his despair and become a prophet?

3. What was happening in the wider world during this time? Who, specifically, was Cyrus? What had he accomplished at the time of Second Isaiah's call? What might have been the response of the Babylonians to these events? Of the Judeans who had been deported there? What might have been happening among Second Isaiah's contemporaries during their long stay in Babylon?

19

His Message and Its Relevance

A. Message

1. The Core

Seen against the background of the prophet's life and times outlined in the previous chapter, the core message of Second Isaiah can be characterized as a relatively simple one. In oracle after oracle he lets it be known that the advent of the Persian conqueror Cyrus on the scene of history is no accident. Yahweh has raised him up in fulfillment of a previously revealed plan. This is what is meant by the references at the beginning and end of this collection to "the word of our God" which "remains for ever" and "will not return to me unfulfilled" (40:8; 55:11). Yahweh is fulfilling a plan.

What plan? Those who have studied the prophecies of Jeremiah and Ezekiel, as we just have, need hardly ask. It is the one *they* had outlined regarding the fate of Babylon and the Judean refugees there. A time would come—in about seventy years, Jeremiah had predicted—when Babylon would fall and the Judeans there would be liberated. Then Yahweh would restore his people to their homeland, give them a new heart and a new sense of unity and security under Davidic leadership, and return in "glory" to a new temple in their midst to be their God forever. And so at last not only Israel, but the whole world would come to know that Yahweh is God.

The time appointed for these things to occur has arrived, Second Isaiah says in effect. The sovereignty of Babylon is now nearing an end. The hour has struck for Israel's restoration. Jerusalem has received double punishment for all its crimes (40:1–2). Babylon's downfall is imminent (chs. 46–47). A new exodus is about to occur, one that will make the exodus from Egypt pale by comparison (43:16–20). Jerusalem is about to be rebuilt and its temple restored (44:28). As these events transpire the whole world will see it and know that Yahweh is really

213

God (45:14–25). It is in this way that his glory will be revealed and "all humanity will see it together" (40:5).

This is the core of the message Second Isaiah brings to his people, and, as intimated, his enthusiasm in doing so is in part the result of his seeing all this as a fulfillment of a plan previously announced by the prophets who had preceded him. "Who has acted thus, who has done this?" he asks with rhetorical boldness (41:4). It is none other, he answers, than the One who calls the generations from the beginning: "I, Yahweh, who am the first and till the last I shall still be there." How does he know this to be true? Because, he declares in 42:9, "See how former predictions have come true" (compare 41:26; 43:9). What Yahweh had earlier said through his prophets *would* happen *is* now happening. Only a God who is totally in charge of the historical process (hence Lord of history) could predict such events as these and then bring them to pass!

Second Isaiah is the first of the prophets to point in this way to the fulfillment of prophecy as a proof of the greatness of Yahweh. It is this which fuels his polemic against idolatry and inspires his magnificent orations on the greatness, oneness and sovereignty of his God (40:12–26).

> As I told you about it long before,
> before it happened I revealed it to you,
> so that you could not say, "My statue did it,
> my idol, my metal image, ordained this."
> You have heard and seen all this,
> why won't you admit it? (48:5–6a)

2. New Things

But Second Isaiah not only proclaimed the *fulfillment* of prophecy, but prophesied of "*new* things" as well:

> Now I am going to reveal new things to you,
> secrets that you do not know;
> they have just been created, not long ago,
> and until today you have heard nothing about them . . . (48:6b–8a).

That this would be the case is only to be expected. As a prophet in his own right he sought to interpret the events of his time in the light of his own unique insight and inspiration. This new or plus element of his vision can be sensed in his thoughts regarding three themes in particular:

- his prophecies regarding Cyrus and Cyrus' role in the restoration drama;
- his radically new interpretation of the Davidic oath (or covenant), and hence his perception of the role Davidic kings would play in the future scheme of things;
- his growing consciousness of the role he himself would play, as prophet, in the unfolding drama of salvation—a sense of things that was endorsed and deepened by his disciples in their remarkable testimony regarding him, in Isaiah 53.

The unique contribution of this last of the major prophets of the Bible will be evident as we look more closely now at each one of these truly novel thematic developments.

(a) Second Isaiah's Words Concerning Cyrus

It will be remembered that when Jeremiah and Ezekiel had looked into the future and had tried to discern what was going to happen to the Judean refugees in Babylon, both foresaw that Babylon's sovereignty would come to an end before long (in about a generation, Jeremiah had said) and that then the Israelites there would be able to leave and return home. Neither, however, was specific as to how this would be accomplished, although Ezekiel had suggested (in ch. 34 of his book) that there would be two stages: first, Yahweh himself (like a great and good shepherd, he had written) would intervene to gather and purge scattered Israel (Ez 34:11–22); then, once restored to its homeland, Davidic kings would again be put in charge of the community there (34:23–31).

It is against this background that we can identify the "newness" of what Second Isaiah has to say about Cyrus. In specifying that Yahweh *himself* would act as a "shepherd" to restore Israel, Ezekiel had left open the question of how, concretely, Yahweh would do this. In what way, specifically, could one imagine Yahweh undertaking this task? What Ezekiel had left vague at this point Second Isaiah made explicit. *Cyrus,* he declares, is the Yahweh-appointed "shepherd" through whom all this will be accomplished (44:28). It is *he* who is going to bring an end to the sovereignty of Babylon and release the Judean captives there. It is *he* who is going to fulfill Yahweh's "entire will" by seeing to it that Jerusalem and the towns of Judah are rebuilt and inhabited once again by their rightful residents (44:26–28a).

It might be thought that in putting forward such an interpretation of Cyrus Second Isaiah is only following in the footsteps of his prophetic predecessors. They too had seen the rise of powerful nations under the leadership of pagan kings like Cyrus as events which Yahweh had designed to accomplish his purposes. However, according to the earlier prophets such nations had been raised up to *punish* Israel, whereas now it is being said that Yahweh is using a pagan king to *restore* Israel. In the initial exodus and entry of Israel into its homeland a Yahwist leader, Moses, had been chosen to accomplish this liberation, and another Yahwist leader, David, was raised up to build Jerusalem and establish the security of the Judean towns. What is new here is that in this new exodus and settlement such Yahwist leaders are being bypassed altogether and a *pagan* ruler assigned this role. To him are now assigned the titles and honors of "My shepherd" (44:28) and "anointed one" once attributed to men like Moses and David (45:1)—even though Cyrus does not even know or acknowledge Yahweh as yet (45:5b).

The novelty and audacity of this interpretation of contemporary events can be gauged by the fiercely negative response it seems to have aroused among Second Isaiah's Judean contemporaries (see 45:9–13).

(b) Second Isaiah's New View of the Oath Sworn to David

A second "new thing" in Second Isaiah's prophecies is his handling of the traditions associated with David. If to Cyrus was assigned such a lofty role in implementing the restoration, what is there left for the Davidic dynasty to do? As we have seen, Ezekiel had also pondered this problem and resolved it by predicting that even though Yahweh would bypass Davidic leadership when gathering his people to their homeland, once there, this dynasty would be restored as the leader of the restoration community (Ez 34:11; 37:20–26).

Was this also what Second Isaiah had in mind? Scanning his book for an answer we are puzzled not to find even a hint there of such an idea—not even a single reference to the Davidic dynasty at all—*until* we reach the very last chapter of his book, in ch. 55. There, beginning with verse 3b, we encounter these remarkable words (and they help to explain this strange silence):

> I shall make an everlasting covenant with *you*
> [the community of the new Jerusalem]
> in fulfillment of the favors promised to David.

Here Second Isaiah seems to be saying that the everlasting covenant made with David has been transferred to the entire restoration community! This suggests that he foresaw a future for his people *without* the political form it had taken under David, indeed, without the Davidic dynasty operative there at all (regarding this astonishing, unanticipated theological innovation, see especially Mays, *Ezekiel, Second Isaiah*). And yet, he goes on to promise that just as under David Israel had become a powerful witness of Yahweh's greatness to the surrounding peoples, so will it again—not now, however, as in David's time, through military expansion and nation building, but through a development that might be characterized as a *missionary* witness of sorts.

> Look, I have made him [David] a witness to peoples,
> a leader and lawgiver to peoples.
> Look, *you* [the new Jerusalem] will summon a nation unknown
>   to you,
> a nation unknown to you will hurry to you
> for the sake of Yahweh your God,
> because the Holy One of Israel has glorified you (55:4–5).

That a missionary type witness is in fact what Second Isaiah is alluding to here seems apparent from several earlier oracles of his where he exuberantly declares that a process has already begun (in the events that are now transpiring) that will eventually bring about the worldwide recognition of Israel's God as God. So, for example, he prophesies in 44:5 that a time is coming when "one person will say, 'I belong to Yahweh,' another will call himself by Jacob's name. On his hand another will write, 'Yahweh's' and be surnamed 'Israel' " (44:5). And in 45:22 it is as though he were himself beginning to *be* such a missionary to the world when he announces:

> Turn to me and you will be saved,
> all you ends of the earth,
> for I am God, and there is no other.

In summary, Second Isaiah appears to have come to the insight that the future of his people would be one in which the prior structures of nationhood under Davidic leadership would be phased out in favor of some alternative form or structure of existence. The restoration itself would occur through Yahweh's servant Cyrus, and once restored the entire community would experience those special favors once bestowed upon the Davidic family alone, so that through them collectively "a witness" would go forth to "the peoples" and "a nation unknown to you will hurry to you for the sake of Yahweh your God" (55:5).

But, one might ask, how realistic is this? Granted Cyrus will liberate this people and bring about their restoration, what is going to happen once it is restored, if the Davidic dynasty is no longer functioning? Where will it get the leadership, inspiration and energy it needs to do the remarkable things Isaiah predicts will be accomplished at this time? Insofar as there are answers in the writings of Second Isaiah themselves to questions such as these they may be found in those remarkably condensed (at times cryptic) passages I referred to earlier as the Songs of the Suffering Servant. In them, I suggest, we are brought face to face with Second Isaiah's own developing sense of his role as prophet within the new age now dawning. This is the third point at which Second Isaiah has some remarkably new things to say.

(c) Second Isaiah's Deepening Awareness of His Own Role Within the Unfolding Plan of God

There are four passages in Second Isaiah that were first singled out as possibly unique and interrelated in a famous commentary on Isaiah by Bernhard Duhm (published in 1892). These passages are commonly referred to as "Songs of the Suffering Servant," even though, as noted earlier, this is a misnomer of sorts since none of them are songs (as we think of songs today) and only two of them refer to suffering on the part of the individual involved.

The first of these, Isaiah 42:1–4, appears to be a Yahweh oracle or message; the second and third, Isaiah 49:1–6 and 50:4–9, are first-person memoirs in which certain experiences are related (in the personal reportorial style that has become familiar to us by now from our study of the earlier prophets); the fourth, Isaiah 53, as earlier suggested, is a communal testimony, having to do with the sufferings and death of someone who though unjustly treated bore it stoically and is now honored for this by those who had earlier despised him. The argument has been made that the man referred to here was none other than Second Isaiah himself and that those who are speaking are those who had become his disciples through the events they are describing. Indeed, although these four texts have provoked a mass of studies with often diverse conclusions, there is a growing awareness among students of this book that all may have to do, in one way or another, with key phases of Second Isaiah's own personal pilgrimage (see especially Whybray). Without assuming that this is the only possible approach, I will try to suggest, briefly, what can be learned by looking at these "Songs" from this point of view.

As a first step in doing so it will be important to note again those passages where Second Isaiah's prophetic consciousness *generally* comes to expression (apart from what we learn regarding him in these Servant Songs). It was earlier observed, for example (see previous chapter), that Second Isaiah not only thought of himself as a prophet (a bearer of divine messages; see 40:1–8), but as a prophet living in a time when the words of prior prophets were coming to fulfillment (40:8; 55:11). Furthermore, he believed he was standing, not on the threshold of a catastrophe, but at the dawn of an age of salvation similar to that of the time of Moses and the exodus from Egypt at the beginning of Israelite history (see Is 43:16–21; 48:21; 52:12). Like Jacob-Israel in Egypt, the main body of Israelites was now in Babylon, far away from their Israelite homeland. But as of old, Yahweh was about to liberate them. A new exodus, he believed, was about to begin, only this time it would be an even greater event than the previous one—so great in fact that the earlier exodus would come to be thought of as insignificant by comparison (43:18).

What does all this imply regarding the self-understanding of this prophet? It would indicate, I suggest, that he may have thought of himself as a second Moses—someone called by God to lead his people on a new exodus of potentially even greater significance than the first one. For Yahweh, he believed, was about to bring about, not only the restoration of Israel to its homeland, but a revelation of himself to the whole of humanity (40:5). It is, in any case, fully consistent with this that like Moses of old, in 48:20 and 52:12, he summons his people to get ready to "come out from Babylon," promising them that as they do so they need not hurry or flee like fugitives, for "Yahweh marches at your head and the God of Israel is your rearguard" (52:12). As a result their journey will be accompanied by miracles (48:21) and their journey's end with a degree of success that will astonish the kings and peoples of earth (49:7; 52:13–15).

Declare this with cries of joy, proclaim it,
carry it to the remotest parts of earth.
Say, "Yahweh has redeemed his servant Jacob" (48:20).

In summary, what we sense regarding Second Isaiah's self-understanding, *apart* from the Servant Songs, is that he saw himself in the tradition of Moses. However, his mission was an even greater one than that of Moses in that it was his calling to lead Israel in an exodus through which not only Israel would be restored to its homeland, but knowledge of Yahweh would be revealed to the whole world.

With this as a background, let us look now at what is intimated regarding yet additional developments in the self-understanding of this remarkable prophet, as these are revealed in the so-called Servant Songs, beginning with 42:1–4.

(i) First Servant Song (Is 42:1–4)

In this first of the Servant Songs the speaker is Yahweh—in other words, the text here should be in quotes, as are the "voices" Second Isaiah heard at the time of his call (40:1–8). The one referred to in the opening line is identified as Yahweh's "servant." "Here is my servant whom I uphold, my chosen one in whom my soul delights" (42:1). Who is this "servant" and "chosen one"? A few verses earlier, in 41:8–9, *Israel* is explicitly identified as such. The words that follow are to be understood, therefore, as a revelation regarding Israel and the mission to which it is now being called. However, as an Israelite himself, Second Isaiah no doubt regarded these words as a description of *his* mission as well.

What kind of mission was this to be? The answer alluded to here is mind-boggling. Yahweh's servant Israel, the text states, is being empowered by Yahweh's spirit "to bring fair judgment *to the nations.*" "To bring" here would appear to allude to a preaching or teaching mission of some sort, and "fair judgment" may be interpreted to mean all that is involved in that enlightened way (of torah or law) of which earlier prophets had spoken so often. What is so astonishing is that Israel is here described as being empowered to testify of this to the *whole* world, and is said to be doing so *without* fanfare or violence (42:2–3a)—and yet so "faithfully" (42:3b) that he will not "grow faint" or "be crushed until he has established fair judgement on earth . . ." (42:4).

As we have seen, other prophets had envisioned the nations of the earth as coming to some kind of recognition of Yahweh in the wake of what Yahweh would do in restoring Israel to its homeland (Ez 36:36). Also, in one famous passage it is even anticipated that these nations will one day seek Israel out and send their representatives there to have their disputes settled on the basis of Yahweh's word and law (Is 2:1–5). But here, by contrast, the movement is in the other direction. Israel does not wait passively for the nations to come to it, but goes out to them. Here Israel is envisioned as empowered for a mission outward, so that precisely in *this* way "fair judgment" will be established on earth (42:4).

Is this really what this prophet is saying, however? Were this his thought would he not be anticipating the missionary movements of Judaism and Christianity by several centuries? Is that possible?

(ii) Second Servant Song (Is 49:1–6)

The second of these Servant Songs makes quite explicit what the first one only alludes to. As noted, this one is autobiographical. In it Second Isaiah appears to be relating something quite personal regarding himself and the experiences he has recently had, both at the time of his call (49:1) and later on during his prophetic mission (49:2–4).

Remarkably, the audience to which he addresses this personal report is not his own people (his fellow Israelites in Babylon), but "distant peoples" (49:1). That an Israelite prophet should direct a message to foreign peoples is not unusual. That he should address them in such an evangelical, personal manner *is* surprising. Yet, this is fully consistent with that enlarged consciousness of worldwide mission alluded to in 42:1–4, as well as with what he goes on to relate in this memoir. For the substance of what he wants to tell the "distant peoples," he informs us, is quite simply the story of how (despite discouragement and lack of success) the focus of his mission was shifted from his being merely Yahweh's servant "to restore the tribes of Jacob" (49:5a, 6b) to that of being "a light to the nations so that my salvation may reach to the remotest parts of the earth" (49:6b).

Thus, a second time in these Servant Songs we are told of Second Isaiah's growing conviction that Israel's mission (and his), at this critical juncture of its history, was not simply its reconstitution as a people in its homeland, but to bring knowledge of Yahweh to the whole earth—and to do this not by making "his voice heard in the street" or breaking "the crushed reed" (42:2–3), but through inspired personal testimony such as we see him employing in this Second Song.

(iii) Third Servant Song (Is 50:4–9)

This Song too is autobiographical in style and content. This leads us to expect that it also (like the second Song) will inform us of important personal developments in the mission of this prophet. We are not disappointed. The passage begins with a beautiful allusion to Second Isaiah's prophetic vocation. It was his experience, he says, that "morning by morning" Yahweh "makes his ear alert to listen like a disciple,'' so that he knows ''how to give a word of comfort to the weary'' (50:4). From this we learn how pastoral he felt toward his people. Day by day he waits before Yahweh for some fresh word of encouragement for them.

But we quickly learn as well that in the particular instance being reported on in this memoir (the revelation for that morning, so to speak) he was encouraged to face openly without fear ''those who struck'' him, tore at his beard and covered his face with ''insult and spittle'' (50:5–6). In verse 8 it is intimated that his very life may be at stake, for someone was apparently threatening to take him to court and put him on trial. Second Isaiah, it seems, had become the target of extreme animosity and violence. But who was it that might have been threatening him (and his disciples also, possibly; see 51:12–13) in this manner?

In earlier chapters (chs. 40–48) we read of fellow Israelites who do not agree with this prophet and oppose his preaching (45:9; 48:1). Nowhere, however, is it ever intimated that they persecuted him or put him on trial, nor, as aliens in this region, would they have had the right to do so, one conjectures. Possibly then the opposition here is from certain officials or authorities within Babylon. It is clear in any case that his preaching regarding the imminent overthrow of Babylon by the Persians would have been, from their point of view, seditious and reason enough for them to want to bring him to trial for treason (50:8).

But the main point of his memoir was not so much to tell us of this, as to give testimony to his willingness as a disciple of Yahweh to face the impending ordeal with calmness and courage:

> Lord Yahweh has opened my ear
> and I have not resisted,
> I have not turned away.
> I have offered my back to those who struck me,
> my cheeks to those who plucked my beard;
> I have not turned my face away
> from insult and spitting (50:5–6a).

He could do this, he goes on to testify, because of his absolute confidence that during the approaching ordeal Yahweh would come to his rescue and vindicate him (50:8–9).

(iv) Fourth Servant Song (Is 53)

The sequel to the events alluded to in Isaiah 50:4–9 is hinted at in Isaiah 53, a passage many Christians rightly regard as the supreme prophecy of the atoning death of Jesus. It should be noted, however, that this text is not a prophecy, strictly speaking. It is rather the testimony of a group of people who relate something they "have heard" (53:1) regarding a certain individual who was initially repugnant to them (53:2–3), but whom they now view in an altogether different light because of the remarkably quiet, steadfast manner with which he suffered during a trial and execution (53:7–9). It was their own complicity in his sufferings, they tell us (53:4–6), which was now in retrospect especially painful to them, for they apparently had not lifted a finger to defend him (53:8), even though they now see that his execution was unwarranted and unjust (53:9). Nevertheless, they go on to testify, they have derived some surprising benefits from this whole experience (and this is undoubtedly the main reason for their having put all this into writing). Heretofore they were each going their own way like straying sheep (53:6), whereas now they have been "healed" of this and are penitent in the realization that it was really because of *their* "rebellions" that he suffered (53:5). They are also full of hope now regarding the future. They firmly believe that the healing they experienced many others will experience as well (53:11–12).

The language of this insightful testimony is difficult at points and many conflicting interpretations have been offered. However, it is hard not to see some connection between what we are told here about a trial (53:8) and the allusions to an *impending* trial in the previous Servant Song (50:8). Does this testimony not reflect what subsequently happened to Second Isaiah himself? And are those who speak not, perhaps, a growing circle of his disciples whose faith was awakened by precisely that confidence and faith to which we learn Yahweh had called him in that pivotal revelation he himself recorded, in 50:4–9?

With this possibility in mind, I will try to summarize now what we have learned both here and elsewhere regarding this unusual prophet. Although initially depressed (as were many of his contemporaries), Second Isaiah, through his prophetic call, came to believe that Yahweh was bringing to fulfillment the dawn of the new age prophesied by his predecessors. Cyrus, whose conquests of Media and Lydia had shocked the ancient world, was the God-appointed leader to make it possible for Israel to return to its homeland. But deeply convinced as he was of this, Second Isaiah (in the first period of his mission) had great difficulty in convincing others. His efforts at getting his Judean contemporaries ready for the new exodus fell on deaf ears (49:4). In the midst of his discouragement, however, he heard divine words declaring that Israel's mission (and his) was to be directed now to the whole world (49:6). Not through political might, but by means of gentle, spirit-inspired testimony true justice would one day be established worldwide (42:3–4). But then, as he undertook to begin this mission, he became the target of persecution (perhaps because his words were interpreted as treason by certain Babylonian authorities) and was subsequently arrested, put on trial and executed, without any of his fellow Judeans coming to his defense.

As it turned out, however, his death accomplished what his life had not, for inadvertently, it seemed, it brought about that inner change he had been trying to encourage all along through his preaching. And those who experienced this testified that they were sure that this was only the beginning of the spiritual transformations that would occur because of him. "After the ordeal he has endured," they wrote at the conclusion of their communal confession, "he will see the light and be content. By his knowledge, the upright one, my servant, will justify many by taking their guilt on himself" (53:11).

B. Ongoing Relevance

No prophet before him (and few since) have had more moving things to say about Yahweh than Second Isaiah. In his words a monotheistic vision was born of truly revolutionary proportions. There is one God and one God only and his glory will soon be revealed to all humanity. It is on this note that his book of prophecies opens in the first chapter (ch. 40).

But is this not sheer idealism? How will such a thing ever take place? As we have seen, Second Isaiah saw this happening in conjunction with the restoration of Israel to its homeland through Cyrus. But even that, he foresaw, in and of itself, would not bring about this universal revelation. This, he came to see, will come about only through the power of gentle speaking and fearless suffering (42:1–3; 50:4–9). Already earlier Ezekiel had begun to sense something similar. If the dead bones of Israel in Babylon were ever going to live again, there would have to be *prophecy*—there would have to be pastor-sentries attending to the needs of individuals through wise hopeful words (Ez 37:1–14; 33:10–20). But even Ezekiel had not quite grasped what Second Isaiah foresaw with the passion of a revelation: namely, that the prophets will not only need to play the decisive role in gathering and renewing *Israel* (49:5a), but in converting the *world* as well (49:6).

No other prophet saw more clearly than Second Isaiah the greatness of Yahweh. But none realized so acutely that this greatness would be communicated to the world not by might nor by power—not by a "great nation" under Davidic leadership or spectacles of nature (at least not in this way only)—but through thoughtful people bearing witness faithfully to "fair judgment" (torah) by means of gentle words and actions (42:2–3).

Here, in this vision of things to come, prophecy replaces messianism, spirit replaces violence, thought replaces spectacle as the chief means by which salvation will dawn for our world.

Is this not the pathway both Judaism and Christianity have traveled in their finest hours since then? Is this not the way that Jesus walked? Is this not the wave of the future? I shall have more to say on this theme at the conclusion of the next chapter where we trace the outlines of the prophetic movement in the century immediately following this prophet.

Questions for Review

1. Summarize the core message of this prophet. In what sense did he believe himself to be living in a time of "fulfillment"? What use did he make of this concept in his preaching? What did it contribute to his mission?

2. What role does Cyrus play in Second Isaiah's interpretation of the events of his time? How does this compare to the thinking of earlier prophets? Why might his contemporaries in Babylon have objected to what he had to say in this regard? What role did he foresee the Davidic dynasty playing in the future?

3. Which passages in Second Isaiah have been identified as the Songs of the Suffering Servant? Characterize these in terms of their literary form. Why on this basis alone are two of these Songs thought to have an autobiographical reference to Second Isaiah himself? On what basis might Isaiah 53 be interpreted as also referring to him? What might be said about the self-understanding of Second Isaiah apart from these Songs? What is added when we take these Songs into consideration?

4. Compare the future expectations of this prophet with those of Ezekiel or Jeremiah. In retrospect how realistic was his vision of things to come? Did any of it come to pass? What relevance might it have for an interpretation of Jesus and Christianity? Prepare your own assessment of the relevance of this prophet generally for our time.

20

The End of an Era: Third Isaiah, Haggai, Zechariah, Malachi, Joel, Jonah

We are nearing the conclusion of our study of the biblical prophets and their writings. After Second Isaiah the prophetic tradition entered upon a period of rather precipitous decline for reasons that I will hope to make clear in this chapter.

More particularly, I will try to do two things in the remaining pages: first of all, survey the story of prophecy during the post-exilic period (that is, the period after the Judean restoration to the homeland in 538), and then, secondly, look back on our study as a whole and try to say something in conclusion regarding the overall relevance and importance of the prophets we have been studying.

A. Prophecy After 538

To understand what happened to the prophetic tradition in the period following Second Isaiah it is important to note, to begin with, that the events that occurred when Cyrus did finally conquer Babylon in 538 were not completely consistent with the predictions of *any* of the Israelite prophets. True, Cyrus did overthrow Babylon, precisely as Second Isaiah had predicted he would, and he did permit the captive peoples there (including the Judeans) to return to their homelands, as Ezekiel and Jeremiah also had said would happen (see Ezr chs. 1–2, and 6:1–12 for the biblical record of his role in these events). But these developments did not prove to be the momentous world-changing events that the prophets had thought they would be. The glory of Yahweh was not revealed to all humanity, as Second Isaiah had anticipated; nor, as it turned out, was it even possible, right away at least, to build him a temple (see Ezr chs. 1 and 2) or establish a Davidic kingdom, as Ezekiel had expected would happen. Above all, there was little immediate tangible evidence of that inward transformation that Ezekiel (and Jeremiah before him) had prophesied would occur at this time: the new heart and new covenant.

In short, while the restoration itself was a remarkable confirmation of *some* of the earlier prophetic predictions, much of what the pre-exilic and exilic prophets had said would happen at this time did *not* occur. Or to put it another way: while the prophets of the previous centuries had been remarkably successful in predicting the shape of approaching *disasters* and in analyzing why they were coming, their prophecies of what was to take place now that Israel had been destroyed seemed far less realistic. On the question of how Israel and the world might eventually come to know God and live in justice and peace, the prophets, it seemed, had reached an impasse.

This was not, of course, the first time that eschatological frustrations of this nature had arisen. Already in the days of Isaiah of Jerusalem, as we have seen, expectations of a spiritual renewal in that city were disappointed (Is 22). The prophets Nahum and Obadiah thought this renewal would occur with the fall of Assyria (Neh 2:1–2; Ob vv. 16–21), but that hope too failed to materialize.

However, the disappointment of these earlier periods cannot be compared to what occurred in the period after 538, for never before had the prophetic expectations of world salvation been so high or so concentrated upon a specific moment and a particular set of events. With the fall of Babylon and the restoration of the Judeans to their homeland it was thought that world-transforming events would take place, but these did not occur, not at least in the manner envisioned.

The story of prophecy during the subsequent decades may be characterized as a series of explorations as to *why* this was so and how and when the fulfillment of Yahweh's plan for the world *would* come to pass.

The prophets who arose in the community of the restoration to address these issues were the following: Third Isaiah (Is 56–66), who may be dated to the very earliest period after the restoration; Haggai and Proto-Zechariah (chs. 1–8), whose oracles are carefully dated by the books themselves to the second year of Darius (522); Malachi, who is generally thought to have prophesied after the completion of the temple in 515, but before the arrival in this community of Ezra and Nehemiah (c. 450); Joel and Jonah (some time later).

During still later periods the prophetic books were increasingly read, interpreted and edited, with the result that a new form of prophecy appeared: prophecy based primarily on the inspired *study and interpretation* of prophecy (now in the form of prophetic writings or books). In some instances prophetic interpretations of this kind were then appended to already existent *older* prophetic collections, as in the case of Ezekiel 38 and 39 and Zechariah 9–14 (note the reference to earlier prophecies in Ez 38:17). In other instances they emerged as separate books in their own right, as in the case of the prophecies of Joel (see below).

These and other prophetic-type writings of this genre reflect an ongoing preoccupation with the enigma of the non-fulfillment of earlier prophecies and what, in this light, may still be hoped for. Problems at this point arose with special intensity during the persecution of the Jews in Palestine at the time of the Helenistic occupation in the second century B.C. (see 1 and 2 Maccabees). The terrible sufferings then experienced raised especially serious doubts about the relevance of the prophets and gave rise to what scholars term "apocalyptic" or "endtime" theologies. In these the earlier prophetic visions of a perfected world were regarded as still valid, but needing yet further clarification as to the time and manner of their fulfillment. In general, it was thought that God himself would have to intervene in some totally unprecedented manner if evil were to be eradicated and righteousness established in the universe. The time when God would do so, the apocalyptists believed, was very near.

The chief biblical example of literature of *this* type (full-blown apocalyptic literature) is the Book of Daniel. Its author (or authors) was not a prophet, but from the circles of the "wise" (11:34–35; 12:3) who were "versed in every branch of wisdom" (Dan 1:4) including the study of the prophets. In Daniel 9:1–2 the author of the vision there is described as puzzling over the meaning of a certain word of the prophet Jeremiah in particular. Here we can see very clearly the transition noted above from prophecy to the study of prophecy as a way of interpreting the future. After Malachi prophecy of the earlier intuitive type came to an end, by and large, and this apocalyptic genre began to take its place.

Against this backdrop, we will conclude our survey of the Hebrew prophets by taking a brief look yet at the most important of the *intuitive* prophets of this final period, after 538. To repeat, these are Third Isaiah, Haggai, Zechariah and Malachi. Each of them tried to address the conditions that existed among those Judeans who returned to Palestine after their liberation from Babylon. What did they say?

B. Major Post-Exilic Prophets

1. Third Isaiah (Is 56–66)

The name of this prophet is unknown to us, but he appears to have been a disciple of Second Isaiah living among those Judeans in Babylon who returned to Palestine soon after the conquests of Cyrus in 538. So we refer to him as Third Isaiah. The conditions in Judea at the time he was prophesying are graphically portrayed in his prayer in Isaiah 64:8–10.

> Yahweh, do not let your anger go too far
> and do not remember guilt for ever.
> Look, please, we are all your people;
> your holy cities have become a desert,
> Zion has become a desert,
> Jerusalem a wasteland.
> Our holy and glorious Temple,
> in which our ancestors used to praise you,
> has been burnt to the ground;
> all our delight lies in ruins.
> Yahweh, can you restrain yourself at all this?
> Will you stay silent and afflict us beyond endurance?

From this we can gather how earnestly Third Isaiah hopes that these terrible conditions will be rectified. In 63:19–64:2 he prays that Yahweh would tear open the heavens and come down, working "unexpected miracles" so that Yahweh's name might be respected among the nations. Words such as these clearly identify this prophet as someone who shared the exuberant hopes of Second Isaiah that the Judean restoration would be a time of events that would reveal Yahweh to all humanity. In 61:1–9 he writes that when Yahweh appointed him to be a prophet, he commissioned him to announce that Jerusalem would soon be rebuilt and a people established there so glorious that it would be famous throughout the world (61:9).

> For as the earth sends up its shoots
> and a garden makes seeds sprout,
> so Lord Yahweh makes saving justice and praise
> spring up in the sight of all nations (61:11).

The admonition that opens his book sums up Third Isaiah's message: "Make fair judgment your concern, act with justice, for *soon* my salvation will come and my saving justice be manifest'' (56:1). Salvation has *not yet* dawned, but soon it will, *if* the community upholds justice (note his moving words regarding this in ch. 58). And he is confident that the salvation he speaks of will be a momentous one, bringing about not only the transformation of Israel, but of the nations as well, for at the beginning and end of his book are again oracles stressing that foreigners too are going to share in the new heavens and new earth Yahweh is creating: ''. . . my house will be called a house of prayer for all peoples'' (56:7; compare 66:18).

In summary: within the difficult conditions and disappointments of the first years of resettlement in Judah, Third Isaiah sought to keep alive the great hopes Second Isaiah had awakened of a universal revelation of Israel's God to all peoples.

2. Haggai and Zechariah 1–8

Yet, year after year went by without any indication that anything of this magnitude was going to happen. Haggai 1:5 alludes to some of the difficulties this restoration community was facing in the second decade of their return: ''Think carefully about your behavior. You have sown much and harvested little; you eat but never have enough, drink but never have your fill, put on clothes but feel no warmth. The wage-earner gets his wages only to put them in a bag with a hole in it.'' Wind-blast, mildew and hail were additional problems (Hag 1:15–16). Under these adverse conditions, it seems, a mood of fierce individualism threatened to take over. From Nehemiah (a generation later) we learn that some became extremely wealthy, while others were forced to sell themselves into debt slavery (see Neh 5).

Clearly something was wrong. Far from salvation dawning for the whole earth, it did not seem to be coming even for tiny Israel.

The prophets Haggai and Zechariah were convinced that they knew why this was so and began sharing their thoughts on the matter in the second year of the Persian ruler Darius (520), successor to Cyrus (Hag 1:1; Zec 1:1)—a time of uprisings throughout the Persian empire. It was now eighteen years since the first members of this community had returned to Judah from Babylon, and yet Yahweh's temple there (in Jerusalem) was *still* unbuilt. *This,* these prophets said, is what is wrong—this is what is preventing Yahweh from reappearing there in his glory and bringing to pass the unexpected miracles that will bring about the new age.

Therefore, they preached, if there is going to be a change for the better, renewed work on the temple must begin at once, for not until the temple is rebuilt will Yahweh return to Zion (Zec 4:8–9; 8:3) and be glorified there (Hag 1:6–8). Only then will the curse now resting on the land be removed (Zec 5:1–4), and vine, fig tree, pomegranate and olive again bear fruit as of old (Hag 1:19). Only then will Jerusalem flourish and nations gather there to Israel's God (Hag 2:7, 15). But then, indeed, all this *will* happen: pagan powers will crumble and Zerubbabel, Yahweh's anointed in Jerusalem (along with Joshua the high priest, Zechariah adds) will become Yahweh's chosen world ruler (Hag 2:20–23; also Zec 6:9–14; however, note the textual changes in this latter passage due to the non-fulfillment of this prophecy).

Needless to say, while the exuberant promises of these two prophets succeeded in reawakening the expectations of their Judean contemporaries to the point that the task of rebuilding the temple was in fact undertaken and completed during the next several years (by 515), once again these hopes were disappointed. The nations were not shaken, their wealth did not come pouring into Jerusalem, Zerubbabel did not become world ruler—there was no change for the better at all, so far as we know. Indeed, things may have gotten worse, for it appears that Darius had Zerubbabel removed from office at this time and Judah politically and permanently downgraded—just because, perhaps, of the messianic expectations aroused by these two prophets. From this moment onward, in any case, leadership of the restoration community passed from the hands of kings to governors, priests and teachers.

3. Malachi

The deplorable conditions that prevailed in Jerusalem in the wake of yet another eschatological disappointment of this nature are reflected in the prophecies of Malachi. In ch. 1 of his book we read that worship at the now restored temple of Yahweh in Jerusalem had quickly become a pathetic affair, with mostly sick or crippled animals being offered there as sacrifices (1:8). Also the priests in charge are characterized as corrupt, causing many to stumble (2:8–9). In the community at large men were callously divorcing the wives of their youth (2:14–16) and marrying foreign wives (2:11). Yahweh seemed distant and uncaring (1:2). Many were openly cynical. "Where is the God of fair judgment now?" people were asking (2:17). "It is useless to serve God" (3:14), some were concluding, for "the evil-doers are the ones who prosper; they put God to the test, yet come to no harm!" (3:15).

In the face of all this, Malachi (not a name but a title meaning "my messenger") presents what he believes to be compelling evidence that Yahweh still loves Israel—he points to how badly things have gone for

Edom in comparison with Jacob (1:2–5). Then in 3:1–5 he renews the prediction that Yahweh will yet return "suddenly" to the temple, and, when he does, will purify the sons of Levi and give testimony against all who deviate from his ways (sorcerers, adulterers, perjurers and those who oppress the wage earner, the widow and the orphan and rob the foreigner of his rights). When this happens, he declares, the difference between upright and wicked will once again be evident (3:18–20).

Notable here is the fading of post-exilic hopes for a restoration of the Davidic empire—without, however, forfeiting the expectation that Yahweh would yet act somehow to vindicate those who are faithful to him. Notable too is the return here to insightful ethical critique as a way of fulfilling the prophetic calling, as in the earlier pre-exilic prophets. A Levite himself, perhaps, Malachi reactivated the instructional techniques of his heritage (the dialogue form especially) and brought them to bear upon the life of a community in the grip of discouragement and cynicism.

4. After Malachi

It is clear, however, from conditions in this community when Nehemiah and Ezra visited it a short time later, that Malachi's words had done little to rectify matters. The trend toward intermarriage continued unabated (Ezr 9–10), morale remained low (see Neh 1–6), social problems of one kind or another were pervasive (see Neh 5). Third Isaiah, Haggai, Zechariah and Malachi had undoubtedly contributed much to keeping faith alive among smaller groups who shared their futuristic expectations. But to many their words promising a soon-to-be-revealed transformation of the world must have seemed increasingly incongruous. Indeed, even those who still believed in the words of the prophets (many of which were now lovingly assembled on scrolls) must have struggled greatly with the issue of when and how the things they read of there would ever come to pass.

A growing conviction among some was that a great war between Israel and the nations still lay ahead before God's *final* act of restoration for Israel and the world would occur (see Ez 38 and 39; Jl 4; Zec 12–14). Others were yet hopeful that the missionary vision of Second Isaiah might yet be fulfilled in a more pacifistic manner, if only Israel would break out of its stereotypical thinking about paganism and get on with the task (the little book of Jonah may reflect the convictions of those who kept this hope alive; see Jonah 4:11).

But with Malachi, it seems, the period of the great intuitive prophets of Israel had come to an end. From this point onward other approaches to the problems facing this community would be needed and leaders of another type (such, for example, as Nehemiah and Ezra proved to be). The prophets had by now said and done all that they could on the basis of the inspiration they had received.

C. Overview and Relevance

Before terminating our study, however—with this final chapter of the story of biblical prophecy in mind (the story of the prophets of the post-exile)—we want to ask once again what the significance and relevance of the prophets we have studied in this volume both was and is.

So far as what their relevance *was* is concerned—for their contemporaries and for those in the years immediately following—there can be no doubt that to these prophets belongs a good bit of credit for enabling the Yahwistic people to survive during the period of the destruction of the Israelite and Judean kingdoms, in 721 and 586, and during their captivity in Babylon. By predicting this destruction and the restoration that followed *before* it happened, and by interpreting these events as actions of Yahweh, they turned what might well have been a final catastrophe into a revelation. In the light of their prophecies the events of this period could be seen as evidence of Yahweh's power and righteousness. Out of this ordeal of judgment and renewal, thanks to these prophets, a people was born who would never again forsake this God, whom they now understood as the true and only God of the whole earth.

The *ongoing* relevance of these prophets, I suggest, is linked to six certainties born of their messages and now integral to the outlook of both Judaism and Christianity (also Islam, to some extent):

1. there is one God and one God only watching over the affairs of this world—the incomparable Yahweh;

2. basic decency counts more with this God than anything else (justice in economics, fidelity in marriage, caring toward the weak); where this is lacking there is no substitute—neither temple, nor sacrifice, nor sacred theologies can make up for its loss;

3. when decency *is* missing and cruelties multiply, disastrous consequences must follow—there is a limit to what even the gracious Yahweh can overlook and permit to happen on this earth;

4. hence, the destiny of a people is determined, not by might nor by power, but by their sensitivity to right and wrong, their instincts for community building;

5. even those who lose their way in this regard can begin again,

for it is Yahweh's will that none shall perish but that all shall live and find fulfillment;

6. a good future awaits the whole world.

On this last point, however, there were and still are problems. As noted, the prophets we have surveyed were far more successful at critiquing and predicting disasters than at envisioning the shape that hope might take during the restoration. As a result, many of their "salvation" prophecies proved to be wrong and this increasingly gave rise to disappointment, cynicism and an end to the prophetic movement itself.

The problem of failed (or unfulfilled prophecy) remains for both Jews and Christians one of our more difficult unresolved theological issues. A traditional solution has been to suggest that even though the era of universal salvation and peace to which the prophets pointed has not yet been fulfilled, it still will be one day—when the Messiah comes, orthodox Judaism would say; when Jesus returns, orthodox Christianity would say.

As already intimated, another solution might be to recognize that the Hebrew prophets, while inspired, were also human and fallible. Among the pioneers of our race in seeking to envision what the world's future might be like, their achievements (as to be expected) are both provocative and puzzling, both inspiring and problematic. It would be a mistake either to idealize them or reject them out of hand. Even from the vantage point of our place in history, twenty-five hundred years later, their futuristic visions, although imperfect, might still have much to teach us.

The following are a few thoughts that have occurred to me as I have tried to assess their futuristic visions in this light:

1. Collectively, these prophets believed that the period of time in which they lived (the eighth to fifth centuries B.C.) was a turning point in world history. Through the destruction and renewal of Israel, they said in effect, God was doing something by means of which he would reveal himself to the whole world.

Looking back on what did in fact happen at that time (and since then), might it not be argued that in *this* at least they were approximately right? The revelation of God to the whole world did not, of course, happen precisely *when* or *as* they had anticipated. But is it not true that from that time onward knowledge of Israel's God has *in fact* been spreading abroad in the world—first through the witness of diaspora Judaism, then through Christianity and Islam (which is also rooted in prophetic faith)—so that today, even though Isaiah's vision of the glory of God being revealed to all humanity is still not completely fulfilled, millions of people throughout the earth do now have a share in the prophetic values and hopes associated with this God and worship him and none other?

In this sense, I suggest, the time of the prophets was indeed a watershed in history so far as the revelation of Yahweh is concerned. Knowledge of Israel's God has, from that time onward, become progressively the heritage of the whole world (regarding this impact of the prophetic witness on the modern world, see our earlier comments at the conclusion of chs. 4 and 10, and again Willis Glover, *Biblical Origins of Modern Secular Culture*).

2. A particularly painful point of non-fulfillment of prophecy in the post-exilic period, as we have seen, had to do with the demise at that time of the dynasty of David. Hopes for a revived Jewish state led by Davidic kings were dashed and with then, slowly, the expectation of a theopolitical form to Judaism. While the Yahweh temple was restored and a community of Judeans reestablished in and around Jerusalem, except for a brief and abortive experiment with statehood, following the Maccabean revolution of the second century B.C., Israel remained an occupied land from 586 (when Jerusalem was destroyed by Babylon) until the founding of the modern Jewish state in this century.

It is well known that instead of statehood, during these centuries, the predominant form taken by the Jewish community was that of depoliticized communities living in the diaspora and centered in synagogues. Increasingly Jews began living as political pilgrims and strangers in the wider world, where sabbath by sabbath they gathered, not to a temple or king, but to a place where scriptures were read and rabbis presided. When Christianity arose, it adopted this selfsame mode of existence. It too spread into the wider world chiefly through its ability to bring all kinds of people into small communities or congregations led by pastor-teachers.

With this development in mind we should recall that not all of the prophets envisioned the future salvation in terms of a restored Jewish state. Already, as we have seen, Jeremiah and Ezekiel began to deemphasize the role of the Davidic dynasty in their visions of the future, and highlighted instead the role of prophecy itself in bringing about that inner renewal without which anything else would be useless. And one prophet in particular, the Second Isaiah, in a daring insight, appears to have foreseen the end of the Davidic covenant altogether—or rather its benefits, he suggests in one notable passage (Is 55:3), are going to be transferred to an entire people. And it was he too who envisioned Israel's destiny as involving, not merely a restoration to its homeland and the temple there, but as also directed outward in a missionary action that would bring knowledge of Yahweh *to* the nations (Is 42:1–4).

Has not subsequent history demonstrated that on these points, at least, Second Isaiah was closer to the truth regarding the future than his prophetic peers?

3. And yet others too may not have been completely wrong in sensing that for such a development to take place (such a missionary action outward, as Second Isaiah envisioned it) a time of preparation would be needed during which a base in Israel would be necessary and a temple community there. So, even Haggai and Zechariah were (in retrospect) not altogether off the mark, it seems, when they insisted that the building of the temple was an essential step, if the coming world transformation was to take place. They simply did not see that other things would be needed as well before this could happen and that this would not happen as quickly as anticipated.

Nor, it might be added, were Haggai and Zechariah altogether mistaken either, even when they pointed to Zerubbabel as the future world ruler. Of course, their thought that God would reestablish the Israelite state at this time and that it would be in some sense a world power (along the lines of the original Davidic state with a Davidic type leader ruling it) was mistaken. This did not happen, nor is there any indication that it is going to happen, even in the modern Jewish state.

However, there is an element of truth, surely, in their intuition that a leader of very special qualities and closeness to God would be needed for God's rule on earth ever to be realized.

As it turned out, however, that leader was not so much a Davidic type figure, but a missionary leader of the kind we sense that Second Isaiah himself must have been. In Jesus of Nazareth, the founder of the worldwide Christian movement, and leaders of this type, what is decisive is not political power, but those qualities that we have come to see marked the lives of the greatest and best of the Hebrew prophets themselves: ability to distinguish right from wrong, intuitive insight into the right way ahead, humility and inspiration from God, courage and the ability to express themselves and give testimony to the truth they have received even to the point of giving one's life. It is leaders like this, we now realize, who are more effective than any others in bringing about that human transformation and knowledge of God on earth without which there can be no lasting peace.

With these few thoughts I bring to a close this chapter and this study, keenly aware as I do so of how much more there still is to say.

I hope, however, that what we have done will have laid a good foundation for continuing reflection and study.

Questions for Review

1. In what sense were the events that transpired after 538 a confirmation of earlier prophecies? In what respects was this not the case? What effect would the non-fulfillment of prophecy at this time have had? How was this problem dealt with in the so-called apocalyptic writings?

2. List the major post-exilic prophets of the intuitive type. What in general was their message? Why did the prophecies of Haggai and Zechariah prove to be especially problematical for their followers? What shifts in perspective does one notice in the prophecies of Malachi?

3. What might be some of the reasons for the cessation of prophecy after Malachi? Overall what has the prophetic movement contributed that is of permanent ongoing value and significance? Can biblical prophetic hopes for the future still help us in shaping and fashioning our hopes? In what sense? Write a one page summary of what this study of the prophets has contributed to your own thinking, personally. What convictions have grown stronger? What new insights have become yours? What questions has it aroused which you might hope to pursue further?

Study Resources

A student of the prophets needs: (1) a good translation; (2) a set of maps of the ancient Near East; (3) a few good introductory studies and commentaries to refer to from time to time for background and help in understanding specific issues or texts.

A. Translations

As indicated in my opening "Note to the Reader," the translation used throughout the previous study is the *New Jerusalem Bible* (1985), a thoroughgoing revision of *The Jerusalem Bible* by a team of Roman Catholic scholars. My choice of this version was determined by the fact that it is geared primarily to students (rather than for reading in church or synagogue) and is the only recent translation that transliterates (rather than translates) "Yahweh," the divine name to which the prophets so frequently refer. Other excellent translations are: the *Revised Standard Version* (1973), endorsed by Protestant, Roman Catholic, and Eastern Orthodox representatives, and also issued as the *Common Bible* (1973); *The New English Bible* (1970), a lucid translation by British scholars; *The Torah, The Prophets, The Writings: A New Translation of the Holy Scriptures According to the Masoretic Text* (1962–1967) by a team of Jewish scholars; *The New American Bible* (1970), a translation by members of the Catholic Biblical Association of America; and *The New International Version* (1978), an "evangelical" translation. Not recommended as a study Bible are *Today's English Version* (1976), a somewhat simplified translation designed for readers with limited formal education, and the *Living Bible, Paraphrased* (1971). This latter is not a translation at all, but a restatement of what the author believes the text to be saying in his own words. Also the *King James Version,* although a classic, is outdated in English usage and scholarship.

B. Maps

One of the best collections of maps for studying the prophets (because of the detail with which it displays the historical context) is *The Macmillan Bible Atlas*. Other excellent atlases have been published by the Broadman, Eerdmans, Oxford, Penguin and Westminster presses.

C. Histories, Introductions, Commentaries

Articles and books about the biblical prophets are legion. Almost any Bible dictionary or one-volume commentary will be of assistance to the enterprising student and help locate additional resources. The five volumes of *The Interpreter's Dictionary of the Bible* (Nashville: Abingdon Press) are an especially authoritative source of information. For a one volume supplementary resource, the recently published *Harper's Bible Dictionary* (Harper & Row, 1985) is especially noteworthy.

The following annotated list is just a sampling of some of the more important book-length works on the prophets. Each of them will contain additional bibliographical suggestions for further study.

1. General Works

BLENKINSOPP, Joseph, *A History of Prophecy in Israel: from the Settlement in the Land to the Hellenistic Period* (Philadelphia: Westminster Press, 1983). A comprehensive and thoroughly researched survey that pays special attention to the social setting of the prophets. Especially valuable for the advanced student.

BOADT, Lawrence, *Reading the Old Testament: An Introduction* (New York/Mahwah, N.J.: Paulist Press, 1984). Clear, well-written, up-to-date introduction to the literature of the whole Old Testament, with a helpful overview of the biblical prophets.

COGGINS, Richard, PHILLIPS, Anthony and KNIBB, Michael, editors, *Israel's Prophetic Tradition: Essays in Honour of Peter Ackroyd* (Cambridge University Press, 1982). A collection of authoritative essays treating various facets of Israel's prophetic heritage by leading biblical scholars. A stimulating resource for the advanced student.

EFIRD, James M., *The Old Testament Prophets: Then and Now* (Valley Forge: Judson Press, 1982). Provides basic information about each prophet and the prophetic movement as a whole. A good introduction for the beginning student.

EPSZTEIN, Léon, *Social Justice in the Ancient Near East and the*

People of the Bible (London: SCM Press, 1986). A lucid, provocative, wide ranging discussion of a theme central to prophetic thought; puts this issue in its wider historical, cultural and legal context.

FRETHEIM, Terence E., *Deuteronomic History* (Nashville: Abingdon Press, 1983). Characterizes the *biblical* histories on which we rely so heavily in our study of the prophets, and looks at selected passages.

GLOVER, Willis B., *Biblical Origins of Modern Secular Culture* (Macon: Mercer University Press, 1984). An incisive, wide ranging account of the way prophetic thought has penetrated western consciousness and is now providing the basis for a world culture.

GORDON, Dane R., *The Old Testament: A Beginning Survey* (Englewood Cliffs: Prentice-Hall, 1985). Another well-written, up-to-date survey of the Old Testament, including the prophets, with excellent notes and references.

KOCH, Klaus, *The Prophets* (2 vols.; Philadelphia: Fortress Press, 1982, 1983). Intriguing approach to the prophets as "thinkers" with a unique "metahistorical" perspective on world events; for the advanced student.

HESCHEL, Abraham, *The Prophets* (2 vols.; New York: Harper and Row, 1962). This "classic" by a famous Jewish scholar emphasizes the passionate, emotional side of the prophetic experience and message.

JAGERSMA, H., *A History of Israel in the Old Testament Period* (Philadelphia: Fortress Press, 1983). A compact but informative account of its subject—a good reference work for understanding the historical background of the prophets.

JASPERS, Karl, *The Origins and Goal of History* (New Haven and London: Yale University Press, 1953). A pioneering work which highlights the importance of the worldwide intellectual awakening of "the axial age" to which the prophets belonged for modern thought.

LIMBURG, James, *The Prophets and the Powerless* (Atlanta: John Knox Press, 1977). A simply written, yet authoritative study of one of the major themes in prophetic literature.

LINDBLOM, Johannes, *Prophecy in Ancient Israel* (Philadelphia: Fortress Press, 1962). Puts the prophets in their cultural context within ancient Israel and relates them to analogous figures in other times and places in history.

LOEWE, Michael, and BLACKER, Carmen, editors, *Oracles and Divination* (Boulder: Shambhala, 1981). A fascinating collection of essays on the "divining" practices of various cultures, ancient and modern, with an astute essay on the prophets of Israel as seen in this light.

OLAN, Levi, *Prophetic Faith and the Secular Age* (New York:

Ktav Publishing House; Dallas: Institute for Jewish Studies, 1982). A pioneering study that seeks to bridge the gap between the world of prophetic thought and our own; has a fascinating chapter on the prophets as poets.

ROWLEY, H. H., *Prophecy and Religion in Ancient China and Israel* (New York: Harper & Brothers, 1956). A leading Old Testament scholar who spent a significant part of his life in China draws astute comparisons between the message of the prophets and the thought of Chinese sages and philosophers of approximately the same historic period.

THOMPSON, William, *Christ and Consciousness, Exploring Christ's Contribution to Human Consciousness* (New York/Ramsey/Toronto: Paulist Press, 1977). Amplifies the seminal insights of Jaspers noted above and shows how Jesus may be viewed as mediating prophetic thought to the modern world.

VOEGELIN, Eric, *Order and History, Israel and Revelation,* Vol. 1 (Louisiana State University Press, 1956). An insightful analysis of the eschatological tensions introduced by the first wave of prophecy, and the shift that occurred in Jeremiah and his successors toward a more anthropological focus.

VON RAD, Gerhard, *The Message of the Prophets* (Harper & Row, 1967). Another "classic" that focuses on the way the prophets both were influenced by and shaped their inherited theological traditions.

WILSON, Robert R., *Prophecy and Society in Ancient Israel* (Fortress Press, 1980). A pioneering work that uses anthropology to obtain a sharper focus on the social setting and role of the prophets generally and of individual prophets. Especially valuable in highlighting the role that the disaffiliated Levitical communities in Israel played in nurturing prophetic dissent.

WINWARD, Stephen, *A Guide to the Prophets* (Atlanta: John Knox Press, 1969). One of the better overviews of the prophets and their books; factual and forthright.

2. Commentaries and Books on Individual Prophets

Amos

MAYS, James Luther, *Amos,* Old Testament Library (Philadelphia: Westminster, 1969). Careful, thorough, balanced—the best commentary for the general student.

WOLFF, Hans Walter, *Joel and Amos,* Hermeneia (Philadelphia: Fortress Press, 1977). First published in German in 1969 (second German edition, 1975), this is an exhaustive, erudite, yet theologically sensitive work. It may be too technical at points for the beginning student.

Hosea

ANDERSON, Francis I. and FREEDMAN, David Noel, *Hosea,* Anchor Bible (New York: Doubleday, 1980). Thorough but excessively technical and prolix at points. Useful for the advanced student.

MAYS, James Luther, *Hosea,* Old Testament Library (Philadelphia: Westminster, 1969). Like the author's commentary on Amos, well-written and illuminating. The best commentary for the general student.

WOLFF, Hans Walter, *Hosea,* Hermeneia (Philadelphia: Fortress, 1974). Initially published in German (1965); like its companion volume on Amos, this is a gold mine of information.

Isaiah 1–39

SCOTT, R. B. Y., "The Book of Isaiah, Chs. 1–39, Introduction and Exegesis," *The Interpreter's Bible,* Vol. V (Nashville: Abingdon, 1956), pp. 151–381. None of the more recent commentaries have surpassed this one in basic good sense.

CLEMENTS, Ronald E., *Isaiah 1–39,* New Century Bible (Eerdmans, 1980). Well-written and solid, but its author's unique hypothesis regarding the way the book was edited is still untested.

HOLLADAY, William, *Isaiah Scroll of a Prophetic Heritage* (Grand Rapids: Eerdmans, 1978). Does an excellent job of leading the reader through the intricate web of developments that led to the formation of this amazing book.

Micah

MAYS, James Luther, *Micah,* Old Testament Library (Philadelphia: Westminster, 1976). Comparable to the author's well-written, judicious commentaries on Amos and Hosea.

WOLFF, Hans Walter, *Micah the Prophet* (Philadelphia: Fortress, 1978). Essays for a general audience; especially insightful regarding Micah's background world and social role in it.

Jeremiah

BOADT, Lawrence, *Jeremiah 1–25* Old Testament Message, Vol. 9; *Jeremiah 26–52, Habakkuk, Zephaniah, Nahum* Old Testament Message, Vol. 10. (Wilmington: Michael Glazier, 1982) Simply written for those with no previous biblical studies background; a theologically sensitive segment by segment commentary.

BRIGHT, John, *Jeremiah*, Anchor Bible (New York: Doubleday, 1965). Solid and clear, with a new translation; especially helpful in establishing the chronology of Jeremiah's prophetic activity.

HOLLADAY, William, *Jeremiah*, Vol. I (Philadelphia: Fortress, 1986). Extensive, erudite treatment of the first twenty-five chapters; for advanced students.

MARTENS, Elmer, *Jeremiah* (Scottdale: Herald Press, 1986). Along with a segment by segment commentary provides helpful suggestions for seeing the text in biblical context and in the life of the Church today.

SKINNER, John, *Prophecy and Religion* (Cambridge University Press, 1922). Another "classic"—essays on the key themes of the book still highly regarded for their insight and clarity.

THOMPSON, J. A., *The Book of Jeremiah* (Grand Rapids: Eerdmans, 1980). An encyclopedic, yet readable verse by verse commentary with a fresh translation; an excellent reference work with numerous bibliographical suggestions.

Ezekiel

EICHRODT, Walther, *Ezekiel*, Old Testament Library (Philadelphia: Westminster Press, 1970). A bit ponderous but still the best commentary for the general student. Eichrodt is a leading Old Testament theologian.

ZIMMERLI, Walther, *Ezekiel*, Hermeneia, 2 vols. (Philadelphia: Fortress, 1979, 1983). An exhaustive, comprehensive work that will be the standard for many years. A valuable resource for the advanced student.

Second Isaiah

MCKENZIE, John, *Second Isaiah*, Anchor Bible (New York: Doubleday, 1968). A solid treatment along traditional lines.

MAYS, James, *Ezekiel, Second Isaiah* (Philadelphia: Fortress Press, 1978). Not a commentary, but a superb discussion of important themes and issues—clearly written and insightful.

WHYBRAY, R. N., *Isaiah 40–66* (Grand Rapids: Eerdmans, 1975). A lucid, verse by verse commentary; advances the hypothesis that Second Isaiah himself was the servant of the Servant Songs.

Index